The Essence of
Business Process
Re-engineering

The Essence of Management Series

Published titles

The Essence of Total Quality Management
The Essence of Strategic Management
The Essence of International Money
The Essence of Management Accounting
The Essence of Financial Accounting
The Essence of Marketing Research
The Essence of Information Systems
The Essence of Personal Microcomputing
The Essence of Successful Staff Selection
The Essence of Effective Communication
The Essence of Statistics for Business
The Essence of Business Taxation
The Essence of the Economy
The Essence of Mathematics for Business
The Essence of Organizational Behaviour
The Essence of Small Business
The Essence of Business Economics
The Essence of Operations Management
The Essence of Services Marketing
The Essence of International Business
The Essence of Marketing
The Essence of Managing People
The Essence of Competitive Strategy
The Essence of Financial Management

Forthcoming titles

The Essence of Public Relations
The Essence of Business Law
The Essence of International Marketing
The Essence of Women in Management
The Essence of Mergers and Acquisitions
The Essence of Industrial Relations and Personnel Management
The Essence of Influencing Skills
The Essence of Services Management
The Essence of Industrial Marketing
The Essence of Venture Capital and New Ventures

The Essence of
Business Process
Re-engineering

Joe Peppard
and
Philip Rowland

Prentice Hall

New York   London   Toronto   Sydney   Tokyo   Singapore

First published 1995 by
Prentice Hall International (UK) Limited
Campus 400, Maylands Avenue
Hemel Hempstead
Hertfordshire, HP2 7EZ
A division of
Simon & Schuster International Group

Typeset in 10/12pt Palatino by
Keyset Composition, Colchester

Printed and Bound in Great Britain by
Hartnolls Limited, Bodmin, Cornwall.

Library of Congress Cataloging-in-Publication Data

Available from the publisher

British Library Cataloguing in Publication Data

A catalogue record for this book is available from
the British Library

ISBN 0-13-310707-8

---

1 2 3 4 5   99 98 97 96 95

Contents

Preface

Over the past few years the level of interest in Business Process Re-engineering has exploded. Increasingly, however, we are concerned that mixed messages and hype are reducing the value of this powerful philosophy. This book is intended to help people understand Business Process Re-engineering (BPR), whether they are working or studying, and lift some of the fog which is obscuring the subject.

The book is divided into three parts:

Part 1 Chapter 1 examines what is meant by the term Business Process Re-engineering and compares it with other philosophies. In Chapter 2, the reasons why organizations are increasingly turning to BPR as a way of improving their performance are explored.

Part 2 This part is divided into three chapters which analyse the underpinning elements of an organization: processes, people and technology. Chapter 3 focuses on product and service delivery systems. It begins by looking at the market and customer requirements which a process must satisfy, according to the chosen strategy of the company. From this starting point the chapter then explores some of the basic principles in process design. Chapter 4 reviews the management of people and emerging organizational forms of specific relevance to BPR. In Chapter 5, the increasingly vital role of technology in enabling business processes is discussed, together with some of the changes which advances are bringing about.

Part 3   Chapter 6 builds on the preceding chapters to explore how
organizations can redesign their processes, highlighting two
main approaches to BPR. Chapter 7 then takes a step back
and examines the wider requirements of a BPR initiative,
and in particular, of managing change. A framework for
re-engineering is presented with a step-by-step guide to the
main issues to be addressed. Chapter 8 outlines some dos
and don'ts associated with BPR and brings together the
lessons learned from BPR and other improvement philosophies.

We have enjoyed putting this book together and are grateful to
our colleagues at Cranfield School of Management for their input
which, as ever, was insightful, informed and to the point.

Joe and Phil
August, 1994

Business Process Re-engineering

What is it?
Why are organizations doing it?

1

What is Business Process Re-engineering?

We trained hard, but it seemed every time we were becoming to form teams we would be re-organised. I was to learn later in life that we tend to meet every situation by re-organising and a wonderful method it can be for creating the illusion of progress, while producing inefficiency, and demoralisation.

Gaius Petronius Arbiter[1]

c AD 65

Reengineering is new and it has to be done.

Peter F. Drucker[2]

c AD 1993

Introduction

Business Process Re-engineering (BPR) has become a popular concept for organizations in recent years but is it just hype; the latest management fad? Many organizations are currently engaged in re-engineering initiatives though their experiences are mixed. When such performance improvement programmes succeed, significant benefits are realized. All too often, however, many companies fail to achieve the expected leaps in performance. In this chapter, we examine what the term BPR means, where it has come from, what distinguishes it from other improvement philosophies and why it has captured the imagination of so many managers.

3

Illustration 1.1: Re-engineering Ford's accounts payable department.

Ford buys in about two-thirds of its car parts from outside suppliers.

Before re-engineering, Ford employed about 500 people in the accounts payable department in North America. Management thought that, by rationalizing procedures and installing new computer systems, it could reduce the headcount to 400. Then Ford discovered that Mazda, in whom they had a 22 per cent stake, did the same job with only 5 people! Even after allowing for scale differences between the two firms, the gap was enormous.

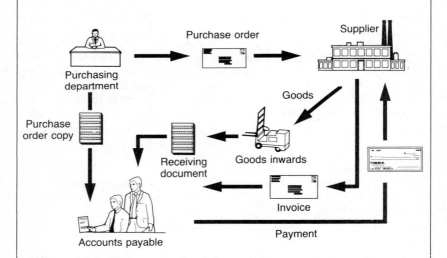

Ford's accounts payable department used to be sent copies of the purchase order, receiving document and the supplier's invoice. It then attempted to match these together, looking at 14 different items of data, however much of its time was taken up with items that did not match. After re-engineering, no invoice was required at all, the number of items to be matched was reduced to three and the purchase order and receiving confirmation was input to a computer system and matched electronically. As a result, Ford achieved a 75 per cent reduction in headcount in accounts payable, not just the 20 per cent it would have gained had the original plan gone ahead.

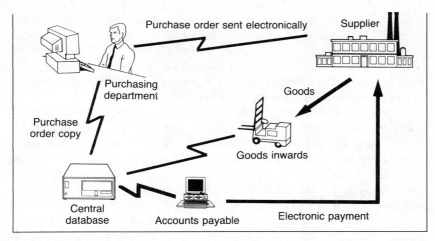

Source: Michael Hammer, Reengineering work: don't automate – obliterate, *Harvard Business Review*, July–August, 1990, pp. 104–112; Butler Cox Foundation, *The Role of Information Technology in Transforming the Business*, Research Report 79, London, January, 1991.

Perhaps the most famous example of business process re-engineering is that of the Ford Motor Company outlined in Illustration 1.1. The company made significant improvements to their accounts payable operation by examining the processes by which it bought and paid for its supplies. Other organizations have begun to use this approach to improve the whole way in which they do business. In particular, financial service companies are using this approach to dramatically reduce the time and cost of processing an application for their products, such as a mortgage or life assurance. One company found that it took 22 days to process an application for insurance, even though it was worked on for just 17 minutes! In an ideal world the customer would need to wait only a few minutes, not even the full 17 minutes. For example, ordering a telephone line, which used to be a lengthy process, can now be done in a couple of minutes over the telephone. Redesigning processes then, as a means to improving performance, can be very powerful. It can, however, call into question the way in which many companies are organized for work.

The traditional organization

Look at your own organization. Does it have different departments such as sales, marketing, finance, purchasing, production, information systems, personnel, product development, logistics? Are people recruited into one of these 'functional' specializations, and is promotion gained almost solely within these functions? What happens to customer orders, or during the development of a new product or service? Does each department do 'its bit' and then hand over to the next department in the chain?

In most organizations this is exactly what happens. Each department is responsible for undertaking one part of a larger whole. Take, for example, the fulfilment of a customer's order in a made-to-order manufacturing firm. Typically the order is taken by the sales department and passed on to the production department for scheduling and fabrication. Any raw materials needed are procured by the purchasing department. The product is then made and the finished good shipped to the customer by the logistics department. The accounts department bills the customer as well as paying suppliers. The customer service department then handles training and support of the product while it is in use.

This 'chain' of linked departments allows for specialization where the overall task is broken down and people with specific expertise can be applied as required. Such specialization of labour, whether on the manufacturing shop floor or within offices has been a normal way of working for a long time. 'Levels' of seniority evolve within these functions to form the organizational hierarchy. This model is so widely established that it is rarely questioned. That is all changing now. Business Process Re-engineering, BPR for short, is questioning this 'functional' way of thinking and is making 'processes' a main focus for organizations. This shift is illustrated in Figure 1.1.

A process focus means looking at the way a customer order is fulfilled, a new product created, or a marketing plan developed, without concern for functional boundaries or specialization. For example, when requesting repair of a telephone fault, the customer is not interested which department the engineer works for, whether he travels by taxi, or if he buys any spare parts in the local hardware store, as long as the service is restored.

So what exactly is a process? The Oxford English Dictionary defines process as *a continuous and regular action or succession of actions, taking place or carried on in a definite manner, and leading to the accomplishment of some result; a continuous operation or series of operations.*[3] In its simplest form a process has an input and an output and is made up of a sequence of individual tasks through which this input passes to become an output. The process itself can be anything which transforms, transfers or merely looks after the input

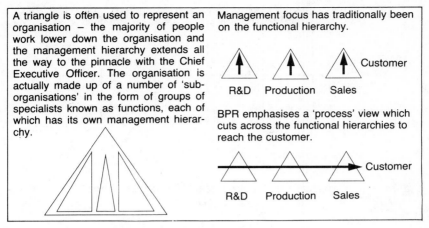

A triangle is often used to represent an organisation – the majority of people work lower down the organisation and the management hierarchy extends all the way to the pinnacle with the Chief Executive Officer. The organisation is actually made up of a number of 'sub-organisations' in the form of groups of specialists known as functions, each of which has its own management hierarchy.

Management focus has traditionally been on the functional hierarchy.

R&D   Production   Sales   Customer

BPR emphasises a 'process' view which cuts across the functional hierarchies to reach the customer.

R&D   Production   Sales   Customer

Figure 1.1 Functions and processes

and delivers it as output.[4] Organizations adopting a process approach find that, for example, many of the steps in their order cycles have nothing to do with delivering the required outcomes. It is sometimes difficult to identify why some steps exist at all. Often it

Box 1.1 The strengths and weaknesses of functions

Functional structures have a number of strengths, providing:

- A pool of expertise, vital for specialization of labour benefits and can mean fewer specialists may service the needs of a number of areas.
- A means of taking the latest thinking in particular areas into the organization.
- The means to develop careers which enhance specialist excellence in a particular field, such as Marketing, Production, IT or Human Resources.

. . . and some weaknesses

- The focus of the organization can be the 'boss' not the customer.
- No one has control over the 'horizontal' processes and co-ordination is weak. While business strategy gives focus to the functions each still has its own agenda.
- No single point of contact with organizations. If a customer has a query with an invoice they must contact the accounting department; sales, for example, only deal with questions relating to sales.
- Unproductive work exists because of functional boundaries which result in many tasks being done simply to satisfy the internal demands of the company's own organization.

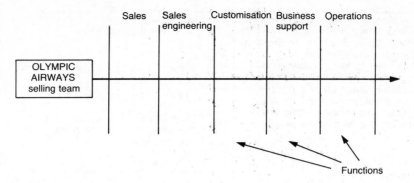

Figure 1.2 Organization of selling team for British Aerospace Regional Aircraft division

is for no better reason than because they always have! Getting rid of all these unnecessary steps means quicker customer service at considerably lower cost. This is all very well, but doing this usually cuts across the functional departments.

Initiatives in British Aerospace clearly illustrates the cutting across of functional boundaries. Process-based multi-functional teams come together to provide a solution to customer requirements. One example of this is the former Regional Aircraft Division of BAe. As Figure 1.2 illustrates, the selling team for Olympic Airways was made up of people from different specialities within the company to ensure that the customer was satisfied in the most efficient manner.[5]

The notion of strengthening the processes in an organization is certainly not new. Perhaps one of the best known models of business is the 'Value Chain' framework developed by Harvard Business School professor Michael Porter[6] who referred to processes as chains. Porter defined two types of activities which firms engage in: primary activities and support activities. Primary activities are those activities through which a company 'adds value' to its inputs for its customers who are prepared to pay for its output. Supporting activities are those required to support the primary value-adding activities both now and in the future. In delivering product to the customer it is vital that the 'chain' of primary activities have strong linkages facilitating the smooth flow of material and information between each. In and between each activity the emphasis is on value-adding to the customer, ensuring that the price increment which can be obtained through each action is greater than the cost of performing it. The 'internal value chain' of an organization is shown in Figure 1.3. A summary of value chain activities is contained in Box 1.2.

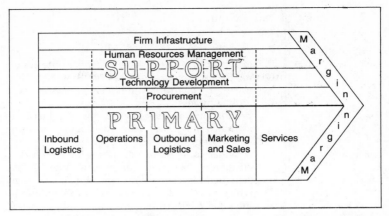

Figure 1.3 The internal value chain

It is nonetheless no coincidence that the names Porter gives to the generic activities correspond to the 'functions' found in many organizations.

Each organization adds value in the context of a contribution to a supply chain or external value chain, as illustrated in Figure 1.4.

Processes can be considered along the dimensions of scale and scope. The scope of a process is concerned with the extent to which it crosses organizational units, i.e., departments or functions. A process with a narrow scope usually takes place within a single department or function. A process with a broad scope is likely to cross a number of functions or departments.

The scale of the process depends on what it is performing, which could be a very simple set of tasks or a highly complex set of interrelated activities. Using Porter's value chain as a base, we can see in Figure 1.5 the scope and scale of a process as shown by the arrows, with the length showing the scope as it spans different departments, possibly across different firms, and the thickness of the arrow depicting its scale.

Identifying and understanding processes is not as simple as it might at first seem. In the delivery of most products and services, companies operate a highly complex set of processes. Identifying them is complicated because they cross departmental and hierarchical boundaries. In a factory one can at least follow the flow of incoming material through to the point of departure of the finished product. This may be complicated, with many materials being combined into one; however, the physical flows are visible and can

Box 1.2 Summary of value chain activities

Primary activities	
Inbound logistics	activities to receive, store and distribute inputs to the product, such as material handling, inventory control, warehousing, and contacts with suppliers.
Operations	production activities to create the product such as machining, assembly, packaging, printing and testing.
Outbound logistics	activities to store and distribute the product to customers, including warehousing.
Marketing and sales	activities associated with providing a means by which buyers can purchase the product, and be intended to do so (advertising, selling, pricing, merchandising, promotion).
Service	activities for providing service or maintaining product value, including installation, repair, parts and training.
Support activities	
Procurement	purchasing capital goods, production and non-production.
Technology development	facilities, machines and computers and telecommunications.
Human resources	activities involved managing the people resources of the organization, such as, recruiting, training, development, and remuneration of staff.
Infrastructure	general management, finance, strategy development, planning, quality assurance. The infrastructure supports the whole value chain.

be understood relatively easily. In services and office environments it is much more difficult to understand a process such as paperwork, and other forms of communications, such as telephone calls, electronic messages and information, must be followed. Many people in the process often have little idea how much of the output they create is used, or even why it is produced.

Yet despite these difficulties, organizations are increasingly turning to processes to deliver quantum increases in performance. In his book *Head to Head: The Coming Economic Battle Among Japan, Europe, and America*,[7] Lester Thurow comments

In the past economic winners were those who invented new products. But in the twenty-first century sustainable competitive

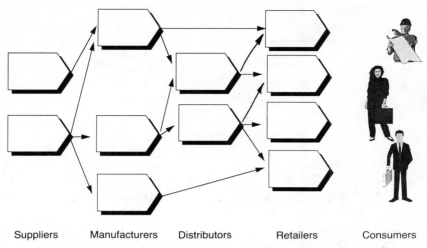

Suppliers   Manufacturers   Distributors   Retailers   Consumers

Figure 1.4 An example of an external value chain (after Porter[6])

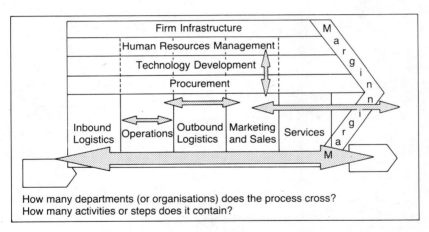

Figure 1.5 Scale and scope of processes

advantage will come more out of new process technologies and much less out of new product technologies. Reverse engineering has become an art form. New products can easily be reproduced. What used to be primary (inventing new products) becomes secondary, and what used to be secondary (inventing and perfecting new processes) becomes primary.

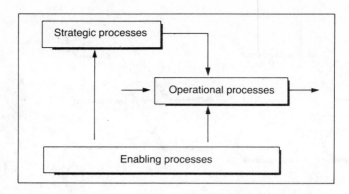

Figure 1.6   High-level organizational processes

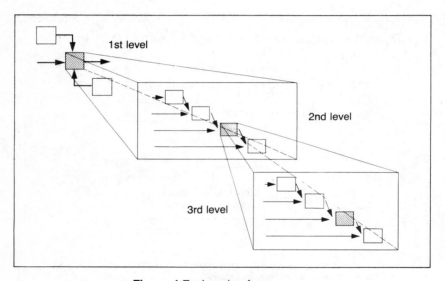

Figure 1.7   Levels of processes

In examining organizational processes we classify a basic set of high-level processes, which we believe apply to all organizations. Figure 1.6 illustrates this classification.

- **Strategic** processes are those processes by which the organization plans for and develops its future. Included here are Strategy Planning, Product/Service Development and New Process Development processes.

- **Operational** processes are those by which the organization carries out its regular day-to-day functions, such as 'winning' the customer, satisfying the customer, supporting the customer, cash and treasury management, financial reporting.

- **Enabling** processes are those which enable strategic and operational processes to be carried out, such as human resource management, management accounting and information systems management.

These three types of organizational processes can thus be broken down into more detailed sets of processes. These processes in turn can also be broken down into further level of detail and so on until we reach the level of the individual task. Figure 1.7 illustrates this idea of 'levels' of processes. BPR is all about redesigning these processes to gain significant improvements in performance.

Business Process Re-engineering – just the latest management fad?

Is BPR, though, really offering new insights into business and how to improve it, or is it just the repackaging of a series of failed or tired management fads?[8] What, for example, does BPR offer the three-letter-acronym-weary manager over other business philosophies such as Just-In-Time (JIT), Total Quality Management (TQM), Time Compression Management (TCM), Fast Cycle Response (FCR), and so on . . . the list seems endless. The confusion is increased by the growing number of companies who, wishing to be seen as keeping up with perceived best practice, claim a re-engineering element in all their initiatives whatever their form. Similarly, many consultancies have seized on the term to describe their approach and expertise. Hugh Macdonald, who has charted many management ideas claims that BPR is now at the 'feeding frenzy' stage with many consultancies introducing BPR into the range of services they offer clients.[9] Indeed, some have even been tempted to claim BPR is, at last, the panacea or 'snake oil' the business world has been waiting for.

To identify what messages lie behind all the hype it is necessary to examine the cornerstones of the BPR philosophy and the elements of other ideas which it has adopted. Like many of the ideas preceding it, BPR builds on the body of existing knowledge and utilizes it with a new and particular focus. TQM programmes, for instance, highlighted the role of processes in delivering quality. One of the most famous quality gurus Dr W.E. Deming stated that 'I should estimate that in my experience, most troubles and most possibilities for improvement add up to proportions like 94% that belong to the system and 6% to special causes.'[10] The system in this case being very much synonymous with process – the way things are done, notably not who does them. TQM programmes, however, have often placed greater stress on the people and techniques aspects rather than on the process elements. Implementations of TQM programmes, in addition, have often re-inforced functional boundaries, overlaying the concept of the 'internal customer' as a means of improving the process interfaces between departments.

As far as process-based teams go, again, organizations have been using them to manage projects for launching new products for some time. Simultaneous Engineering, or Concurrent Engineering as it is known in the USA, is a process-based organizational form for the design and manufacture of new products. Just-In-Time as a manu-facturing philosophy also placed great stress on the process: optimizing material flow through the plant by simplifying processes and eliminating the causes of inventory such as poorly performing work centres and suppliers. However, neither Simultaneous En-gineering or JIT have had much impact on services. When talking about BPR with many production managers it is clear that they cannot understand what all the fuss is about: they have been doing it for years. Yet talk to office bound executives in the same organization or managers in service industry and the concept seems new and exciting. In a sense BPR has come about because other improvement programmes, despite some successes, have failed to deliver the scale of improvement required, and now the whole organization needs to get involved. The ever faster pace of change also means that, however successful past initiatives have been, further improvement must be made. This was the situation faced by AT&T's Universal Card Services division who 'found itself winning a Baldridge Quality award one day and reengineering for its life the next'.[11]

That many of the 'rules' of BPR are common to other programmes which have gone before makes sense: they work. As each philoso-phy has elements which have proven to be useful over time, so subsequent philosophies build on that body of experience. As each new 'fad' comes and goes it is important to distil the valuable elements of each and thereby assemble the appropriate 'toolkit' for improvement from the complete body of knowledge available to business. Proponents of BPR have done this and many of the elements of BPR can be identified as being proven methods from other, earlier philosophies. Table 1.1 outlines the main elements of a number of philosophies.

Although we think that Table 1.1 is a useful starting point to put BPR into context with these other philosophies, we must point out that we are, to an extent, mixing apples and pears here. JIT, TQM and Simultaneous Engineering (SE) are all philosophies governing the way an organization, or part of an organization works. While implementing these ways of working will serve to improve performance in leaps and bounds if done well, they are not improvement philosophies in the same way that Fast Cycle Response and BPR are. FCR and BPR have no prescriptions for the way organizations should work day to day but rather are concerned with how organizations can get shift performance based on one way of working to another.

- **Focus** – the clear focus of BPR is processes and the minimizing of the non value-added content in them. This may result in the reduction of time, but it is not the main focus as it is in FCR/TCM. TQM focused on quality and getting things right first time, JIT focused on inventories, waste elimination and through-put, and SE focused on new product development and, specifically, the reduction of time to market and increased quality.
- **Improvement scale** – while each philosophy preaches improvement, it is apparent that some have become associated with incremental improvement and others with more radical improvements. We shall return to this topic later in the chapter.
- **Organization** – both FCR and BPR emphasize the role of processes within an organization. SE is also process based, although it is specifically the new product development process around which any organizational change is directed. TQM, in many cases, has not changed the existing organizational structure although it has often brought common goals between areas. JIT, closely allied with TQM, has meant organizational changes on the shop-floor and team or 'cell' structures have often been the result. Many of these shop floor structures are now being applied to office environments as we shall see in later chapters.
- **Customer focus** – BPR is quite clearly focused on the outcome of the process. For operational processes, these are primarily for the customer; while for strategic processes such goals will be driven by medium- to long-term business needs. It would be true to say that the other philosophies also focus on outcomes,

Table 1.1 Business philosophy comparisons

ELEMENT	Total Quality Management	Just-In-Time	Simultaneous Engineering	Time Compression Management/Fast Cycle Response	Business Process Redesign/Re-engineering
Focus	Quality Attitude to customers	Reduced inventory Raised throughput	Reduced time to market Increased quality	Reduce time (time = cost)	Processes Minimize non-value-added
Improvement scale	Continuous Incremental	Continuous Incremental	Radical	Radical	Radical
Organization	Common goals across functions	'Cells' and team working	R&D and Production work as a single team	Process based	Process based
Customer focus	Internal and external satisfaction	Initiator of action 'pulls' production	Internal partnerships	Quick response	'Outcomes' driven
Process focus	Simplify Improve Measure to control	Workflow/Throughput efficiency	Simultaneous R&D and Production development	Eliminate time in all processes	'Ideal' or Streamlined
Techniques	Process maps Benchmarking Self-assessment SPC Diagrams	Visibility Kanban Small batches Quick set-up	Programme teams CAD/CAM	Process maps Benchmarking	Process maps Benchmarking Self-assessment IS/IT Creativity/out of box thinking

however their emphasis is slightly different. Closest is TQM which emphasized quality but also introduced many more customers into the process with the concept of the internal customer. FCR was focused solely on becoming quicker in response to the customer, similar in many ways to JIT's treatment of the customer as the initiator of action. This obsession with time compression has more recently received some criticism from one of its main proponents. George Stalk talked about the competitive advantage of time compression in 1988[12], but more recently has highlighted the problem of indiscriminate action and preached the need for customer focused action.[13] SE's focus was more, though not exclusively, about internal partnerships to raise quality and reduce time from concept to market launch.

- **Process focus** – BPR seeks to generate 'ideal' processes either from a 'clean sheet' design, or from systematic redesign of existing processes. We shall return to these two approaches in Chapter 6. SE has a specific process focus ensuring that Marketing, R&D and Production work together, and in parallel, on new product introduction. TQM's process focus was towards control and measurement so that variation could be eliminated and quality raised. FCR sought to eliminate time from the process and JIT similarly focused on throughput efficiency (explained in Chapter 3) and work flow.

- **Techniques** – not all the techniques associated with each philosophy are shown in Table 1.1. Though there is some commonality it is not apparent in the Table just how common the techniques used are. Certainly TQM, FCR and BPR are similar but many of JIT's techniques are employed in FCR and BPR as a matter of course. One major difference is the role of Information Systems (IS) and Information Technology (IT). BPR has often been defined as the redesign of processes to make the most effective use of IT.[14] We disagree. BPR is about improvement and not about IT for the sake of it. Many BPR projects may actually strip out IT rather then deploy it. Hammer's original message 'Don't automate – obliterate' clearly illustrates the pitfalls of applying IT without first getting the processes right.[15] Having said that, it is clear that IT can, and does, have a major impact on the way business is done. In particular, it allows work to be performed in ways which are not possible manually. We shall explore the potential of IT in Chapter 5.

The message from Table 1.1 is really that the philosophies are similar in many ways and 'borrow' techniques from each other to good effect. *What matters most is not what the initiative is called, but what it delivers.*

Value engineering applied to processes

In many ways BPR is value engineering applied to processes rather than products. Value engineering was developed by General Electric in the 1940s and is essentially a technique to improve product performance through redesign. With this approach, an existing product's design was scrutinized to ensure that every aspect was necessary to deliver the utility of the product. Anything that did not directly contribute to this utility was eliminated. In effect, the product was redesigned to deliver or enhance its value, in customer terms, in the most cost-effective manner possible.

An example of value engineering illustrates well the savings that can be made by questioning basic design assumptions. American Airlines saved a great deal of money by implementing a suggestion to adopt a non-painted livery on their aircraft. You will see that their aircraft are silver, with the exception of the strip of colours, and this is because unlike other airlines, American does not paint all of the aircraft's body. Many tonnes of paint are required to cover a jumbo jet, and savings come not just from the elimination of paint and labour, but most significantly from the saved fuel through the reduced weight.

Continuous improvement versus radical improvement

A main area of debate and indeed some contention is whether BPR is concerned with radical change only while other philosophies, such as TQM, focus on continuous incremental change. For us this debate seems a distraction from the central issues at best, and at worst a damaging message which seeks to promote only high-risk radical change.

Proponents of the 'BPR is about radical change' camp are usually to be found in places without direct responsibility for the change, often in academia, consultancies or support functions with everything to gain and little to lose by such projects. They may also quietly admit that most re-engineering projects fail but that managers should not let that distract them from the central task of BPR which is radical change. This is rubbish in our opinion and we have heard it many times. The point of BPR is *improvement* not change for its own sake. It may be that to effect radical improvements a company ends up having to make radical changes to both its processes and its organization, but this does not necessarily follow. As many in manufacturing know, a great deal can be achieved through continuous incremental improvement based on small changes throughout the firm. Companies such as Toyota and Nissan have shown that this approach is often far more effective than the 'complete overhaul' approach that many western companies followed for so long, often at great cost and with little success.

Even where radical changes are required, it is important that the focus remains firmly on the improvement and that the changes are seen only as a mechanism for achieving it. We will return to this topic in Chapter 7 and at this stage it is sufficient for us to say that we associate BPR with *radical performance improvement* for any given process. Such radical performance improvement on a local department's process will not yield, on its own, radical performance improvement for the organization as a whole. However such a local departmental initiative replicated many times throughout the organization as part of continuous improvement across the whole company may well yield such organizational radical performance improvement.

It is important to understand the potential improvement which might be gained from re-engineering. The potential gains will relate to the scale and scope of the processes. If the scale and scope are small, you should not expect a huge pay-off. Similarly, if the scale and scope are wide ranging, a greater payoff should be expected (though this may be achieved by small changes being made to the processes, but a lot of them which in sum become significant). Figure 1.8 shows a broad means of categorizing the scale and scope of improvement which can be expected given the scale and scope of an *individual* process re-engineering initiative. The 'scale of potential bottom line improvement' relates to the possible pay-off from a project at an enterprise level.

Of course this diagram is a general rule only for there are other considerations. Take, for example, a project whereby a company seeks major improvements in the performance of its procurement processes. This project may involve the re-engineering of a highly complex process, involving many suppliers, yet may not actually impact the company's own customer service very much. While the improvement of the processes may be significant it may be difficult to track such gains back through to the bottom line. In contrast, smaller scale and scope changes to the company's own customer

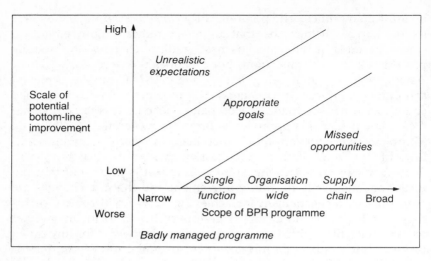

Figure 1.8 Expectations for improvement

facing processes may yield significant improvements in customer service leading to higher customer loyalty, higher customer spending and an increased number of customers as they switch from competitors. Such a project's impact on the bottom line is likely to be much easier to trace. We are not saying that only customer facing processes should be re-engineered, although it may be the best place to start, simply that gaining an idea of expected benefits and tracking them is not always easy.

So what is BPR?

We define it as follows:

> BPR is an *improvement* philosophy. It aims to achieve step improvements in performance by redesigning the processes through which an organization operates, maximizing their value-added content and minimizing everything else. This approach can be applied at an individual process level or to the whole organization.

If that is nothing new it does not matter. There may be little new in each element of BPR, but for many it has brought a valuable set of tools and techniques together which can be readily applied to their situation. It has captured the imagination of managers in many organizations and has made them aware of the power of a process focus and has thus proven to be extremely valuable.

Summary

Traditional organizational structures have been built around functions and hierarchy. While these have served enterprises well in the past, they have proven slow and cumbersome in responding to the needs of today's competitive environment. Business Process Re-engineering challenges many of the assumptions on which organizations have been built and puts processes firmly on the management agenda. By redesigning these processes it is possible to effect step improvements in the performance of these processes to revitalize the competitiveness of the business.

We end this first chapter with a further illustration of BPR, NKL of Norway (Illustration 1.2), and although less well known than the Ford example referred to at the beginning of the chapter, it nonetheless demonstrates the power of process understanding.

Illustration 1.2 NKL (Norway)

> Norway's wholesale co-operative NKL, which commands 25 per cent of the market, is one of the pioneers of business re-engineering. The company began its first pilot project in 1991 and completed it a year later, halving the supply lead time from production to point of sale. They achieved this in partnership with one of their largest suppliers, a paper products manufacturer.
>
> 'The actual time was cut from 70 days to 33 days over an eight month programme', said NKL's project manager Dag Schoyen, who is responsible for the company's entire logistics operation.
>
> NKL, which has a turnover of around 8 billion NOK and profits of some 200 million NOK, is growing and improving performance year on year. Its nine warehouses, located around the country, supply all co-operative stores.
>
> Senior managers from NKL and the paper products manufacturer were inspired to tackle the project jointly after attending a presentation by a leading US consultant on the concepts of process improvement. Although not called BPR, they later came to realize it was in fact the same idea without the current label. NKL embarked on the project after a major reorganization and management changes, triggered by a serious business decline in the late 1980s. The action reversed NKL's fortunes and provided the platform for further progress.

In 1992, after the success of the pilot, the business began to look for new tools to help in making business improvements and hit on business process re-engineering. 'We realized that we had already applied many of the ideas in our pilot project, which gave us a flying start, but BPR provided a more structured framework', said Dag Schoyen.

In the next round of activity, NKL selected their biggest suppliers and asked them to collaborate in extending the cuts in lead time achieved in the pilot project to their own business. Eight suppliers took part, accounting for 35 per cent of total turnover. The goal was to achieve a three per cent improvement in profitability mainly through the economies from reduced stock thanks to shorter lead times.

This time, however, the project also involved partnering with co-operative retail chains as well as suppliers. It was agreed that any savings achieved would be shared equally, providing an added incentive for project success. 'We have found it easy to achieve stock reductions of 50 per cent, simply by finding better procedures and changes to our routines such as putting our warehouses in direct touch with suppliers', he said.

Everything achieved so far has been done without changing electronic or computer systems. The next phase of the programme now underway, however, will involve computerization developments, explains Dag Schoyen. These will focus on areas such as improvements to EDI and access to point-of-sale information. The latest project to achieve a 15 day supplier lead time – a further reduction of 50 per cent – is being piloted in partnership with the same company involved initially. The goal is to achieve this by the end of 1994.

NKL is assuming the role of intermediary in the communications flow with responsibility for taking information from retailers and passing it on to suppliers. Again, stock reduction is a key enabler in achieving the goal. 'We have seen that by reducing lead times, two further benefits result. First, we see an improvement in service quality because people acquire greater knowledge of how the process works. Second, we have experienced an increased level of innovative ideas generated by people looking for more improvement opportunities.'

Several of these have already been implemented, reducing transportation costs and improving the efficiency of logistics procedures. In addition, reducing lead times has an added spin off in simplifying operational planning.

In future, NKL is looking to involve more of the 1400 workforce in BPR projects. So far only 20 or so employees have taken part, but the company needs a wider platform to extend into new areas. 'The overall goal is to get the whole organization to work in a better way', says Dag Schoyen.

He is, understandably, satisfied with the achievements so far, especially when compared with a failure rate for BPR projects often quoted as 70 per cent. And yet, he adds, ambitious as the targets might seem, he believes they could have been set even higher and still have been achieved.

NKL is sharing its knowledge and experiences with co-operative movements in other countries through Interco-op, the European association. Most are considering the possibilities for BPR in their organization while co-op businesses in the UK, Denmark, Finland, Italy, and Sweden are actively pursuing the idea.

> To companies contemplating embarking on a BPR project, Dag Schoyen cautions that although BPR may sound simple, it actually demands commitment that should not be underestimated. 'We have learned that it's a lot more complex than it seems on the surface', he said, 'and it took longer to achieve than expected. It really is a major adjustment to the whole way of thinking and working.'

Source: International Business Systems/IBS ONLINE. No. 5, Brussels, 1994.

References

1. From Petronii Arbitri Satyricon, AD66, attributed to Gaius Petronius, a Roman General who later committed suicide.
2. Quoted in 'Reengineering: the hot new management tool', *Fortune*, 23 August 1993, p. 33.
3. *The Oxford English Dictionary* VIII, 1408, Oxford: The Clarendon Press, 1978.
4. For an interesting perspective on business processes see Allan M. Scherr, 'A new approach to business processes', *IBM Systems Journal*, 32, no. 1 (1993), 80–98.
5. Presentation by Tim Scott-Wilson, Director Engineering and Quality, Regional Aircraft Division BAe, Cranfield School of Management, November, 1992.
6. Michael Porter, *Competitive Advantage*, New York: The Free Press, 1985.
7. Lester Thurow, *Head to Head: The Coming Economic Battle Among Japan, Europe and America*, London: Nicholas Brealey Publishing, 1993.
8. For further views on this question, the reader may wish to refer to Chris Edwards and Joe Peppard, 'Business Process Redesign: Hype, Hope or Hypocrisy?', *Journal of Information Technology*, 9, no. 1 (1994); and Michael Earl and B. Khan, 'How new is business process redesign?', *European Management Journal*, 12, no. 1 (1994), 20–30.
9. Personal correspondence with K.H. Macdonald, who was ICL Representative on MIT's *Management in the 1990s* research project.
10. W. Edwards Deming, *Out of Crisis*, Cambridge: Cambridge University Press, 1986.
11. George Harrar, 'Baldridge notwithstanding', *Forbes ASAP*, 28 February, 1994, pp. 44–57.
12. 'Time – the next source of competitive advantage', *Harvard Business Review*, July–August (1988), 41–51.
13. George Stalk and Alan M. Weber, 'Japan's dark side of time', *Harvard Business Review*, July–August (1993), 93–102.
14. For example, Tom Davenport sees BPR, or process improvement, as he refers to it, as a 'revolutionary new approach that uses IT and HRM to dramatically improve business performance', *Process Improvement: Reen-*

gineering Work Through Information Technology, Boston, Mass.: Harvard Business School Press, 1993. The Butler Cox Foundation views 'information systems . . . [as] the fundamental ingredient of redesigned business processes . . .', *The Role of Information Technology in Transforming the Business*, Research Report 79, London, January, 1991.

15. Michael Hammer, 'Reengineering work: don't automate – obliterate', *Harvard Business Review*, July–August (1990), 104–112.

2

The imperative to re-engineer business processes

Secretary Dulles told Premier Yoshida frankly that Japan should not expect to find a big US market because the Japanese don't make the things we want. Japan must find markets elsewhere for the goods they export.

Minute 802
National Security Council
12 September 1954

After World War II, a British commission on modernizing government discovered that the civil service was paying a full-time worker to light bonfires along the Dover cliffs if a Spanish Armada was sighted. The last Spanish Armada had been defeated some years before – in 1588 to be precise.

US Vice-President Al Gore
National Performance Review
7 September 1993

There are three routes to disaster: Gambling is the quickest, sex is the most enjoyable and technology the most certain.

Georges Pompidou

Introduction

In this chapter we examine BPR's rise against a background of increasingly intense competitive pressure, world-wide economic recession and the search for a way to realize the benefits of Information Technology following the highly expensive disappointments of the 1980s.

25

Competitive pressures on Western industry reached new heights during the 1970s and 1980s as markets globalized. The trend looks set to continue with the European Union (EU) becoming a reality, North American Free Trade Agreement (NAFTA) signed, and talk of free trade within the Association of South-East Asian Nations (ASEAN). This globalization brought new competitors for most companies, most notably from Japan. These new arrivals in both the US and European markets brought with them a new philosophy of business, management and operational strategy.

The new market-place – the war zone

In Japan the world of business is more akin to the world of war. The war is relentless and the large *Keiretsu* groups of companies slug it out in a daily fight for market share. When Yamaha threatened Honda's number one spot in the motorcycle market Honda responded with a startling battery of new product launches: 81 new motorcycle models in Japan in just 18 months, against Yamaha's 34. Prior to this frenzied action, each had only 60 models in their entire line-up.[1] Yamaha was finally forced to concede, on that occasion, but no group in Japan can rest on its laurels. In the West, companies in many traditional markets such as shipbuilding, car manufacture and consumer electronics had not thought of the market-place in the same terms. For them, the market-place was not seen as a war zone but as a place, often contained within national borders, where a group of people meet to trade with one another, each had his stall and did not encroach on the holding of the others. Unfortunately for many Western companies, the Japanese business war machines began arriving in their market-place. Discounted as not much of a threat at first, soon such names as Caterpillar, General Motors, and Harley-Davidson were beginning to realize that they were under attack.

In the high-technology world of computers and telecommunications the fights between companies in the domestic US market have recently been just as ferocious as any in Japan and this has given the USA great strength in this area.[2] The USA has seen small companies such as Microsoft and Intel rise to challenge the now not so mighty IBM. Sun Microsystems has transformed a niche market for workstations into a significant market, with high performance workstation technology replacing mainframes for some applications. Predictions of an American surrender in computers, made even as recently as 1989, now look hasty.[3] The assault on the Japanese PC market by Dell Computers, Compaq and Apple Computers has been highly successful with demand far outstripping supply. Even in the more traditional industries Japan's victory no longer seems so certain as it once did. Chrysler seems to have effected a major turnaround with the development of a range of exciting new products, such as the *LH* and the *Neon*, known as the 'Japan car killer' in Japan, development with Japanese style speed in just 33 months.[4] Even Ford and GM cannot be ignored and some Ford plants can now hold their heads up with the best in the world. The USA is still the most productive nation in the world and leads the Japanese in nine key manufacturing industries by 17 per cent.[5]

If the Japanese have failed to steal the crown of productivity king from the Americans, they have succeeded in doing so in cars, steel and consumer electronics. Only a fool would discount the threat the Japanese present to traditional Western companies, and in particular the Europeans. Unfortunately, such a threat is no longer restricted to the Japanese. It is unlikely that the world market will ever be the same again, with cosy, protected markets as existed in Europe up until very recently. France can no longer afford to prop up its industry, which must now become as good as its competitors or die. Germany, having enjoyed economic prosperity despite its workers being the highest paid, with the longest holidays and working the shortest week has been shaken by the scale of its recession and the costs of re-unification. In the United Kingdom, the decline of the manufacturing infrastructure has been enormous with some sectors such as shipbuilding, which once dominated the world, almost ceasing to exist.

In tomorrow's markets, surviving and beating Japan may only be the beginning. China and India are emerging as strong economies. Korean *Chaebol*, the large industrial groups are now well established in many Western markets and the other 'Tigers' of Singapore, Taiwan and Hong Kong are not just exporting a great deal but are developing into significant markets in their own right. Exports from these low cost countries are rising and foreign investment is becoming increasingly significant. Even markets which have been dominated by the West, such as software, are moving in part to this area of the World. German electronics giant Siemens is looking to India to source some of its software, recognizing that country's growing prowess in the field.

Processes – a weapon of war

The Japanese arrival in the USA and more latterly in Europe, was noted not just for an assortment of new products and coach loads of smiling photographers, but also for the arrival of new ways of working. Just-In-Time, Lean Manufacturing and Fast Cycle Response broke many of the 'rules' of traditional manufacturing methods and gave Japanese manufacturers a significant competitive advantage over Western rivals in superior quality, lower costs and shorter product development lead times. This was not the Japan people remembered from long ago, with a reputation for shoddy workmanship and poor quality.

After World War II, the main objective of Western manufacturers was to produce sufficient volume to meet rising market demands. The huge industrial might of America, built up during the war without the disruption of bombings, gained the USA the unquestioned pre-eminence it had sought. The UK faced the world as a diminished kingdom with the end of its empire assured. Germany and Japan, who had been significant industrial nations pre-war, were literally reduced to rubble and were dependent on US help and financial support as they rebuilt their industrial base. The Cold War ensured that such help and finance was forthcoming. Such was the fear of communism that the USA reversed its policy of breaking up the pre-war industrial groupings, or *Zaibatsu*, in Japan and sought to use them as one further bulwark against the 'evil empire' of the communists. During the 1950s, Japanese industry saw some of the worst industrial disputes in that country's history. Lock-out strikes affected many major producers with Toyota and Nissan experiencing strikes lasting many months. Eventually the companies were victorious, beating the militant unions and forming their own company groupings. Workers' wages were reduced and the working week extended. In return for this deal and the workers' dedication to working the company's system, some firms promised never again to reduce wages or to make redundancies. This social contract ensures the dedication of all the workers to continually improve the efficiency of the company, eliminating waste and thus many jobs, knowing that they will be found other work within the company. Several times in their history the Japanese car companies have sent factory workers out to sell cars door-to-door when the companies experienced problems. This seemingly desperate act, however not only made better use of the labour which could not be shed but also brought the workers building the cars into direct contact with the customers. The importance of quality was further emphasized and the role of the production worker in delivering customer satisfaction made clearer.

As Japan rebuilt its industry it sought to learn from the Western nations and proved to be highly receptive to the quality message which was emerging from the USA. It is no mistake that the quality award in Japan is named after an American, W.E. Deming. Together with Juran and others, Deming spread the quality message in Japan to a highly receptive audience. Process control and other techniques, widely adopted by US industry during World War II but later abandoned in many plants, were transplanted to Japan where they helped greatly in transforming the poor quality of goods in the 1950s and 1960s, to the world class standards of the late 1970s through to the present day.

One of the fundamental approaches on which the Japanese built their Just-In-Time philosophies was to understand and simplify every step in the manufacturing process. They 're-engineered' the manufacturing processes of the West to capitalize on their strengths and reduce the impact of their weaknesses. The Japanese car companies could not, for example, afford the costs of the inventory which the Americans took for granted as necessary to the manufacturing process, so they reduced it to a minimum. Simple, visible means became the way to control shop floor material movement through the use of Kanbans (explained in Chapter 3).

While the Japanese were sharpening their process weapon, Western manufacturers paid scant attention to the quality message and, as computer technology advanced, sought to handle the increasing complexity of manufacturing through ever more sophisticated computer systems. Techniques such as Materials Requirements Planning (MRP) and Manufacturing Resource Planning (MRP II) were developed to help companies reduce inventory and boost capacity utilization. While these have proven highly successful in scheduling supplier deliveries they have not worked so well in controlling the actual work at a shop-floor level. It is ironic that as many of the champions of Computer Integrated Manufacturing are stripping out their centralized computer scheduling systems and restoring factory control to the plants themselves, the Japanese are implementing the best features of the MRPs building on an efficient process base. MRP-type systems can bring great benefits to firms; however, those that succeed do not use computers to try and fix problems which are better solved by other means.

Services – a new battleground

The globalization of markets has by no means been restricted to manufacturing. Services have grown significantly from being primarily national enterprises to regional and global. Banking, financial services, transport, telecommunications, entertainment, information, all have become the focus of fierce international competition.[6] Deregulation and the political move to freer markets has spurred huge growth in cross border service trade. Many companies with household names have failed to survive, such as Pan Am and Airtours in the airline industry.

In Europe, the United Kingdom is actively promoting deregulation in many industries. The arrival of American Airlines and United Airlines to Heathrow signalled the start of a major increase in competition not just for British Airways, but for Europe's other national flag carriers. The scramble to form alliances in the industry is an indication of how far reaching the eventual changes could be. In telecommunications, the UK market is now the most deregulated in Europe. It has also become the key battle ground for a new range of services to be delivered to the home and office and many US companies are now setting up networks in the UK as pilots, not only for the larger continental markets in Europe, but also for their own home market. The area of retail shopping in the UK is also seeing a significant increase in competition loom on the near horizon as the large US discount shopping stores, such as CostCo, move into Sainsbury's and Tesco's markets.

In the new battleground of international services, processes are once again emerging as a key weapon. During the early 1970s Toyota realized that while it took only a matter of days to build a car it still took several weeks to process orders. The company turned to its processes for the answer and used many of the techniques it employed on the factory floor to considerably speed up its order cycle. The lesson was not lost. Process management was just as effective in an office or service environment as it was on the shop floor. It was not until very recently that recession combined with deregulation and the liberalization of markets forced companies to take action and upset the *status quo*. That stunning performance improvement in some processes have been reported is an indictment of the lack of improvement for so long. According to leading management thinker Peter Drucker, the most pressing social challenge, not only for companies but for society, is to raise the productivity of service work.[7] He believes that it will determine the very fabric of society and the quality of life in every industrialized nation. BPR, at least for the moment, is proving highly popular as a way of meeting that challenge.

The public sector

In the public sector the pressures for improvement have become almost as severe as in the private sector. In many OECD nations, governments have begun to inject a 'free market' environment into the public sector as a means of inducing operational improvements, both in terms of cost and service. The UK's National Health Service (NHS), Europe's largest employer, is perhaps indicative of this trend. Recent changes have seen the development of a quasi-market for health care with hospitals competing for contracts from General Practitioners and Health Authorities. The government has also sought to increase the power of the local organization through the granting of Trust status to hospitals and fund-holding status to GPs.

Outsourcing of many facilities and services has forced all organizations, including the armed forces, to take a hard look at how they do business and how they can improve. Six staff to change a light bulb in a hospital in the UK[8] is as unacceptable as the bureaucracy created in the federal government of the USA. The recent US *National Performance Review* highlights the potential which BPR offers in dramatically improving the performance of its public sector. The following extracts clearly illustrate the existence of what BPR seeks to eradicate:

A Cure Worse Than The Disease . . .
     The federal government is filled with good people trapped in bad systems: budget systems, personnel systems, procurement systems, financial management systems, information systems. When we blame the people and impose more controls, we make the systems worse . . . many are now afraid to deviate even slightly from standard operating procedure.
     Yet innovation, by its nature, requires deviation.
     Unfortunately, faced with so many controls, many employees have simply given up. They do everything by the book – whether it makes sense or not. They fill out forms that should never have been created, follow rules that should never have been imposed, and prepare reports that serve no purpose – and are often never even read. In the name of controlling waste, we have created paralyzing inefficiency. It's time we found a way to get rid of waste and encourage efficiency.[9]

The notion of 'market forces' is no longer a stranger to most public sector organizations in the developed world. In the UK, the Citizen's Charter led to the development of a number of public service bodies' own charters: the Patient's Charter, the Passenger's Charter, and so on, where the organization specifies the customer service level which people have a right to expect and for which, in some cases, compensation can be obtained when these levels are not met. Since the mid-1980s, Canada has had a programme entitled

Public Sector 2000, which has as its essential objective management by results rather than by rules. The National Performance Review in the USA is part of a similar drive to raise the service levels offered to American Citizens and cut costs. Savings of US$108 billion are projected if all the recommendations of the review are implemented. That such savings can be projected is a measure of just how vast is the Federal Bureaucracy. In the UK the public sector workforce still accounts for some 20 per cent of the total workforce, even after a decade of aggressive sell-offs to the private sector.

BPR will have a major impact in the public sector and in some cases is already doing so. From healthcare to tax collection the message of processes and BPR is being sounded loud and clear.[10] Illustration 2.1 describes how Karolinska Hospital in Stockholm is organizing itself around the patient flow.

Economics

The great recession of the late 1980s and early 1990s only served to heighten the problems faced in both the private and public sector. As consumers began to rein in their spending so price competition intensified in all sectors. Quality and image were no longer enough to guarantee sales as people worried about the threat of unemployment and loss of value in their properties. A one per cent drop in price will slash operating profit by 12.3 per cent for the average Standard & Poor's 1000 company, assuming that costs and volume remain the same.[11] As companies sought to cut costs to survive in this situation they inevitably perpetuated the cycle. In the longer term companies could no longer afford to develop products and expect to recover costs without taking into account the lower market prices. Some companies are now working back from the price which they can expect to sell a product, identifying the required profit and then determining how much can be spent on each feature. In general, customers today are more discerning and demand high-quality goods at low prices. To achieve this, they are stripping away costly features, redesigning products for ease and speed of manufacture, forging closer links with customers and accelerating new product development. Illustration 2.2 describes how PC manufacturer Compaq designed its Prolinea and Contura ranges.

Illustration 2.1 Karolinska hospital: reorganizing around the patient flow.

Think of a car going down a production line. Then picture a patient going through a hospital. Can the two be compared? And can management techniques to improve efficiency in the manufacturing sector be used with success in services such as healthcare? If Sweden's Karolinska hospital is anything to go by, the answer is yes.

The Stockholm hospital was facing a severe budgetary squeeze as part of a sweeping reform of the country's healthcare system. An 18-month time-based management project at the hospital has cut costs and waiting lists without affecting staff morale. The hospital is one of the first healthcare organizations in the world where manufacturing techniques have been applied so systematically.

'What we have done is organize ourselves according to how the patient moves through the system', says Jan Lindsten, the hospital's chief executive. 'The process is not quite the same as in the car industry but there are great similarities.' The hospital feared that a 'cheese slicing' approach to its 45 departments would endanger their capacity to function effectively. It decided to reorganize itself around the patient flow.

One of the first revelations was just how much patient and hospital time was wasted by inefficient investigation procedures, which sometimes required the patient to make up to five visits for different tests. Now nurse co-ordinators arrange for all tests to be made during a single visit. The second big area of inefficiency discovered was the operating theatre, where an average of 59 minutes was being lost between the end of one operation and the start of the next. The changes have cut the figure by more than half.

The overhaul has placed far more stress on efficient preparation for operations and bottlenecks have been reduced. Patients are pre-anaesthetized outside the operating theatre so that less time is lost before the operation begins. There is also less emphasis on having certain operating theatres dedicated to particular types of operations while those of a similar length and complexity are carried out in the same theatre. The changes have enabled the hospital to close four of its 16 theatres, while increasing the number of operations.

The project has led to more efficient use of operating nurses and surgeons; but it also revealed that the hospital did not have enough anaesthetists and that their time was used inefficiently. More anaesthetists have been employed and an out-patient clinic for anaesthesiology has been set up. There has also been a significant re-organization of the hospital's functions. Separate medical and surgical departments and different tests have been brought together to facilitate patient flow.

Source: Reprinted with permission from Christopher Brown-Humes, 'Production line treatment for patients', *Financial Times*, 7 January 1994.

Illustration 2.2 Compaq: designing to price

After being battered for several years by low-cost personal computer rivals, Compaq struck back in 1992. It now builds computers that cost up to 60 per cent less through what it calls 'design to price'.

Here is how it works: a design team comes up with specifications for a new computer. It sits down with marketing, manufacturing, customer service, purchasing, and other departments. Based on a price target set by marketing and a profit margin goal from management, the team determines what the costs will have to be. To achieve target costs, engineers design products with fewer parts, and re-use parts from existing designs. Compaq's factories have been overhauled to crank out products more cheaply. And supplier contracts have been re-negotiated, cutting material costs by U\$212 million in 1992 and U\$425 million in 1993.

The first products manufactured under the new pricing system, the Prolinea personal computer and the Contura notebook computer, came out in less than eight months. Since the third quarter of 1992 year, Compaq's sales volume has skyrocketed 64 per cent and profits have nearly doubled.

Source: 'Stuck!', *Business Week*, 15 November 1993, 41.

The rise of quality

Organizations around the world have well and truly woken up to the message of quality. While some still have a long way to go in improving their operations using TQM those who have had many years experience in this field are increasingly searching for a way of re-juvenating their improvement efforts. BPR is often seen as a way of doing this.[12] Motorola, IBM, Ford and a host of other leading organizations are turning to BPR to build on their quality successes and take them to a new level of business performance. Rank Xerox, for example, established it's *Leadership Through Quality* programme in 1983 to move towards a total quality company. This strategic initiative led to fundamental changes in the culture of the corporation and has become a way of working for all employees. The programme integrates all employee efforts into a comprehensive method designed to enable them to reach goals, meet or exceed targets and achieve objectives. Late in 1990, they recognized that a functionally aligned hierarchical organization was sub-optimal when viewed from the perspective of the customer because it had delays and, when compared with a business process aligned structure, was more expensive and less efficient to operate. As a result of BPR, many of the company's processes now take substantially less time. For example, specialized individual contracts (for customers requiring, say, special payment or leasing terms) take less than two days to process instead of 100.[13]

The IT 'black hole'

Although less directly associated with increasing business rivalry, technology is a further reason why BPR is proving so popular. The rapid pace of technological advancement offers opportunities to perform work in new and innovative ways. Progress, it seems, knows almost no bounds yet investment in technology, particularly Information Technology (IT) has in all too many cases brought disappointment and merely depleted company reserves without realizing the benefits sought.

During the 1980s, U$1 trillion was spent on IT by US businesses, U$800 billion of it by the service sector.[14] Yet, white-collar productivity remained virtually unchanged throughout the decade despite such enormous investment. Statistics for the US shows that while the number of blue-collar workers decreased by 6 per cent between 1975 and 1985, real output increased by 15 per cent. This gives a productivity gain of 21 per cent. During the same period, the number of white-collar workers increased by 21 per cent but real output only increased by 15 per cent, for a productivity loss of 6 per cent.[15] While measures of the effectiveness of this investment are fraught with difficulty it is widely accepted that this spend failed to realize the benefits which were promised in all but a few cases. Economists spoke of a *productivity paradox*. Many companies feel that their money simply disappeared into a 'black hole'.[16] This is particularly worrying as spending on IT now exceeds spending on other capital goods.[17] Yet the potential of IT to transform business is not in question; it is how to unlock that potential that is the question and BPR seems to be providing one answer.

One of the many reasons why IT had failed to deliver its potential is that it had been applied to old and existing ways of doing things. Rather than concentrate their attention on how work should be done, and then consider how technology might help with this, most companies sought merely to automate existing tasks so that efficiency savings could be gained. Nowhere was this more true than in the office where many of the so called 'office productivity' systems turned out to be just the opposite. Dreams of a 'paperless office' soon gave way to the realization that IT actually enabled the rapid generation of greater amounts of paper. Regardless of their value, reports were produced to ever more exacting standards. Wonderful drawings that took days, if not weeks, to create suddenly became a necessity if one was to get senior management 'buy-in' to the project. Because it was so easy to change documents and drawings, so they had to be changed to keep each and every layer of management happy. How many versions of documents are normal in your company – several per management layer is not uncommon. One company's executives were so startled when they found out how long it took to prepare reports for them, that they ordered that no more than three iterations could be worked on. But who was to say how many there had been? The executives had no idea how to really check and even if they had the creators could have got round the checks. In this company the only thing that changed was that the problem was sunk, hidden from view, with junior staff resenting more and more their unreported time being taken up with endless re-writes.

In the delivery of customer service, automation sometimes caused problems too. Automation of existing but wasteful tasks often locked those tasks into the process most firmly. They now had to be performed as required by the computer not the customer; while it was often recognized that a change to the process would be beneficial, all too often it was shelved as the required changes to the computer systems were too costly and time consuming. IT all too often became a cause of inflexibility rather than flexibility and organizations sought to understand why and how IT could be better exploited. Some organizations combined their efforts with academia and perhaps the best known study into this vexing problem was run at the Massachusetts Institute of Technology (MIT) called *Management in the 1990s*, running from 1984 to 1989 with some follow up work until 1991. The programme examined the impact that information technology was having on organizations of all kinds.[18] During this project, researchers such as Thomas Davenport, James Short and John Rockart[19] observed that successful organizations were using IT systems in ways which were more advanced than the traditional automation of clerical and operational tasks. Venkatraman[20] elaborated on these observations and identified five levels of what he referred to as IT-induced business transformation. Illustrated in Figure 2.1, these are explained below.

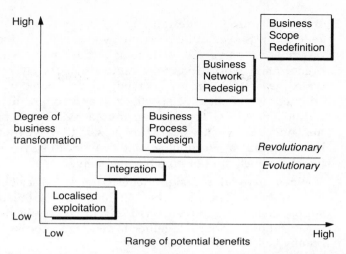

Source: From The Corporation of the 1990's: Information Technology and Organizational Transformation by Michael S. Scott Morton, editor. Copyright © 1991 by the Sloan
School of Management. Reprinted by permission of Oxford University Press, Inc.

Figure 2.1 The five levels of IT-induced business reconfiguration

Level 1: Localized exploitation The application of IT to different
parts of an organization in isolation from one another.
Using computers, often different types, to make the management of accounts, customer records and stock, more
efficient are examples of how IT has been exploited at a
local level.

Level 2: Internal integration As organizations matured in their use
of IT they recognized the need to link the 'islands of
automation' which had been formed through localized
exploitation, e.g. design and production systems were
integrated through the sharing of data.

Levels 1 and 2 are evolutionary in that they are a natural
development. It is likely that they will occur over a period of time
from the introduction of IT. Unfortunately, while some benefits
undoubtedly accrue at these stages they are not generally enabling
organizations to make the best use of IT. Levels 3, 4, and 5 are
revolutionary in that they start, not with the existing order and then
apply IT, but rather concentrate on the work and then identify IT
capability to support new ways of working.

Level 3: Business process redesign. The term business process redesign was used quite precisely by the MIT researchers to describe the use of IT to transform the way in which an organization works internally rather than simply to automate the way it already worked. In this book we have adopted a broader perspective. We recommend using technology where appropriate, thus a redesigned process may not entail the use of IT. Having said that, we must also bear in mind that technology allows work to be performed in ways which are not possible manually.

Level 4: Business network redesign. Redesign of processes between organizations. The likely benefit in terms of the overall supply chain's performance is likely to be greater through organizations working together to redesign processes than on any isolated firm in the chain.

Level 5: Business scope redefinition. Extending the scope of business that the organization operates in through the use of IT. New products/services to new or existing markets, or existing products/services to new markets are possibilities.

The ideas of BPR were further popularized by Michael Hammer in his seminal article 'Re-engineering work: don't automate – obliterate' which appeared in *Harvard Business Review* in 1990.[21] He warned against paving the cow paths with IT and suggested that organizations should rethink their business by capitalizing on the opportunities provided by the new information technologies. He re-enforced the message that before implementing IT, organizations should first ensure that the process is right. Hammer has been instrumental in promoting the message of BPR across the world and has done much to bring the topic to the attention of all levels of management up to the most senior levels in business and government.

Illustration 2.3 describes how IT has been used as a crucial enabler in simplifying the job of filing tax returns in the US.

Deciding on BPR

Is BPR right for you and your organization? Answering this question will depend on a number of factors and it is useful to use a framework such as that developed by Nolan Norton & Company.

Illustration 2.3 Re-engineering the tax collection process

Taxes are never good news. For US corporate taxpayers and state revenue departments, a new service promises to simplify the job of filing returns. The Federation of Tax Administrators, a nonprofit organization representing all 50 US states, has set up a new division, called TaxNet Government Communication Corporation to operate the service which will allow companies to electronically file most types of tax forms with participating states. The service is called TaxNet.

Before implementing the technology, the process by which firms and tax authorities interact was examined and a decision made to redesign this process. This change also required both bodies to redesign a number of their own internal operations to make the most benefit for the new streamlined operation. The new way of operating is illustrated below:

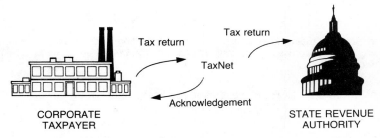

CORPORATE
TAXPAYER

STATE REVENUE
AUTHORITY

1. A company files its return through TaxNet and at the same time electronically authorises payment of taxes either as a credit through its bank to the state's bank or as a debit.

2. TaxNet sends an acknowledgement back to the company and passes the return to the state, as well as processes the debit or credit data with the state's bank.

3. The state accepts the return and processes the payment either by collecting on the debit or receiving the credit.

Combined, all the states receive approximately 325 million tax returns per year, giving the possibility of 3.6 billion transactions per year among banks, tax payers, and state revenue agencies. The advantages for participating states and companies include reduced costs associated with handling and mailing paper forms and reduced errors caused by re-keying information.

Source: Lynda Radosevich, 'States to plug in EDI', *Computer World*, 18 October 1993.

This framework, illustrated in Figure 2.2, plots the business need for re-engineering against the organizational readiness for change.

Positioning in a quadrant is a first-cut look at how to proceed. Quadrants I and II represent the Critical Zone, where a BPR effort needs to be launched as soon as possible. Quadrants III and IV

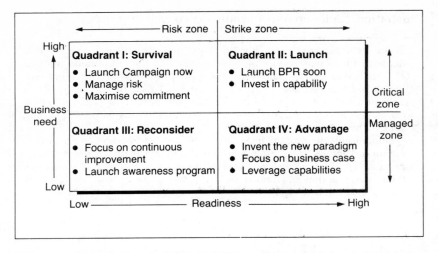

Source: Rocco W. Belmonte and Richard J. Murray, 'Getting ready for strategic change: surviving business process redesign,' *Information Systems Management*, Summer (1993) 23–29.

Figure 2.2   BPR business need/readiness analysis framework

represent the Managed Zone, where there is less urgency for business process redesign and any effort should in fact be approached carefully. Quadrants I and III represent the Risk Zone, where significant effort should be focused on preparation and managing risk. Quadrants II and IV represent the Strike Zone, where launching a BPR effort has a high probability of yielding strategic advantage.

- Quadrant I **Survival**: Indicates it is critical to improve business performance as soon as possible. Quadrant I endeavours are high risk and require maximum sponsorship commitment.

- Quadrant II **Launch**: Indicates it is critical to improve business performance. As it is only a moderate risk to engage in BPR, companies will benefit from investing in the development of BPR capabilities and launching an effort soon.

- Quadrant III **Reconsider**: Indicates the company is healthy and has a low need for dramatic improvement at this time. Companies in this quadrant also not well equipped for BPR. Such companies should reconsider launching BPR and instead focus on continuous improvement.

- Quadrant IV **Advantage**: Indicates that although there is no urgency for dramatic improvement, there would be a strategic advantage in undertaking a BPR initiative. Companies in this quadrant are prepared for BPR, but undertaking such an effort requires an aggressive vision that seeks to create new paradigms.

We find that where organizations have previously been engaged in quality initiatives there is a more ready acceptance of BPR. Some would see BPR as actually being an element of their wider quality programme, others as distinctly different. That does not mean that organizations who have not been engaged in quality programmes before cannot be successful in re-engineering, merely that they may have more preparatory work to do in initiating the programme and that the time taken before improvements are achieved may be longer.

Summary

The rise of BPR and the interest in processes stems from a number of different roots. Increased competition, deregulation, recession, the maturing of TQM and the disappointments of IT have all led to a search for ways to achieve step improvements in effectiveness, efficiency and adaptability. Processes, long ignored by management, have provided a common focus for many disciplines and the words 'business process re-engineering' have proved very popular. We believe the global competition element to be very important and a differentiating factor in this recession. Benchmarking has taken place on a scale never done before and has simply broken the assumptions of many companies. Previously, organizations shed labour in the bad times and took it on again in the good. During the leaner years it was accepted that many things would suffer due to poor manning. As companies peered deep into the operations of one another, and in particular at the Japanese, they realized this cycle was not necessary. By changing the processes through which they operated step improvements in efficiency could be made without a knock-on degradation in customer service. One consequence of this is that as the economies trundle out of recession, unemployment is not swinging upwards as it has previously done, further prolonging the uncertainty, price pressure and the need to re-engineer.

References

1. James C. Abegglen and George Stalk Jnr, *Kaisha: The Japanese Corporation*, New York: Basic Books, 1985.
2. Michael Porter, in his theory of national competitiveness, states that the competitiveness of the home market is one of the corner stones of national competitive advantage. See M.E. Porter, *The Competitive Advantage of Nations*, New York: The Free Press, 1990.
3. Simon Caulkin, *The New Manufacturing*, Economist Intelligence Report, 1989.
4. *The Independent*, 10 January 1994, p. 24.
5. Christopher Farrell, *Business Week*, 27 June 1994, quoting a recent report by McKinsey & Company.
6. For an interesting perspective on the subject see S. Roach, 'Services under siege: the restructuring imperative', *Harvard Business Review*, September–October (1991), 82–91.
7. Peter F. Drucker, 'The new productivity challenge', *Harvard Business Review*, November–December (1991), 69–79.
8. John Langan and Alison McIntosh, 'Investing in change', *Business Change & Re-engineering*, 1, no. 1 (1993), 22–27.
9. US Vice-President Al Gore, *National Performance Review*, 7 September, 1993.
10. The UK Government advisory agency CCTA recently produced a booklet entitled *BPR in the Public Sector: An Overview of Business Process Reengineering* (London: HMSO, 1994).
11. *Business Week*, 15 November 1993.
12. A survey undertaken at the Cranfield School of Management revealed that 84 per cent of all companies engaged in BPR also engaged in TQM and that only 6 per cent of companies doing BPR have no links with TQM. Fifty-six per cent of those engaged in both TQM and BPR treat them as the same or similar programmes. See Chris Edwards and Ian Preece, *A Survey of BPR Activity in the UK*, Working Paper, 1993, Information Systems Research Centre, Cranfield School of Management, Bedford MK43 0AL.
13. Cedric Williams, 'Business process re-engineering at Rank Xerox', *Business Change & Re-engineering*, 1, no. 1 (1993), 8–15.
14. 'The technology payoff', *Business Week*, 14 June 1993, pp. 37–45.
15. H. James Harrington, *Business Process Improvement: The Breakthrough Strategy for Total Quality Productivity and Competitiveness*, New York: McGraw-Hill, 1991.
16. For an interesting perspective on the view of senior managers see Kit Grindley, *IT in the Boardroom*, London: Pitman Publishing, 1991; and *Information Technology Review 1993/94*, London: Price Waterhouse, 1993.
17. 'The information technology revolution: how digital technology is changing the world', *Business Week*, 13 June 1994, p. 37.

18. For a review of the findings of this programme see *The Corporation of the 1990s: Information Technology and Organisational Transformation*, edited by Michael Scott Morton, New York: Oxford University Press, 1991.

19. Tom Davenport and James Short, 'The new industrial engineering: information technology and business process redesign', *Sloan Management Review*, Summer (1990), 11–27. Also, John Rockart and James Short, 'IT in the 1990s: managing organisational interdependencies', *Sloan Management Review*, Winter (1989), 7–17.

20. N. Venkatraman, 'IT-induced business reconfiguration', in *The Corporation of the 1990s: Information Technology and Organisational Transformation*, edited by M. Scott Morton, New York: Oxford University Press, 1991, 122–158.

21. Michael Hammer, 'Re-engineering work: don't automate — obliterate', *Harvard Business Review*, July–August (1990), 104–112.

Underlying principles

Processes
People
Technology

All organizations are built on three main pillars as shown in Figure P2: processes, people and technology. In designing a set of processes these three elements must be aligned to the needs of the market and the customers within it, and with each other. It is imperative that each of these three pillars is considered in turn. We start first with the processes of the firm which must be identified

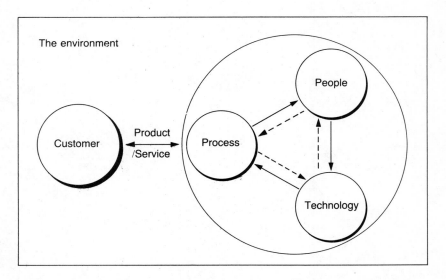

Figure P2 Organizational pillars: processes, people and technology

and designed. We then consider the people who will operate the processes. This stage is iterative: having considered the people it will be necessary to go back and review the processes and then return to people. People can only perform as well as the processes let them and similarly the processes can only perform to the level of the skill, knowledge and motivation of the people who operate them. The third element to consider is the technology to be used to support the processes and people. In technology we include the office and factory technology together with the buildings, the telecommunications and information technology of all types from roladex files to computers. In considering technology it will also be important to revisit the process and people designs as technological opportunities or constraints become apparent.

In the next three chapters we will focus on each of these three pillars in turn. In Chapter 3 we will look at the needs of the market and the product and service delivery processes which must satisfy those needs. In Chapter 4, we will go on to explore people and organizational issues. Chapter 5 will then examine the role of technology, specifically information technology, and how it is transforming the nature of work.

3

Product and service delivery processes

Customers are attracted by promises and retained through satisfaction. Marketing can deliver the promises but only the whole company can deliver satisfaction.

Philip Kotler[1]

Introduction

In this chapter we explore principles which have been adopted by both manufacturing and service organizations over many years. We focus first on the customer and the outcomes which are required from the process, before considering the basic decision areas in designing processes. The structure of the Chapter is outlined in Figure 3.1.

In Chapter 1 we outlined three main types of processes found in organizations, strategic, operational and enabling. We shall not attempt to cover the design or re-engineering of all three types of processes but instead shall focus on operational processes because these have been the main focus of BPR initiatives to date.

The service task

In designing a set of processes to deliver a product or service we must examine clearly the requirements of the market and the

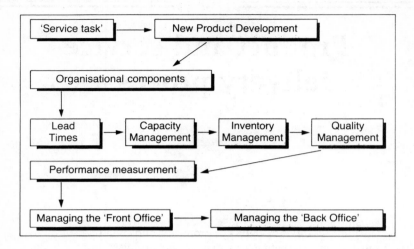

Figure 3.1   Chapter 3's structure

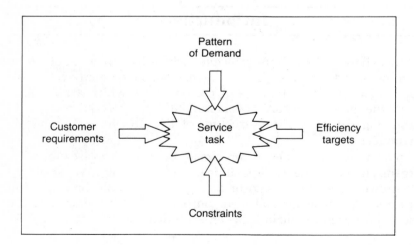

Figure 3.2   The service task

customers within it. However, the process design will be influenced by other factors as well. Overall, four key elements should be considered:

- Customer requirements.
- The pattern of demand.
- Constraints.
- Efficiency targets.

These four elements combine to set the 'deliverables' for a product or service delivery process and we shall refer to these combined requirements as the *service task* (Figure 3.2)[2].

Customer requirements

In designing any process it is important to first direct attention to the market and the customers in it: they, after all, buy the products and services. A number of questions can be asked: What do the customers want today? What will they want tomorrow? What extra things could you do for them which would truly delight them but which they may not, themselves, even have expressed as a need?

Understanding how to satisfy customers is not always as easy as it sounds. People do not always say what they want and many products have failed because researchers failed to understand what their customers really valued. Yet, before any process can be designed or redesigned, its purpose, that is the desired output or outcome, must be clearly understood. Organizations must become oriented to the needs of their customers and decide on what bases they are going to compete (in the public sector absolute levels and improvement targets for customer service as well as costs are now being set by regulators). They should then ensure that their processes, people and technology are aligned to deliver these outcomes and do so at the minimum possible cost.

In general, companies can compete on a range of bases which may be broadly categorized as:

- Quality.
- Flexibility.
- Delivery reliability.
- Speed.
- Price.
- Relationship management.

Quality

It is important to distinguish between two main aspects of quality:

- **Consistency** – How consistently the product or service conforms to what is expected (this can be its specification or from previous experience).

- **Capability** – How well the product or service actually fulfils the needs of the customer, e.g. How fast is it? How long will it last? How comprehensive is it? How is it perceived?

In thinking about what quality means in more detail we find Garvin's eight dimensions of quality the most useful for products.[3] These dimensions are described below using the example of a car:

1. **Performance**: the main operating characteristics of the product, e.g. top speed, fuel consumption, number of occupants who can be accommodated, etc.

2. **Features**: the secondary or supplementary characteristics of the product, e.g. colour range, safety features (increasingly becoming a key performance characteristic), stereo system, etc.

3. **Reliability**: the reliability or dependability of the product. Measurement of this is often of the probability of failure, e.g. the chances of the car failing in some way within the given period.

4. **Conformance**: How closely the product conforms to its specification, e.g. levels of safety and emissions, etc.

5. **Durability:** For how long can the product be used before it becomes prohibitively costly to keep it in use, e.g. the car's life-time.

6. **Serviceability**: How easily the product can be serviced in terms of speed and cost, e.g. on board diagnostics in many newer cars have significantly speeded up the servicing of the vehicle.

7. **Aesthetics**: How a product looks, sounds, feels, tastes or smells, e.g. the styling of the car.

8. **Perceived quality**: Many dimensions of quality cannot be neatly placed in the above categories, yet may be significant to the customer, often the image of the product, and its 'street cred' value will be important factors for a discerning purchaser.

While these dimensions are applicable to both manufactured products and services we prefer the dimensions used by Fitzgerald *et al.*[4] when describing service quality. These are described below with examples of each shown for a bank:

1. **Access**: how easily and pleasantly the customer gains access to the service, e.g. extent of telephone services and parking outside the branch for visits.

2. **Aesthetics / appearance**: how the service outlet appears to the customer, e.g. the branch decor and the tone of the staff on the telephone – are they professional?

3. **Availability**: is the service available when required? Automatic Teller Machines have made a huge impact on the availability of some banking functions – telephone banking has further enhanced availability.

4. **Cleanliness / tidiness**: how clean and tidy the facilities are. Banks typically portray a clean and tidy image, perhaps to reflect an image which makes people more comfortable at handing over their money for safekeeping.

5. **Comfort**: the level of comfort, both physical and mental in experiencing the service, e.g. how comfortable the bank manager makes you feel when asking for a loan!

6. **Communication**: how well the service provider communicates to the customer. This could be through the post, signs or through staff and covers the content of the communication and its style, e.g. how well the bank communicates, the queuing system to its customers and the range of products and services it offers.

7. **Competence**: how competent the service provider is to deliver the service, e.g. vital for a bank as few would leave their money with one they considered to be incompetent.

8. **Courtesy**: how courteous were the service providers. Everyone wishes to be treated with a basic level of 'common' courtesy, e.g. how well the bank staff treat the customers.

9. **Friendliness**: how friendly is the service. This, as do other dimensions, depends very much on the culture of the nation in which the service is being provided and increasingly world class service organizations are taking into account the nationality of the customer. Preferences change and while Americans may like a very friendly service, the French for example may prefer a more detached style.

10. **Reliability**: Is the service reliable, e.g. if the bank say they will

do something, such as forward a cheque book, do they do it, or do you have to chase them?

11. **Responsiveness**: how responsive is the organization to requests – one measure of this is how many non-standard requests are dealt with. This can be extended to include the level of management intervention required to effect this service. At a bank, for example, will they cater for your financial needs or do you have to fit your financial needs to their range of products and services?

12. **Security**: how secure and safe is the service and the service experience? Is your money safe with the bank and do you feel secure and safe when visiting the branch.

Many of these service quality dimensions are 'intangible' and difficult to measure, yet the effective management of them is nonetheless vital for high quality service delivery. Many organizations have both a service and a tangible product content to their offering and may have to consider both dimensions in parallel in order to really form a view of the critical competitive factors.

Flexibility

Flexibility can be applied in three main directions:

- **Design** – To what extent can each product or service be tailored to the requirements of each customer?
- **Volume** – To what extent can the volume of the product produced or the service delivered be adjusted and how quickly?
- **Variety** – To what extent can a variety, or mix, of products or services be offered and how quickly?

It is important that the market requirements for flexibility are well understood and efforts aimed at increasing an organization's adaptability be focused on to the correct direction. As organizations seek to understand their flexibility in each direction it is important to consider different dimensions:

- **Range** – to what extent can the organization respond, for example, can output be doubled?
- **Response** – the speed with which the organization can adapt, for example, how long does it take to double output?

- **Mobility** – How easily can the organization move across the range? What will be the effects of doubling output or changing the mix be on the customers and the organization's resources?
- **Uniformity** – How uniform or constant is performance across the range? As output is increased does quality deteriorate?

Delivery reliability

How reliable or dependable is the delivery of the product or service? The reliability of delivery is crucial in many industries. A ship waiting in dry dock for a part which never arrives is more serious to the customer than the non-arrival of a certain type of chocolate bar is to a retailer (providing other lines are available).

Financial dependability can be key to safeguarding delivery reliability over an extended period of time and the lack of this can result in lost orders.

Speed

Speed has become increasingly important as a basis of competition and can be thought of in two main ways:

- **Delivery lead time** – the time it takes for day to day operations to work, e.g. how long does it take to deliver the product or service to the customer? How long does it take to respond to a request for information, or to a complaint?
- **Development lead time** – the time it takes for tomorrow's products, services and processes to be developed and implemented, e.g. how long does it take to bring new products or services to the market place?

In the pharmaceutical industry it often takes 12 years or more before a compound identified in the research laboratory is developed commercially and results in a saleable product. Add to this the length of time to gain Federal Drug Administration (FDA) approval, often up to three years, and it does not leave much time before the patent expires and competitors can begin to sell rival products. One recent report estimated that reducing the time to market by one day could add one million dollars to the bottom line.

Price

Price should not be confused with cost. A company which has a lower cost base than its competitor can, all else being equal (which, of course, it rarely is), decide whether to lower its price and thus hope to gain market share, or operate at a higher margin. Thus, cost is a factor in considering a company's competitive advantage, but price is a mechanism by which it can compete and manage demand.

Relationship management

Relationship management is becoming increasingly important for competition today. We identify two main areas of relationship management:

- **Partnership** – Companies working in partnership can sustain a customer relationship longer and more profitably than those seeking only a straight contractual arrangement. (Customers and suppliers must be willing to take this approach. Increasingly, companies are selecting suppliers on their readiness to become partners and some even select customers on this basis.)
- **Learning** – Companies willing and able to learn from others, including suppliers, customers and others in different industries can ensure that they do not get complacent and can maintain their competitive edge.

Hygiene factors and order winners

In some markets, and to some customers, performance to very high standards on some criteria are required even to be considered as a potential supplier. In the car industry, for example, to supply Nissan, Toyota or Honda the levels of quality consistency must be very high, as must delivery reliability, and price also must be competitive, i.e. low. Perhaps more importantly the company must be prepared to work with the car companies to build a relationship over a long period of time. This often involves learning from them and implementing change based on the lessons they have learnt over many years. To supply Tesco, Marks & Spencer or Sainsbury, similarly high levels of quality and delivery reliability must be achieved. For companies in the defence industry, having a good product is just the start, while the ability to work with other defence companies and with client countries is the key to winning orders in the international arena. In other words some of these bases for competition are considered *hygiene* factors in some markets or by some customers.

Companies must recognize the hygiene factors in their markets and ensure that they perform up to expectation on these. They should not, however, waste time and effort in excelling in these areas in an attempt to woo customers. Customers will be won and retained by excelling in those factors that the customers seek added value from, not those that are merely 'market entry qualifications' as are hygiene factors. The things which attract customers to buy from one company rather than another, given that each satisfies the hygiene criteria, are called *competitive edge factors* and sometimes *order winning criteria*.[5] Competitive edge factors will change from one market to the next and it is vital that segmentation is done to identify them accurately. Segmentation involves breaking up the market you serve into a number of broad categories based on the needs of different customer groups. This can be done in a number of ways, depending on what makes sense for your business. It involves understanding what is bought, who buys it and why.

To understand hygiene factors, competitive edge factors and segmentation ask yourself what features a pub must have before you will even consider going there, and those features that actually make you decide to go to one, rather than to another. Have these things changed as you have got older and as your circumstances have changed?

The pattern of demand

The demand pattern for a product or service will play a significant part in determining the design and resource provision of the delivery system. It is not just the flexibility requirement of the process which will be determined by the pattern of demand: the very nature of the process will depend on it. Demand for very large volume product or services requires a different kind of process to products and services offered on a low volume basis. Essentially, low volume products or services can be delivered using a classic 'job shop' approach. The process requirements of each product or service are analysed at the time of order taking and scheduling. Higher volume demands a repetitive process design with the service or product being delivered through a standard, practised set of activities. We examine this 'match' of processes to demand later.

As well as absolute levels, we are also interested in the variability of demand. Demand can vary in a number of dimensions:

- Variety.
- Volume.
- Variation in the nature and level of demand.

Variety and volume

In examining variety and volume the notion of Runners, Repeaters and Strangers, as used by Lucas Engineering, is useful.

- **Runners** – are those products or services which the organization provides on a near continual basis. Often a pareto analysis of the products or services demanded in the greatest volume will reveal that 70–80 per cent of orders, or so, are accounted for by only 30–20 per cent of the range. Similarly, 70–80 per cent of the business may be accounted for by only 30–20 per cent of the customers. Processes to deliver the runners should be slick and the delivery without surprises. Repetition gives the opportunity for the process to be perfected over time.

- **Repeaters** – Are those products or services which are demanded reasonably frequently, but not constantly. In a similar way to runners, the volume and frequency of repeaters should allow the organization to perfect a set of processes which can be brought to life easily to deliver high quality at low cost. Often repeaters will be produced in batches by processes which deliver other 'repeating' products.

- **Strangers** – Sometimes customers demand something which is not a standard offering. These 'strangers' are a problem and should be minimized unless the organization specializes in bespoke products or services. They should not be delivered by the same processes that deliver the runners. Strangers are different to the runners and repeaters, and thus processes perfected for the latter categories will not work well with them. Many strangers require a project management approach rather than the activation of pre-determined or engineered processes and should be managed carefully.

Variation

Demand for some goods and services will vary in ways other than volume and variety. Seasonal demand fluctuations affect many industries from ice cream to umbrellas, but some products even have specific days on which demand peaks significantly. Guy Fawkes night on 5 November in the UK, Independence day on 4 July in the USA, and Bastille day on *Le quatorze juillet* in France all account for the majority of fireworks sales in each country. Christmas and Easter in the Christian world also see a significant rise in confectionery sales and, for the post offices, Christmas is a major headache with over 1½ billion items of mail being processed by the UK's Royal Mail during the run up to Christmas.

Managing demand

Fluctuations in demand can prove to be a major headache. There are a number of strategies, however, that organizations can adopt to manage the demand pattern for goods or service in order to make optimum use of the process:

- **Differential pricing** is a common way of manipulating demand. Lower prices for telephone calls in non-business hours means more effective use of the installed capacity which has to deal with the business traffic during the day.

- **Discounts** for early booking of seats on aircraft and for holidays are used to improve the forecasting of demand and thus the provision of capacity.

- **Promotions** are often used to raise demand levels during periods when it would otherwise be slack.

- **Appointments and reservations** are used by many organizations to set the level of demand and manage customer's expectations of service availability.

Constraints

Any constraints on the operation must be included in the service task. Constraints fall into several categories including:

- Government/legislative/regulatory.
- Company policy.
- Financial constraints.

Government or legislative constraints will cover everything from health and safety and the environment to the provision of advice on financial matters. Designing any operational process must of course take these into account. Company policy will further dictate constraints on the process such as the need in many companies to obtain a written customer order before service can commence. In some areas, company policies often go further than legal requirements and some companies, such as the fast growing South West Airlines, even have a policy that work should be fun![6] Financial constraints may be imposed on the process either through company policy or because banks have put certain conditions on loan agreements.

One of the biggest constraints on process design can be 'the way things are done in this organization'. Many processes end up with 'features' which are there purely to satisfy the organization itself and this is a prime target for BPR programmes.

Efficiency targets

All organizations have efficiency targets, though some are, of necessity, more aggressive than others. These efficiency targets will impact the amount and type of resources that can be utilized by the process, including people, machines, computers, facilities, financial resources, and so on. These targets will inevitably affect the design of the process. Many companies use these efficiency targets to bring out innovative low-cost answers to problems. This is particularly true when considering people and technology where companies are asking their managers how they would operate with significantly fewer staff and without large computer systems projects to facilitate the operation.

The four areas of the service task should be examined and the impacts for the organization understood and clearly communicated. The people tasked with the design of the products, services, and the processes to deliver them in particular should have a clear understanding of the task's dimensions.

New product development

Having identified the requirements of the market and other factors impacting the 'service task' the product or service must be designed to fulfil them, if none already exist. Shorter life cycles brought on by increasingly intense competition and greater government controls, especially on the environment and health, have focused much attention on the process of new product and service development. Following the example set in Japan, many companies are now switching to a philosophy of new product development known as *concurrent engineering* (CE) in the USA or *simultaneous engineering* (SE) in the UK, which were briefly outlined in Chapter 1. CE/SE tie the processes of developing new products and of developing new production or delivery systems together. Instead of sequential stages both are performed in parallel. Products are designed to be made, often called design-for-lifecycle whereby the production, distribution and eventual destruction of the product is considered as well as meeting customer needs. The result of this activity, if done correctly, is significantly reduced lead times from concept to customer, and a leap in quality performance. As many quality problems arise from designs which are difficult to make, a product which is designed to be made eliminates the causes of much quality failure.

One telecommunications company uses a simple rule of thumb to illustrate how important it is to get the design of something right first time, that is at the design stage, and not have to 'fix' design problems later. It has a ten stage process for delivering software. If the cost of correcting a fault in the first stage is 1, this cost rises to 10 if the fault is not corrected until the second stage. The cost rises to 100 if the fault is put right in stage 3 and so on. By stage 10, this stage 1 fault costs 1 000 000 000 times more than putting it right in stage 1! Sounds far fetched? Then consider this; in 1990, ten million people's phones were disabled for a period of time in the USA due to three faulty lines of code in a programme of two million instructions.[7] We do not know at what stage in the software development the fault was created, but the costs associated with it are clearly significantly higher than if it had been fixed during the stage of development in which it was created.

Figure 3.3 illustrates the costs incurred in a typical manufacturing operation from design through to final production. It clearly illustrates that any changes made as the product gets nearer to production incur significant penalty.

Manufactured products are an obvious example where the constraints of the production system can only be changed over time. As major new products are introduced, investment in processes may modernize certain areas but it is rare that totally new facilities are built. Getting the most out of existing production process investment, then, is usually the challenge for the designer and the process engineer. Often this can be achieved without any serious degradation in the product's customer appeal, once the ingenuity of the engineers is motivated to find a solution. There is often a 'culture clash' between designers and producers as each accept and adapt to their new roles and it is important that management set a good example and praise early successes which can provide the basis for a powerful new team spirit.

Services must also be designed to be delivered. In an age where millions of pounds worth of IT may provide a constraint on the system's delivery capability, designing the 'offer' to the customer will depend on a mix of researched requirements and organizational ability. By understanding the delivery channel better, new services can be added which build on the existing systems' capabilities and do not require effort in areas of weakness, at least in the short term. To help achieve this, the use of what Richard Heygate calls 'filters' between new systems and old has been successfully used in both telecommunications and financial companies.[8]

Over the medium and long term there are no constraints in the

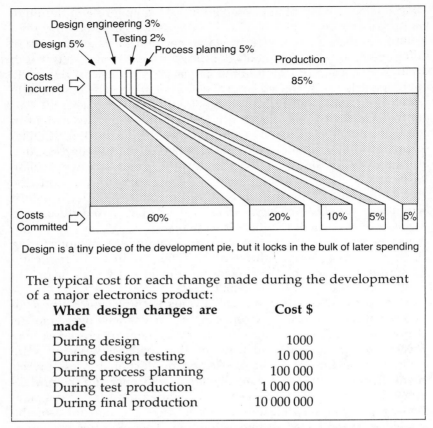

Design is a tiny piece of the development pie, but it locks in the bulk of later spending

The typical cost for each change made during the development of a major electronics product:

When design changes are made	Cost $
During design	1000
During design testing	10 000
During process planning	100 000
During test production	1 000 000
During final production	10 000 000

Source: Dataquest data, presented in *Business Week*, 30 April 1990, p. 64.

Figure 3.3   Focusing on the correct cost drivers

existing production and delivery systems which cannot be changed. Professionals from all areas, not just marketing, should work together to ensure that the company is able to utilize advances in all areas in its mission to serve the markets of tomorrow.

Product variety
In attempting to attract and retain the increasingly illusive and discerning customer, companies are tying to offer highly customized products or services. The strategy of *mass customization* has recently been adopted by a small number of successful companies.[9] At the

same time, organizations are recognizing the downside of product variety and are seeking to reduce the amount of variety they have to manage.[10] Ideally a 'standard' item can be assembled and a differentiating part fitted as the last stage in the process to give the desired market-place variety. The most famous example of this approach is the Swatch watch approach. Car companies have greatly reduced the final product range that they offer to customers, particularly by reducing the range of 'options' which can be specified. Rationalization programmes of this type are finding some surprising levels of variety. Nissan found it had 80 different designs of steering wheel in its *Laurel Sedan*, which it has now reduced to 10.[11]

New product development goals

At the start of any new product or service development two main goals should be specified:

- Product or service requirements as defined by marketing and design professionals
- Process requirements as defined by those charged with the production or delivery of the product or service.

Neither of these can be specified in isolation from the other with any chance of success. Co-operation and teamwork to design products or services and processes together is the key to real competitive advantage.

Components of an organization

It is helpful at this point to take a high level view of the delivery processes running through the organizations. Most can be divided into two distinct elements as shown in Figure 3.4: the front-office and the back-office, also known as the front-room and back-room. While re-engineering and other improvement programmes have changed the perception of how these two parts of an operational system work and interact, they still exist, and it is important to recognize their differences in design and management.

The front-office

The customer and the organization 'encounter' each other in the front-office. It should not be thought of as a physical office or shop,

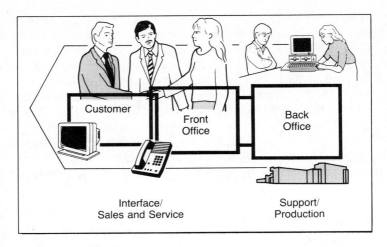

Figure 3.4 Components of an organization

although there may well be a building of some sort where customers visit. 'Encounters' happen wherever the organization and the customers connect. This may be through people or technology. Sales people, telephones and ATMs are all examples of channels for a service encounter. Service personnel maintaining or repairing equipment in customer premises are just as much a part of the front office as the sales personnel in a shop.

In service organizations the front-office will often be the larger of the two elements, while in manufacturing companies it can be the smallest. Whatever the nature of your business running the front-office is different to running the back-office. Whether customer contact is by phone, in their office or in an office belonging to the organization the key ingredients are the customers themselves and the staff who service them. Supporting processes and systems should focus on enhancing the ability of both the customer and staff to achieve a satisfactory exchange.

The back office

The back office is effectively the delivery and support service to the front office. That is not to say it is less important. Neither 'office' can function without the other. In the back office the key ingredients are the schedule or demand information, any necessary materials to produce the required product or execute the service, and the people to ensure that the product is produced or the service is carried out.

Traditionally the back office has been thought of as distant from the customer, 'buffered' from the outside world. This is no longer true and both offices must recognize the role of the back-office.

Front-office/back-office linkage
It is essential that the linkage between the customer and the front-office and in turn the front-office and the back-office are smooth and effective. Where possible the link between the front-office and the back-office should be transparent to the customer. Apart from the more exclusive marques such as Aston Martin, for example, customers may not wish to see their car being made. The customer is also not very interested in any problems between the car dealer, or for that matter the car company's sales force, and the car manufacturing plant. They just want timely delivery of the car they ordered in such a way that it is a pleasant experience; the people are friendly and helpful, the car is clean when delivered and there are no 'nasty surprises'. To effect such a delivery, the supply chain from the dealer to the car maker and within the car maker between sales and manufacturing must be effective. This cycle is not always just a standard process either. As problems arise, they must be dealt with speedily, the customer satisfied and thus retained. It is much more expensive to win a new customer over to your product and service than attract a new one. The figure that is often quoted is that it is five times more expensive to win over a new customer, than to retain an existing one.

There are a number of considerations which are common to all parts of the operational system. These are:

- **Lead times** through the process – how long does it take to fulfil the order?
- **Capacity management** – is there sufficient, yet not excessive, resources?
- **Inventory management** – where should stocks be placed through the process?
- **Quality management** – how should quality be managed throughout?
- **Performance measurement** – how is the process performing and how can it be improved?

We shall examine these areas before focusing in more detail on the front-office and back-office.

Lead time

A principal driver of the process design will be the customer delivery lead time. The complexity, cost and production lead time of the product or service will govern whether the company waits for an order before commencing production or produces stocks to satisfy demand which it forecasts. Broadly there are three choices of operational systems to deliver a product or service:

- **Make for stock/provide for use** – where products or services are produced before they are demanded it is known as 'make for stock' manufacturing. There is no generally recognized equivalent term for services although we call them 'provide for use' services. Examples of the types of products which are made for stock include fireworks, ice creams, many food products, spares for consumer goods, etc.

   In services the concept is a little more complicated. Some services are provided on a near permanent basis, based on forecasts of demand. Services cannot be stored, however, the nature of the service may not allow providers to wait until a firm order is known to schedule delivery. Airline seats, electricity, and hospital beds are examples of provide for use services. Other services are less perishable and a charge is only made when used; some information-providing services, such as the French Minitel system and or Harvest company information database from Dun & Bradstreet, would qualify under this category, though every minute they are not used to full capacity represents potentially lost revenue depending on the supply agreement.

   Making to stock becomes important when availability is a key pre-condition of sale. If a shop does not have any Mars^{TM} bars for example the customer is likely to buy an alternative bar. Ex-stock availability is where the item is available to the customer directly from stock. Companies manage the inventories of stock based on the customer service level they wish to achieve, that is, the amount of requests they wish to satisfy balanced against the cost of holding stock, or a buy instruction being issued to a broker.

- **Make to order/Perform to order** – many products and services are only produced when ordered. Examples include, specific market research, bespoke information systems developments, machine tools, tailored clothes, large construction projects etc. Making goods or producing services in response to a customer order requires greater time than satisfying the demand from stock. Reducing this lead time is a major concern of many companies operating this type of system. For services, the term 'perform to order' may be more apt to describe this mode of operation, for instance, a service call to correct a fault with a product, or, a buy instruction being issued to a broker.

- **Assemble to order** – can be considered a cross between make for stock and make to order. Assembly to order allows a company to reduce the lead time required to deliver the product and also reduces the variety of goods which would otherwise have to be held in stock. Components are made and held in stock ready for assembly when an order is received. Many Personal Computers are assembled to order from a selection of disk drives, chips and assorted peripherals which are held in stock. Some services operate in a similar fashion with pre-prepared material being combined to meet the needs of a particular client. Restaurants are an example where the basic ingredients are held and then either thrown together or combined according to a careful recipe depending on the nature of the establishment.

The approach adopted, and thus the lead time to satisfy customer demand will depend on the exact nature of the product or service and the market requirements. Clearly make to stock provides for the shortest lead time to meet demand. Management attention in this instance is on the lead time to replenish stocks through the supply chain. Minimizing this time will help reduce the levels of inventory which must be held. For the other alternatives it is important that all steps in the delivery process have the minimum possible lead time. In an assemble to order operation, for example, the lead time to take and process the order and ship the product should be minimized, as should the production lead time itself. Just because it is not possible to meet demand off-the-shelf does not mean it is acceptable to take a long time.

Capacity management

Matching supply and demand in operations is crucial for success in the service task and in meeting required lead times. Failure to produce this match results in either higher costs, where there is over-capacity, or reduced service quality, longer lead times and lost business where capacity is insufficient. In operations terms, demand and supply are often known as load and capacity:

- **Load** is the demand placed on an operational system, or the demand that is already committed to the system. Typically, organizations will have an order book or schedule of contracts which represents the demand which they are already committed to satisfying. Load is described in terms of volume (e.g. n units) for a particular good or service.

- **Capacity** is the ability of the operational system to deal with demand, or, the ability to work off load. Capacity is described as a rate (e.g. y units per day). Often an operational unit will have a theoretical or potential capacity and an actual or effective capacity. The effective capacity should always be used for planning purposes as the theoretical capacity suffers from 'leakages' such as staff absence, machine downtime, different skill levels and so on.

- **Output** is the actual rate at which load is being processed. If the company is fully loaded then output will be the same as effective capacity.

In managing capacity, three generic strategies are often applied:

- **Level** – whereby the operation maintains its output at a constant rate and uses stocks and manipulation of demand to balance the load on the system. This strategy is used most often when the resources delivering the added value are expensive or inflexible and their use needs to be maximized in order to reduce costs. The doctors' surgery is an example of a level strategy where the patients queue up to see the doctor and additional doctors are very rarely on standby to help if it gets busy.

- **Chase** – where capacity is variable to meet changes in demand. This strategy is used where capacity resources are flexible and relatively inexpensive. Customer service levels are delivered more consistently in chase strategies within the predicted demand levels. Organizations can manage the supply of people resources in chase strategies with flexible working hours and annual hours contracts.

- **Coping** – One way of managing supply and demand is to 'cope' with it.[12] Every organization reaches a stage of coping at some point. It happens where demand exceeds capacity and those delivering the product or service simply have to cope with the situation. Overloading processes has a detrimental effect on performance and if the strategy for dealing with this situation is not thought through it will be even more damaging. The key to coping is to understand what the system must deliver as a priority and where it can fail with the least effect. Typically safety, above all else, must not be allowed to suffer. Then what should be a priority? Organizations that have thought this event through, know what can go wrong and plan for it to happen, go on to deal with such situations much better than those who do not. A blinding glimpse of the obvious perhaps, but how good are your plans to cope with demand exceeding capacity?

In many situations, a combination of all three strategies is used. Telephone call centres often have to use a number of the above strategies. In the insurance industry a sudden storm, or high winds, can suddenly cause a huge surge in the number of calls being taken and thus careful planning has to be undertaken to avoid a prolonged period where the number of staff is inadequate. Ice cream and chocolate manufacturers operate at a particular level above demand for some periods of the year, thereby building up stocks. They then raise the level of production in peak periods but are unable to raise it high enough to satisfy demand and rely on the stocks built up during the other periods to meet this demand.

During this and the previous section we have discussed the way stocks can be used to manage lead times and capacity. Let us now take a closer look at this area and examine inventory management.

Inventory management

Stocks, usually referred to as inventories in operations management, can be stored throughout the supply chain. Inventories can be used to raise customer service levels, safeguard operations against disruptions in supply, enhance flexibility and take advantage of bulk discounts. The disadvantages are that they: are costly, both in opportunity costs and in administration and handling; slow the progress of material through the system (in some cases material can be obsolescent by the time it gets through the system); and hide many problems in the operation by enabling production to continue when it would otherwise stop. The levels of inventories will be determined by the design of the operational delivery system and by fluctuations in demand and supply, i.e. some level of stock will be purposefully designed into the process and some will occur due to problems inherent in the process. Paperwork can, in many situations, be thought of as inventory and, increasingly, services are taking this view and managing it accordingly. The main types of stock can be categorized as follows:

- **Raw Materials Stock** (RMS) – usually held to safeguard against disruptions in supply; to cope with changes in demand which might then require a different range of products to be produced; and sometimes to take advantage of special offers or bulk discounts. This is a prime area for inventory reduction programmes, yet some raw materials stock is inevitable in all but the most integrated geographical sites. Some spare parts may be thought of as RMS where they have to be worked on prior to replacing existing parts.

- **Work in Process** (or work in progress, WIP) – without WIP there would be no production and while many improvement programmes preach stockless production or zero inventories we prefer the term used by Colin New of Just Enough Desirable Inventory, or JEDI, as it recognizes the need for stocks yet includes the desire that they should, generally, be minimized.[13] WIP can be used to increase scheduling flexibility by providing choices for processing. In job shop manufacturing output is likely to rise, up to a point, as WIP increases, though both the manufacturing lead time and its predictability are adversely affected. It should be noted that the lower the WIP, the faster the throughput time in production. For example:

Batch size/WIP	100	200
Time to process	1 minute	1 minute
Throughput time	100 minutes	200 minutes

- **Finished Goods Stock** (FGS) – held to cope with fluctuations in demand, guard against disruptions in supply, and to meet customer demand 'off the shelf'. In a recession these are usually built up as manufacturers cut capacity only reluctantly and thus production levels are maintained for a period, despite a drop in demand. In meeting demand off the shelf, stock levels will be governed by the targeted customer service level, usually known as *first pick availability*, that is, the proportion of customer orders which are available at the time they are required. Other things being equal, the larger the inventory, the higher the service level. A 99 per cent service level, for example, would mean that 99 per cent of customers on average would be satisfied out of every 100. The cost of raising the service level, however, rises exponentially and increasing the service level from 90 per cent to 99 per cent requires twice the amount of stock. Services also use this technique. Banks, for example, employ statistical and probability algorithms to determine how much cash to hold in branches. Spare parts can also be thought of as FGS.

Stock replenishment is managed in a number of ways.

● **Re-order period** – where a new order is placed at a specific period of time with the order quantity dependent on the current level of stocks

● **Re-order level** – where new stock is only ordered when its level falls to, or below, a pre-determined level, with the order quantity being fixed in advance

These approaches are outlined in Figure 3.5.

● **Material Requirements Planning** (MRP) – is concerned with the time-phased determination of stock requirements based on a disaggregation of a finished product into its component parts. As a starting point, the *Master Production Schedule* (MPS), i.e. the set of orders which are to be produced by the production system in a particular sequence, must be determined. MRP, usually carried out by computer, breaks the MPS down product by product to the components and materials required. The system does this by examining the product's *bill of material* which contains details of the product's structure, components required and quantities. Based on the required components the system works out how much should be ordered, and when, for each component based on lead times and existing stock levels to fulfil a particular set of orders. This technique is used in services as well as manufacturing. Airlines, for example, use MRP techniques to schedule parts for the maintenance of aircraft to gain lower levels of stock while minimizing the time aircraft are not available due to servicing. MRPII, or Manufacturing Resource Planning, takes this concept further and evaluates the MPS for

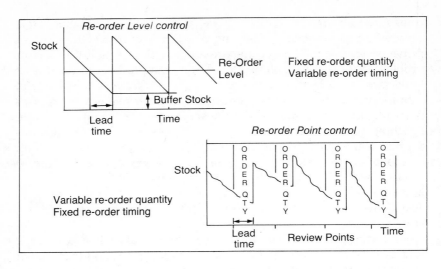

Figure 3.5   Re-order level and re-order point stock control

feasibility within resource capacity constraints. Such systems can be used to model alternative MPS's and evaluate the required range of resources in the future. MRPII also extends to shop floor control, though this is rarely used.

The positioning of the inventory is also key. It is no good an organization having the required form, part or product in stock if it is in the wrong place and there are no processes to move it speedily to the point at which it is required.

Logistics and the supply chain

An important area for all operations to consider is that of logistics. How can the operation best get the required inputs to where they are needed and any finished goods or passengers to the required location. Logistics covers all aspects of the storage and movement of people and materials between countries, sites and within sites. For the manufacturing industry, the task centres mainly on the movement and management of inventories. Raw materials, components and capital goods must all be delivered to the operation so that smooth production can be enabled at minimum cost. Movement around the plant must be managed as well as the distribution of finished goods. For many service industries the location of service parts or the necessary equipment to provide the service is a major consideration. In the City of London, for example, the siting of office equipment spares to provide high levels of responsiveness can prove costly given the cost of land and buildings. To get round this problem companies employ novel methods such as roving warehouses (i.e vans) or store components with small shops.

Smooth and speedy flow is desired at all levels in a logistics network from the point of departure to final destination. Material handling technology, packaging, container design and information capture (often through bar codes) are all essential elements in the movement of materials in-plant and between plants.

Virtual inventory
The holding of inventories used to be managed on an individual storage location level. Often the performance of each stock point would be managed independently of the others – the net result – a lot of stock as each manager sought to achieve the best customer service levels for their own 'operations'. Virtual inventory is a philosophy which has come into its own with information technology. The total inventory of the organization is managed as if it were in a single large warehouse even though it physically resides in a number of geographically dispersed sites. Although the cost of moving some inventory considerably longer distances may have to be borne, the savings overall are claimed to be significant.

Major decision areas centre on who should be responsible for the logistics network at which points. Should an organization outsource the management of its distribution and warehousing operation or is it a source of competitive advantage?

Quality management

Total Quality (TQ)

Total Quality, sometimes called Total Quality Management (TQM), Total Quality Control (TQC), or Total Quality Excellence (TQE) is popular. It has become a priority for many organizations as a means to:

- Improve customer service.
- Reduce costs.

There are many excellent books on quality and we do not intend to cover all aspects of this vast subject here.[14] This section is intended merely to raise awareness of the types of issues to be considered in managing quality through a process and build on the different perspectives of product and service quality discussed earlier.

The cost of quality

Organizations are increasingly estimating their cost of quality in order to provide a deeper understanding of their business and how it can be improved. These costs can be categorized as follows:

1. The cost of **failure** which comprises the costs arising from:
    *   **Scrap and rework** – where products and services have to be worked on for a second time to put right the mistakes made when they were first produced or provided.
    *   **Warranty claims** – where the product or service provided fails to live up to the promises made for it and customers claim recompense through the warranty system which costs money to administer.
    *   **Customer complaints** – when customers complain they consume staff time and resources. The best an organization can hope for is to recover from the failure to the extent that the customer walks away impressed with the organization. Some research would indicate that companies who effectively recover failure situations, can raise the intention of the customer to re-purchase to nearly the same level as if nothing had gone wrong.[15] One very awkward feature of complaints is that only very few customers actually complain, especially in the UK. However, they may go on to tell others, possibly up to ten other people, how bad they found the service. For every complaint received there are probably about a dozen similarly dissatisfied customers who are unlikely to come again and may be telling their friends why.
    *   **Loss of customer goodwill** – where a customer becomes disillusioned with the organization and may be inclined to purchase from a rival in future. It is much cheaper for organizations to retain existing customers than to attract new ones and this side of failure is now seen as a major issue.

2. The cost of **appraisal**
    *   **Inspection** – the costs associated with inspecting the goods to identify their quality levels. Typically this activity ties up staff resources and other costs.
    *   **Measurement** – the costs of actually measuring the quality levels throughout an operation. Typically this is a difficult

thing to do, particularly in a service environment where much of the quality is for intangible things.

- **Testing** – the costs of testing products or services which involves consuming them, sometimes to the point of destruction.

3. The cost of **prevention**

- **Training** – the costs of training employees in the importance of, and techniques of, quality control and management.
- Up front **design** work, which might be perceived as more expensive than that currently done, though, if undertaken correctly, the cost of the product through its life will be reduced by eliminating the causes of failure and thus reducing warranty claims, etc.

4. The psychological or **hassle factor**

Often the most difficult cost to measure is the detrimental effect low quality and its attendant problems can have on staff. Low morale and stressed staff are conditions which are likely to adversely affect service quality.

British Standard BS6143 details the cost of quality as defined by the first three categories above. The estimate of the cost of quality failure usually provides a powerful incentive for companies to improve their performance.

Over the last few decades the view on quality versus other operational objectives has changed. At one time the achievement of high quality was believed to be possible only at the cost of reducing speed and productivity. The experiences of some Japanese and US businesses, though, have proven otherwise. Today, most companies see quality consistency improvement as a way of improving productivity, dependability, speed and flexibility, which in turn may allow the production of more capable goods at lower cost. The European Foundation for Quality's annual awards cover a number of areas in their assessment of an organization's success in quality and apportion the overall marks to these areas as shown in Figure 3.6, including processes and business results.[16]

Quality systems

Many quality systems exist which detail the activities an organization undertakes to provide a basis for improvement. Many manufacturers specify their own quality systems which their suppliers

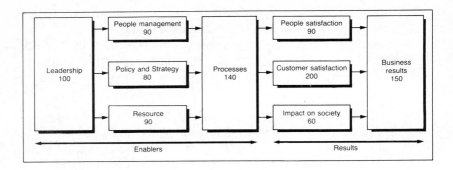

Figure 3.6 European Foundation for Quality Award Criteria

must satisfy in order to become a 'preferred' supplier and possibly to be a supplier at all. The Ford Q1 standard, for example, is awarded to companies who conform to the exacting requirements of the standard covering all aspects of their operations. In the USA, Motorola takes a slightly different approach insisting that its suppliers apply for the Baldridge national quality award.[17] In the last few years a standard for quality systems has begun to take on increased importance as governments and private businesses the world over specify it instead of their own standards. The International Standards Organization details ISO9000 as the international standard governing the operation of a company's quality system.

A quality system is a set of policies, standards and procedures by which a company controls and monitors its operation and the quality of its output. Achieving ISO9000 registration does not in itself improve the quality of the output of a company, but does provide the measurement mechanism necessary to evaluate it. There are a number of standards, 9001, 9002, 9003 and 9004, covering different types of manufacturing and service businesses. The number of companies registered or seeking registration has grown enormously in recent years although there is currently much controversy about the benefits and costs of this standard in the UK, where it is covered by the British Standard BS5750, and increasingly in other parts of Europe (EN29000). For existing companies wishing to register for ISO9000 we would advise them to re-engineer their processes first and avoid the drain of having to generate the procedures and documentation on processes which are about to change. Some companies however do find that ISO9000 acts as an incentive and a driver for change and improvement through the organization.

Statistical Process Control (SPC)

Statistical Process Control puts the emphasis on the process, rather than on the product and its main role is to provide feedback on a process's operating condition, thereby allowing any errors in the process to be eliminated. It was first used to a significant extent by the USA during World War II to improve the quality of the war material delivered to its troops. After the war SPC's use dwindled in the West and it was in Japan that it found supporters before being repatriated back to the USA. SPC involves the monitoring of process characteristics critical to the production of quality products. Products and services are often monitored too, using *samples* to check that the process is operating as it should. This monitoring takes many forms from paper charts plotted by the workers responsible for that part of the process to sophisticated on-line computer systems which not only monitor and provide information but often directly control the process.

SPC is a powerful tool to ensure quality consistency is high and many firms have used it to significantly improve their performance in this area, training a large number of production workers in these techniques who can then take genuine responsibility for the quality of their output. Screens or boards showing the numbers of products produced have been common in plants for many years but SPC charts provide some of the information to make sure that this output is good output.

A key element of quality management is measurement. This should be done on all critical aspects of product or service production and delivery. Results should be analysed and then acted on. Remember it is the **process** that is likely to be at fault, not the people.

Performance measurement

All organizations aim to be highly *effective*, i.e. satisfy and delight its customers, *efficient*, i.e. do so at minimum cost; and *adaptable*, i.e. ensure that they can be effective and efficient in response to changing market needs. While effectiveness is about 'doing the right things' and efficiency is about 'doing things right', ideally a company should be 'doing the right things, right'. It is most crucial to be effective, but efficiency too is important. Two companies competing equally well in customer terms, that is, with the same level of effectiveness, will make different profits depending on their

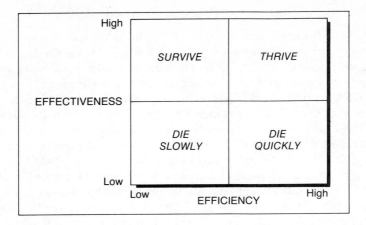

Figure 3.7 Effectiveness/efficiency matrix (after Drucker[18])

costs of operating, that is, their efficiency. The company with the lower cost base can choose to enjoy higher profits and thus have better opportunities for investment, or it may opt to lower its price, thus gaining market share at the expense of its competitor or forcing its competitor to cut prices and operate at a lower margin.

The effectiveness/efficiency matrix, illustrated in Figure 3.7, demonstrates the expected results of company performance when measured in terms of efficiency and effectiveness.[18] Companies which are highly efficient yet poor in terms of effectiveness are the first to die in the market place; they simply have no fat to lose as a means of delaying death.

Measuring your performance is key to being effective and efficient. If you are not measuring you are not managing.

Measures and targets

Performance measurements should provide a basis for understanding what is happening within an organization and provide a means to focus efforts on certain factors or areas for improvement in effectiveness, efficiency and adaptability. Targets are an important element in motivating performance and improvement efforts. They should emphasize the need to continuously improve and innovate, and thus annual improvement targets should accompany any absolute measures. It is also important to understand the impact of efficiency targets on other targets for the system such as quality levels. Reducing staff costs in a shop, for example, may result in a drop in customer service as there is insufficient staff to deal with the volume of customers. In this situation some customers may get fed up and take their business elsewhere. The problem will then be perceived as fixed: however, the resulting profit reduction will trigger further cuts and so on, possibly resulting in the closure of the shop.

Everything that happens through a process can be placed in one of two categories – it is either:

- **Value adding.**
- **Non-value adding.**

This simple distinction is often forgotten as new steps are added to a process over time. Clearly an organization wants to focus all of its resources on value-adding activity. It should also seek to perform this value-adding activity as efficiently as possible. For operational processes value adding can be expressed in terms of what customers are prepared to pay or other agencies, such as government, are prepared to fund. By this definition some tasks may be classified as non-value adding yet be justified on economic grounds. Consumers are not usually concerned in the short term, for example, whether a company checks their credit worthiness and yet this may be vitally important in minimizing the financial risk to the firm. Having said this it is important, nonetheless, to recognize that they do not add customer value and such steps should be minimized. For a strategic and enabling process the determination of value-added is less easy but equally necessary; the contribution of each step to the overall process outcomes must be assessed. In designing any new process the organization should attempt to ensure that its value adding activities are performed efficiently and that the process has a minimum of non-value adding activities. A useful measure to be applied in designing a process to monitor its performance is that of throughput efficiency.

Throughput efficiency
Throughput efficiency is a key indicator of an organization's value adding efficiency and is defined as:

$$\text{Throughput efficiency} = \frac{\text{Work content time}}{\text{Total time in system}} \times 100\%$$

While it does not tell us whether or not the value-adding stages are being performed efficiently it does tell us how much of the time is definitely not contributing to the goals of the process. As an example of measuring throughput efficiency and what it indicates, consider the progress of a simple purchase order from the manager in a department to the supplier:`

Action	Time of action	Transit/wait time
Complete purchase order form	10 minutes	
Send to senior manager for signature		1 day
Senior manager signs form	1 minute	
Sends form to finance control		1 day
Finance book spend and sign order	3 minutes	
Sends form to purchasing		1 day
Buyer reviews order form	5 minutes	
Buyer issues order to supplier		1 day
Total times	19 minutes	4 days

$$\text{Throughput efficiency} = \frac{19 \text{ minutes}}{4 \times 8 \times 60 + 12 \text{ (an 8 hour day)}} \times 100\%$$

$$= \frac{19}{1932} \times 100\%$$

$$= 1\% \text{ approximately}$$

In other words 99 per cent of the time that the purchase order spent in the system it is not being worked on. No value is being added! This example is not far-fetched – how many days does it take your organization to process a purchase order on average? How much of that time is spent sitting in in-trays?

Throughput efficiency is one of a number of important measures for a process. A common metric in traditional manufacturing industry is output volume per person. This measures not just the volume of 'good' products produced, but all products including failures. Clearly this measure could give a very misleading impression of the operation's productivity. Producing just one perfect product, however, is also not good enough for most industries, were it even possible, and there must be a balance between quality and productivity. Quality consistency must be continually improved and there is no trade-off in the medium to long term between this and productivity. For quality capability, however, there is a trade-off. Over-engineered products exist in every industry and companies can have a real problem in getting proud workers to achieve the appropriate quality level, without destroying their motivation, and thus ability, to keep quality consistency high. 'Rolls-Roycing' of a product is a term often used to describe this phenomenon in the UK.

Many companies recognize the weaknesses of their existing performance measurement systems and are searching for new ways to measure, and thus improve, performance.[19] In particular, utilization measures should be used with great care. Maximizing utilization, either of human or other resources, is another favourite target, however if this utilization is not directed at immediate customer needs it can result in excessive, and costly, inventories being built up.

Constructing a performance measurement system

Kaplan and Norton detail one technique for constructing a set of performance measures, known as the 'balanced scorecard'.[20] They argue that financial measures, which form the corner stone of most reporting systems, indicate the results of past decisions, and say nothing about the likely future performance. This technique has proved most useful in driving change and is of obvious interest to any BPR initiative. The scorecard, typically of between 15 and 20 different high level measures, is divided into four categories:

- **Financial**: e.g. profitability, cash flow, market share, return on investment.
- **Customer**: e.g. customer satisfaction, delivery performance, customer retention.
- **Internal**: e.g. inventory turns, space used, labour used.
- **Innovation and Learning**: e.g. rate of technological advancement, number of joint projects.

Management should select the key measures in each category by setting goals in support of their business strategy and then setting up measures to support the achievement of these goals.

Other measurements which help focus attention are:

- **Customer profitability analysis** – which customers are the most profitable, and possibly, which lose the company money?
- **Product/service profitability analysis** – which products and services are most profitable (and which lose money)? – this is particularly useful when attempting to reduce product variety.

In general, all targets should be well communicated and achievement towards them fed back to all staff. Feedback can generate performance improvement by giving people something for which to aim.

Managing the front office

Jan Carlzon popularized the term 'moments of truth' to describe the moments when the customer comes into contact with the organization.[21] This service encounter may last for only a few seconds, yet on the basis of that moment the customer will form opinions or judgements about the whole organization. The front-office is the best place to start in designing or for that matter re-engineering business processes which deliver a product or service to the customer. Understanding the service encounter enables a company to work back from this point, through the front-office and back-office to ensure that at every stage in the process the right things are being done and that they are done right.

Customer service
The quality of the customer service can best be thought of as a number of components. The actual product the customer receives, how the customer receives it, i.e. the 'service experience', and the customer's initial expectations.

- **Product quality** and **'service experience'** quality can have a number of dimensions as discussed earlier.
- **Expectations** are important. Customers will either be delighted or disappointed by the quality of the service depending on their expectations. Consistency in both product and service provision quality is important here as is the careful management of expectations. Many theme parks manage customer expectations in queues, for example, by deliberately quoting longer wait time than will be experienced, thereby delighting customers who had decided to make a longer wait.

If you are aiming to delight the customer you must exceed their expectations and thus the equation becomes:

$$\text{Customer service quality} = \frac{\text{What is received} + \text{how it is received}}{\text{Expectations}}$$

If expectations are valued at 1 it is necessary for the sum of the what and how to be greater than 1 in order to delight the customer. If they are significantly greater however, expectations may be raised for future encounters and ideally very small, yet noticeable, increments should be made.

As discussed earlier in the chapter, many of the criteria on which a customer will judge a service operation are intangible yet also vitally important. Perception is everything and never more so than in service delivery. Creating the right service environment is important for both the staff who are expected to deliver it and the customers for whom it exists.

In designing a front-office environment it is important to consider process, people and technology and how these should be combined to deliver the desired outcome. Building on the discussion so far we can thus construct a checklist to ensure we cover the main areas for process design:

- At what points will customers come into contact with the organization? These can be all considered front-offices of a sort.
- What will the customer require at each front-office?
- Are all these front-offices needed and how do they inter-relate?

For each then identify the following:

The service task

- The **customer service dimensions** – what is important to your customer; what are their *hygiene* factors; and what makes them actually buy from you? What do you expect of your customers in the front office and how will they perform these things (e.g. provide information, take their meal to their table, etc.)?
- The **pattern of demand** – volume, variety and variation – how will the process cope with these and what are the runners, repeaters and strangers of the process?
- **Constraints** on the process – what legislative, company policy and financial conditions must the process work within?
- **Efficiency** targets – what resources can be utilized to start with and how much improvement is expected over time?

The process decision areas

- **Quality** management – both *product* and *service* quality, how will it be measured and improved?

- **Lead time** management – how quick does the response to orders need to be? How quick could it be in an ideal world?
- **Capacity** management – how will the process balance load and capacity and what will happen when it becomes overloaded?
- **Inventory** management – how can inventory be minimized and where should it be in the supply chain?

People considerations

It is crucial to identify the type of people needed to perform activities within the process. Ideally staff should be capable of performing any of the required tasks and take responsibility for improving the customer's experience within laid down constraints. Broadly there are two different attributes to consider when evaluating the type of person to recruit:

- **Behavioural** characteristics
- **Technical** skills required

In our opinion, the behavioural characteristics are the most important regardless of where the person is going to work but this is perhaps especially true of the front-office. In a hairdresser customer loyalty is won as much by the personality of the stylist and their ability to 'engage' the customer as by their ability to deliver a good haircut, the same is true for management consultancy.

How will these people be **rewarded** such that it encourages team working towards high customer satisfaction and higher productivity? What will be the staff's **terms and conditions** – will they be part-time, job-sharing or full-time?

We will cover these human resource issues in Chapter 4.

Technology considerations

By technology, we mean technology in the widest possible sense.

- Physically what will the front-office be like?
- Will the customer use a technology interface in some way such as an Automated Teller Machine?
- What supporting information does the customer need?
- What supporting information does the staff need?

- How will other information be collected both for the fulfilment of the immediate customer need and to aid new business opportunities?

Broadly three main areas should be carefully examined:

- Facilities.
- Usable devices and supporting mechanisms.
- Information management (customer and staff).

Performance Measurement

How will the process be measured in terms of both:

- Customer service?
- Productivity?
- Flexibility?
- Improvement?

We will not repeat all the detail covered in previous and subsequent sections, but in designing a set of processes for the front office readers are recommended to use the relevant section as a checklist to get started. In addition, special consideration should be given to service recovery.

Service recovery
Things sometimes go wrong, often when the organization is 'coping' (i.e. where demand exceeds capacity). When they do, organizations have to be able to 'recover' the situation. Research indicates that customers experiencing a problem, complaining and then having their problem dealt with to their satisfaction are only marginally less likely to return as those who did not experience a problem in the first place.[22] No one is suggesting that you actually create a problem and then fix it, but planning to resolve problems can pay off. 'Empowering' the service provider is often said to be the answer and it can be, if managed properly. For further information on empowerment see Chapter 4.

See for yourself
Front-offices are almost infinite in their variety and the best way to design a front-office is to look at others and assess them. Fortunate-

ly, examples of front offices are accessible to us all. Next time you eat in a restaurant, or go shopping, or phone a company, think about how they have, or have not, designed the encounter and how you might improve it. Think about what the implications for the operation would be if they delivered what you wanted. You could even go as far as using the checklists provided in this chapter. It can be fun!

Managing the back office in a manufacturing firm

It is not the purpose of this book to examine in detail the management of a manufacturing facility, but it is crucial that the basics of manufacturing systems design are understood. This is important firstly for those who may be participating in a BPR exercise in a manufacturing environment, but also for those with no experience of manufacturing as the underlying philosophies and techniques are now finding wide acceptance in service businesses and the office. We shall take a look here specifically at manufacturing and in particular focus on some common themes in 'Lean Production',[23] Just-In-Time[24] and the Toyota Production System.[25] These terms are often used synonymously to describe perhaps the most famous of production philosophies. We will use elements of each of these as examples of how to run a manufacturing back office.

Manufacturing process types
Although manufacturing processes span a continuum, there are broadly five main categories which can be distinguished:

- **Projects** – which are suitable for products which are unique or 'one of a kind'. Projects involve a number of discrete steps and sequencing and scheduling are very important. Although there will be similarities between projects, the estimation of costs and times is often a problem as the Channel Tunnel project so clearly demonstrates.

- **Job Shops** – are appropriate where there is a wide variety of products demanded in small volumes. There is a loose interconnection between the various stages as the exact operations to be performed will vary with each product type.

- **Batch Processes** – like job shops except that the volume for each batch is larger and the variety of products produced less. Scheduling is the major task of batch process control.

- **Assembly lines** – are appropriate where there is very high volume and a standard product-type, although there may still be a lot of variety within that product type, such as a car or computer. Assembly lines rely on the division and specialization of labour, with workers each doing a small part of the overall process. Assembly lines are either *worker paced*, where the workers control the pace of the line, or *machine paced*, where the workers have to work to the line's speed. Some lines are fully automated and are called *transfer flow* lines. Worker boredom can be an issue on assembly lines.

- **Continuous** – is a production method, similar to transfer flow, for very high volume standard products. Flexibility is a major problem often associated with these dedicated production lines.

'Fitting processes to products'
It is important that the process selected matches the demands of the market that you are operating in. Use of project or job shop-processes where the volume demanded would justify the use of batch or even assembly line methods would be very inefficient. Similarly, use of an assembly line to produce low volume high variety products would be very costly.

Manufacturing excellence
When we go into a factory there are a number of features which become immediately apparent, one of these is cleanliness. There is no reason why manufacturing, *per se*, has to be a dirty business. If you do not believe that you will have a dirty factory and if you do, it is likely to be considerably cleaner than would otherwise be the case and also a lot nicer to work in. The mindset of the managers and workers will dictate to a large extent what the operation is like. If you accept that things will inevitably go wrong, they will – often, if you believe that your products are costly to make by their very nature – they will be and if you believe things take a long time in your business – once again they will. During the 1950s, when Toyota was beginning to turn around its car manufacturing business, it laid down the three main objectives of its production system and has strived endlessly to meet them ever since. Toyota aims to produce its products:

- To the highest possible quality.

- At the least possible cost.
- In the shortest possible lead time.

Toyota has succeeded in doing all three of these things to a greater extent than its rivals. There are many reasons why, and not all of them have to do with the design of the production system and its management, but we would argue that it is a crucial part. Cars are not the only industry to be implementing these principles. All types of manufacturing processes can benefit from the application of its principles, though some specific aspects will be more applicable than others depending on the nature of the process. Boeing, for example, which for years considered JIT irrelevant to its business, which is so different from cars, is now finding huge savings in implementing the principles and methods that its executives saw at first hand in Toyota and other Japanese companies.[26]

Just-In-Time/Total Quality

Just-In-Time (JIT) and Total Quality (TQ) go hand in hand and it would be impossible to operate JIT without the foundations of TQ. JIT production is about producing the right amount of the product at the time that it is required. It thus aims to reduce inventories and in so doing exposes the reasons for those inventories. Those reasons, then, have to be addressed and as most are problems of dependability, either of labour, machines or suppliers, these sometimes complex issues have to be addressed.

It is a common belief that JIT is all about suppliers, it is not. A company has a great deal to gain by implementing JIT internally and any improvements in the linkages to suppliers is a further benefit to be added to a lean operation.

Key aspects of JIT operation are:

- **Standardization** of components reducing variety and thus complexity. Any company introducing JIT may require some time to achieve greater standardization, depending on the design to production lead time, however because it is likely to be a long lead time item it should be started as soon as possible
- **Total Preventative Maintenance** (TPM) Machines are proactively maintained and the teams do not wait until a breakdown occurs to fix the machine but regularly service it to ensure continued availability. The old adage of 'if it ain't broke don't fix it' is not used, instead it is 'if it ain't broke, make sure it stays that way', recognizing that simple wear and tear causes breakdowns. In

addition, operatives are encouraged to take on responsibility for the normal maintenance and repair of their machines. Maintenance engineers spend more of their time making this easier by modifying machines and training staff as to how to keep them running smoothly.

- **Total Quality Control** (TQC) is one of the principal foundations of JIT. Causes of failure should be identified and fixed, not just the symptoms which might be in the form of faulty components. The emphasis is on eliminating all causes of quality problems. *Pokayoke* or mistake-proofing is a favourite approach where simply designed jigs and fixtures are used to make it difficult or impossible for workers to make mistakes. The principle of *jidoka* should apply, whereby operators stop the line when a faulty component, or any other problem, is identified. The concept of allowing workers to stop the lines to fix problems was a break with Western traditions, which was to keep the line moving at all costs, even if the parts it was producing were no good. These faulty products then had to be put right at the end of the line – never as good as building them 'right' first time.

- **Set up reduction** – One of the causes of quality problems are large batch sizes. With large batches, or lots, problems in production may not be detected until many parts have been made. Smaller lots thus help reduce the cost of quality failure. Smaller lots also reduce the lead time as demonstrated earlier. A pre-requisite to small lot sizes is rapid changeovers for machines and people between one product and another. This also gives considerably greater flexibility. The target is for instantaneous changeover.

- **Plant layout** – It seems common sense that the flow of materials should be smooth, uninterrupted and that movement should be minimized. Plants should be laid out to facilitate this. Many parts of the plant are divided into dedicated manufacturing 'cells'. These cells are laid out to perform the process in the most efficient manner and the workers are responsible for the smooth running of production. Often these cells are laid out in a 'U' shape as described below.

- **Small machines** – The preference is for small, dedicated machines which allows greater flexibility and also do not create a 'reason for being' in their own right as do many highly expensive machines. Companies who have highly expensive machines are loath to leave them idle or do away with their use when the product changes. They also tend to become bottlenecks. That is not to say that large Flexible Manufacturing Systems are not used, they are, but sparingly and only when they offer increased flexibility over people and small machines. This is often difficult as people are very flexible in comparison with a machine.

- **Multi-function workforce** – the operators are trained to a high degree, which enables them to undertake a range of jobs in the plant and on their line. This gives greater flexibility than employing workers who possess fewer process skills
- **Pull scheduling and lot size reduction** – the mechanism for shop-floor control is 'pull scheduling' whereby the use of material downstream 'pulls' material from upstream. Thus, as a product rolls off the line at the final stage so the operators at the last stage 'pull' the next nearly-finished-part from its previous station to theirs. In turn, the workers at the preceding station 'pull' material from the station before them, and so on. The systems used to do this are simple *kanban* systems explained below (Figure 3.8). The size of the lots 'pulled' is, ideally, one, which maximizes flexibility, production lead time and reduces WIP.

- **Visibility/enforced problem solving** – the reduction of inventory through the system via reduced lot sizes forces problems to the surface which had previously been covered up by inventory. Stages which are unreliable, either because of quality problems or machine downtime, quickly become critical problems which must be addressed. Slowly lowering the 'water level' of inventory, exposes the 'rocks' or problems and companies can then, gradually, improve the performance of the overall system by solving problems which were previously invisible.

- **JIT supply** – JIT purchasing and supply seeks to repeat many of the above tenets of JIT between customer and supplier. Smaller lot sizes means more frequent deliveries, and here the Japanese are backing off the ideal of a lot size of one in favour of 'optimized deliveries'. Clogged roads, among other things are to blame for this modification to the basic principle of reducing inventory buffers between supplier and customer to a bare minimum and effecting delivery direct to line side.[27] Often quality inspection is not performed as goods arrive and if a problem occurs the supplier rectifies the problem immediately and pays penalties. On the whole many Japanese companies prefer not to single source, but to maintain competition between approved suppliers which are managed almost as part of its own vertically integrated supply chain.

A two-card kanban system

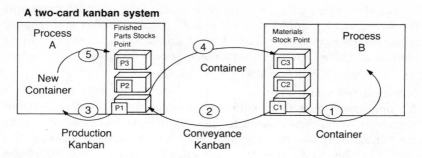

Process B starts to use the contents of container C1. As it does so it passes a 'conveyance kanban' back to the finished parts stock point of process A to request another pallet of items. Pallet P1 is despatched and a 'production kanban' passed back to process A which starts to produce more items which it then stores in the stock point.

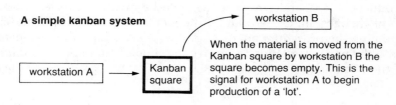

Figure 3.8 Kanban operations

Kaizen or continuous improvement

The Japanese pursue the last 'grain of rice' long after many others have opened up another packet! Kaizen teams work constantly, not as special task forces, to improve every aspect of the operation. Where processes have not been improved for a period of time attention will be focused on these and all workers are expected to contribute ideas as to how operations can be improved. Harrison[28] describes how Toyota's Kaizen efforts are directed towards *muda* or 'waste' in the following categories (see Chapter 6 for further details):

1. Over-production.
2. Waiting time.
3. Transport.
4. Processing.
5. Inventory.
6. Motion.
7. Defective goods.

Toyota has provided help to its suppliers, without which, many of those companies could not have met the strict cost and quality criteria. Other companies have set up similar supplier improvement teams including General Motors (GM) and Volkswagen (VW).

Standardized work
All operators must follow the documented procedure to perform each of their tasks. All work is standardized and procedure boards are placed next to work stations describing how each job must be done. In this way, the task is perfected and quality problems eliminated. That is not to say that these procedures are cast in stone. They must be adhered to, but they are also constantly changed and improved by the workers through the Kaizen teams. The team leaders decide if a particular change will have impacts beyond that production 'cell' and who else needs to be involved in the change. Local changes are carried out by the workers themselves, including updating the procedure board. If problems occur, the support teams go to the workers' station to resolve the problem under the guidance of the team leader.

Teams
Both Nissan and Toyota go to great lengths to foster a team spirit amongst its workforce. Workers will stay in their teams for some years and learn how to perform every job within the team. Often a production 'cell' is the focus for the team, although frequently office staff are put into teams. To enhance the team spirit, single status, uniforms for all and open plan offices characterize the working environment. There are still job status differences of course, but the outer trappings of status and position on the corporate ladder so jealously guarded by many Western managers are not evident. Team leaders are the linchpins of the team-working operation. They are specially selected individuals whose task it is to ensure that their team is working well, cohesively and that the team members have the support required to get their jobs done. In general, recruitment and selection is taken very seriously at Toyota and lots of tests and interviews are conducted. 'Fit' and attitude is more important than industry experience.

Figure 3.9 contrasts the traditional arrangement of stations and workers with the cell aproach. The cell arrangement is not just used for component manufacture but as the optimum arrangement for feeding components and assemblies onto the assembly line at certain points (see Figure 3.10).

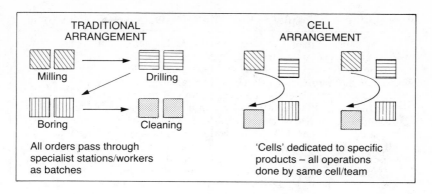

Figure 3.9 Manufacturing cells

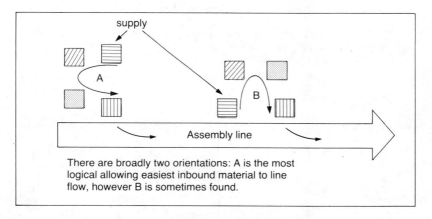

Figure 3.10 'U' shaped cells

Illustration 3.1 highlights the application of this 'cell' arrangement in a small manufacturing company.

Managing the back office in a service firm

Service operations are very diverse and thus the design and management of the back office portions are equally diverse. In manufacturing industry a significant portion of staff can be employed in service functions such as invoicing, purchasing and so on.

Illustration 3.1 Kaizen at Paddy Hopkirk car accessory factory

It takes a brave man to allow consultants to tear up his factory and rearrange it over night. It takes employees who are even more understanding to accept such changes. At the Paddy Hopkirk car accessory factory in Bedfordshire consultants inspired by the Japanese concept of continuous improvement – or Kaizen – did just that.

One morning the factory was an untidy sprawl of production lines surrounded by piles of crates holding semi-finished components. Two days later, when the 180-strong workforce came to work, the machines had been brought together in tightly grouped 'cells'. The piles of components had disappeared, and the newly created floor space was neatly marked with colour-coded lines mapping out the flow of materials.

Overnight there were dramatic differences. In the first full day, productivity on some lines increased by up to 30 per cent, the space needed for some processes had been halved, and the work in progress had been cut considerably. The improved lay-out had allowed some jobs to be combined, freeing up operators for deployment elsewhere in the factory.

'I was expecting a change but nothing as dramatic as this', says Hopkirk, who is chairman. 'It is fantastic.'

Hopkirk wishes he had discovered Kaizen 25 years ago.

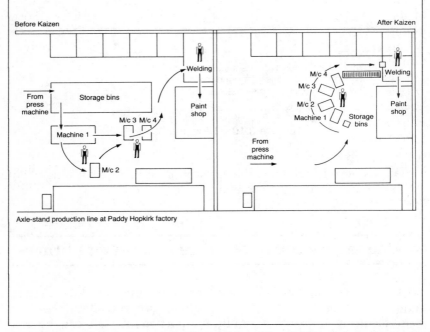

Axle-stand production line at Paddy Hopkirk factory

Source: Reprinted with permission from Richard Gourlay, 'Back to basics on the factory floor', *Financial Times*, 4 January 1994.

Often the service back room revolves around the processing of paperwork and it is here that BPR is having perhaps its biggest impact. Indeed where paperwork has been replaced by computer systems the basic processes, often, were not redesigned and remain ponderous and slow. Workflow and imaging software, where the actual paperwork itself is digitized and then can be manipulated through a 'computer factory process', was the introduction to BPR for many companies (workflow is discussed in more detail in Chapter 5). Consultancies specializing in these fields have been at the forefront of many BPR initiatives, Wang being perhaps the most famous of these.

Traditionally the structure and flow of the back room depended on the number of specialist departments through which the paperwork would have to go and for many companies it still does. Specialization of labour has been a feature of the offices and paperwork as much as it has been in the factory. One key difference in processing paperwork, as opposed to materials, is that it is much harder to follow the flow of paper and see the value-added at each stage.

Having worked out the flow through the process and the best configuration of people, the design of individual tasks and activities in the process must be determined. This is best decided by those doing the jobs plus some help from professionals with experience in the appropriate area. For services that mimic manufacturing production systems the same principles should be applied as described in the section above. Such 'production' services involve all activities where physical goods are transformed in some way. The transformation may not be easy to see or even significant, yet the process must still be designed as a proper production system. The production of reports to a standard format is made considerably easier if everyone on the computer network can access the standard format and possibly an example. Clear means to obtain copies, and binding should be operated, and the number of wrongly copied or bound orders monitored with the reasons being noted to avoid mistakes in the future.

For those services that do not mimic factories, such as professional services, back-room operations are likely to be small compared with customer-facing processes or front office work. Nonetheless effective process design is crucial. Paperwork can get out of control very quickly and leaving mundane tasks, such as report preparation, filing, client information, etc., up to the individual's discretion is a recipe for problems in the future. The organization should have systems for collecting and storing critical information such as client details and work done to date. If it is simpler to file, it is probably simpler to extract, whether on computer or not.

When new staff are employed they should be able to see and understand the process quickly and easily. Continuous improvement to make service delivery efficient and effective is not the preserve of manufacturing and to do this well it is necessary for all staff to have a common view of what happens. Common views and common practices do not happen by accident and improving the delivery of 50 different service delivery systems instead of one is much more difficult.

Any new design of back-office service operations owes much to the 'cell' concept in manufacturing where all the steps in the production process are performed by the same team, rather than each stage being carried out by specialized teams dedicated to that specific task for all orders. Here the distinction between the front office and the back office blurs and a cell, or 'case team' as it is often known in BPR, is formed. The development of IT has also changed considerably what is possible, and this is discussed further in Chapter 5.

An overall process design

Before moving on to consider people considerations, it is now important to firm up on the overall design of the process through the front and back office. Each step through the process should be determined and linked to form a chain. All of the factors covered in this chapter should be considered at and between each step.

In Figure 3.11 we show a set of high level processes used to deliver a product which is manufactured to a customer's order. There is a marketing process which attracts the customer in the first place. The selling process obtains an order. Having placed an order the customer then waits for delivery, although they may wish to make enquiries during and after this period. The organization must ensure that the details of the order are clear and, typically, there is an order management process whereby order details are captured and progress updated. Next, the order must be prioritized and scheduled. Having done this any necessary supplies and raw materials must be ordered and delivery scheduled to meet the required production start date. Once manufactured, the product is then delivered to the customer and an invoice requesting payment forwarded. Assuming all is well with the product the customer then

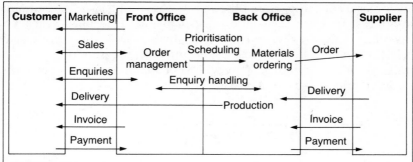

Considerations:
- **Lead times** through the process – how long does it take to fulfil the order
- **Capacity** management – are there sufficient, yet not excess, resources
- **Inventory** management – where should stocks be placed through the process
- **Quality** management – how should quality be managed throughout
- **Performance measurement** – how is the process performing and how can it be improved

Figure 3.11   High-level product or service delivery processes

pays the company. Similarly any suppliers must be paid. Lead times, capacity, inventory, quality and performance measures must be considered in and between each process which combine to form the overall delivery system.

For each process it would be necessary to drop down to further levels of detail and plan exactly what will be done, by whom and when. Process 'maps' are useful in designing these processes and are discussed later in Chapter 6.

Summary

Designing product or service delivery systems is a complex task and this chapter gives an overview of the types of decisions to be made. Essentially, a clear understanding of the 'service task' is critical to developing a process, although enough flexibility must be built in so that as the nature of that task changes, the processes can be realigned to meet the new requirements. We recommend that having started with these customer requirements, designers then draw up an overview of the set of activities which must be undertaken to deliver these, thinking particularly hard about the customer/front office, front office/back office and back office/supplier interfaces. In each case, options for managing lead times, capacity, inventory and quality must be evaluated and the appropriate selections made. An effective performance measurement system must be designed into the process to enable it to be managed and improved on a continuous basis.

References

1. Philip Kotler, *Marketing Management: Analysis, Planning, Implementation and Control*, seventh edition – paraphrased by Tony Millman in *The Emerging Concept of Relationship Marketing*, Presented at the Ninth Annual Industrial Marketing & Purchasing Conference (IMP), University of Bath, UK, 23–25 September, 1993.
2. Colin G. Armistead, 'Service operations management and strategy: framework for matching the service operations task and the service delivery system', *International Journal of Service Industry Management*, 1, no. 2 (1990).
3. David A. Garvin, 'What does product quality mean?', *Sloan Management Review*, Fall (1984).
4. Lin Fitzgerald, Robert Johnston, Stan Brignall, Rhian Silvestro and Christopher Voss, *Performance Measurement in Service Businesses*, The Chartered Institute of Management Accountants, 1991. Alternative dimensions can be found in Leonard L. Berry, Valerie A. Zeithamal and A. Parasuraman, 'Five imperatives for improving service quality', *Sloan Management Review*, Summer (1990), 29–38; Zeithamal, Parasuraman and Berry, *Delivering Quality Service: Balancing Customer Perceptions and Expectations*, New York: The Free Press, 1990; Berry, Parasuraman and Zeithamal, 'Quality counts in services, too', *Business Horizons*, 28, May–June (1985).
5. Terry Hill, *The Essence of Operations Management*, Hemel Hempstead: Prentice Hall, 1993.
6. Forbes, June 1994.
7. Barry James, 'Why this computerised chaos', *International Herald Tribune*, 15 July 1993.
8. Richard Heygate, 'Avoiding the mainframe trap in redesign', *The McKinsey Quarterly*, Fall 1993, pp. 79–86.
9. For more information on the mass customization concept see Andrew C. Boynton, Bart Victor and B. Joseph Pine II, 'New competitive strategies: challenges to organisations and information technology', *IBM Systems Journal*, 32, no. 1 (1993), 40–64; and B. Joseph Pine II, Bart Victor and Andrew C. Boynton, 'Making mass customisation work', *Harvard Business Review*, September–October (1993), 108–119. See also Pat Mullen, *Organising for the 21st Century: How to Make the Necessary*

Transition from a Mass Production to the Mass Customisation Organisation Form, paper presented at POSPP, Winter General Meeting, Los Angeles, California, 28–30 January 1991.

10. See George Stalk and A.M. Webber, 'Japan's dark side of time', *Harvard Business Review*, July–August (1993) 93–102.

11. Alex Taylor III, 'Here come Japan's car makers – again', *Fortune*, 13 December 1993, pp. 63–67.

12. David Clutterbuck, Graham Clark and Colin Armistead, *Inspired Customer Service: Strategies for Service Quality*, London: Kogan Page, 1993.

13. Colin New, *Competitive Edge Manufacturing Workshop*, DTI/Cranfield School of Management, 1993.

14. John Bank, *The Essence of Total Quality Management*, Hemel Hempstead: Prentice Hall, 1992; George Binney, *Making Quality Work: Lessons from Europe's Leading Companies*, London: The Economist Intelligence Unit, 1992; W. Edwards Deming, *Out of Crisis*, Cambridge: Cambridge University Press, 1986; David A. Garvin, *Managing Quality*, New York: The Free Press, 1988; Joseph Juran and Frank M. Gryna, Jr., *Juran's Quality Control Handbook*, New York: McGraw-Hill; John Oakland, *Total Quality Management: The Route to Improving Performance, second edition*, Oxford: Heinemann Professional Publishing, 1989; Mary Walton, *The Deming Management Method*, Mercury Business Books, 1989.

15. Technical Assistance Research Program (TARP), US Research Company.

16. *Total Quality Management. The European Model for Self-Appraisal 1993: Guidelines for Identifying and Addressing Total Quality Issues*, The European Foundation for Quality Management, Building 'Reaal' Fellenoord 47A, 5612 AA Eindhoven, The Netherlands.

17. 'The Quality Imperative', *Business Week*, 2 December 1991.

18. Peter F. Drucker, *Management: Tasks, Responsibilities, Practices*, London, 1977.

19. For an overview of the problems of performance measurement systems and ways they can be improved see the Economist Intelligence Unit research report, *The New Look of Corporate Performance Measurement*, New York, 1994.

20. Robert S. Kaplan and David P. Norton, 'The balanced scorecard', *Harvard Business Review*, January–February (1992), 71–79. See also their article 'Putting the balanced scorecard to work', *Harvard Business Review*, September–October (1993), 134–142. There is also a good interview with Larry D. Brady of FMC Corporation on using the balanced scorecard, see 'Implementing the balanced scorecard at FMC Corporation: an interview with Larry D. Brady', *Harvard Business Review*, September–October (1993), 143–147.

21. Jan Carlzon, *Moments of Truth*, Cambridge, Mass.: Ballinger Publishing Company, 1987.

22. US Office of Consumer Affairs, *Consumer Complaint Handling in America: An Update Study*, Part II, April (1986).

23. James P. Womack and Daniel T. Jones, *The Machine That Changed the World*, New York: Harper Collins, 1991. For an update, see their article 'From lean production to the lean enterprise', *Harvard Business Review*, March–April (1994), 93–103.
24. Alan Harrison, *Just In Time Manufacturing in Perspective*, Hemel Hempstead: Prentice Hall, 1993.
25. Shigeo Shingo, *The Toyota Production System*, translated by Andrew Dillon, Cambridge, Mass.: Productivity Press, 1991.
26. 'Re-inventing Boeing: radical changes amid crisis', *Business Week*, 1 March 1993, pp. 38–41.
27. Richard Halstead, 'Is Just In Time a waste of time?' *Business Age*, February (1994), 31; see also 'I want it now', *The Economist*, 13 June 1992, pp. 90, 95.
28. Alan Harrison (reference 24).

4

Organizing people: new organizational blueprints

Never tell people how to do things. Tell them what you want to achieve, and they will surprise you with their ingenuity.

General George S. Patton

The best executive is the one who has the sense to pick good men to do what he wants done, and self-restraint enough to keep from meddling with them while they do it.

Theodore Roosevelt

Introduction

The management of an organization's people resources is crucial to business success and few underestimate its importance. In this chapter we cover the second organizational pillar of people. Processes can only perform as well as the people who operate them and the organization and management of these people is thus a key element in the design of any set of processes.

Whenever people have come together to accomplish something, an organization has been formed. The tribe, the family, the church, and the military are all examples. Even in their earliest forms, each had its own structure and hierarchy; members performed different tasks, had different roles and different levels of authority. The modern business organization, however, is a relatively recent phenomenon whose evolution can be traced to two important

99

historical inferences: the industrial revolution and changes in the law.

The industrial revolution, which occurred largely in England during the 1770s, saw the substitution of machine power for human work and marked the beginning of the factory system of work. It spawned a new way of producing goods and offered opportunities which saw business increase to a scale never previously possible. The early Company Acts provided limited liability for individuals who came together for business purposes. Both these events led to the emergence of the professional manager, i.e. someone who managed the business but who did not own it. The increase in the scale of organizations required a structure to be put in place to manage the increasing complexity.

Early attempts to formulate an appropriate way to organize for work focused on determining the anatomy of formal organization. This so-called *classical approach* was built around four key pillars: division of labour, functional tasks, structure, and span of control.[1] Included here is the *scientific management* approach pioneered by Fredrick Taylor, which has dominated thinking on how to organize and manage people for many decades.[2] This approach to a large extent treated people as automatons, to be deployed as the needs of the process dictated. Division of labour was articulated as far back as 1776, by Adam Smith.[3] Although initially this concept applied to factory-floor workers, its application spread progressively in most organizational activity.

This mechanistic view was subsequently challenged by an emerging view stressing the human and social factors in work. Drawing on industrial psychology and social theory, the *behavioural school* argued that the human element was just as important. Themes such as motivation and leadership dominated the writings of subscribers to this view.[4] Since then there has been an avalanche of other theoretical perspectives advocating alternative organizational structures and role of the people within them.

Recently the perceived role of people in organizations has undergone a significant shift. Workers have always been employed to perform specific tasks and this will continue. What is changing is the addition of a second major role, that of improvement, previously the preserve of others such as management and staff functions. *Doing* and *improving* now go hand in hand as organizations seek to benefit not just from workers' brawn but from their brains too. The way people are organized and managed must now facilitate both these roles.

When examining the people issues in new process design we would wish to ask the following questions:

- What type of culture are we trying to foster?
- How many people are required by the process(es) and how should they be organized?
- To what extent should they be empowered?
- What behavioural characteristics should they have?
- What skills do they require?
- How can they be recruited?
- What terms and conditions should be offered?
- How should the people be developed?

In the sections that follow we examine these questions and relate them to a process view of the organization. We start with culture as this has a strong influence on the other questions. Few have the opportunity to start building an organization from scratch, although those that do, will need to consider what culture to build from the very outset. Those seeking to work within an existing organization must manage culture as a necessary element in the change process.

Culture

Despite the widespread use of the term in today's management literature, the word culture originates from social anthropology. Studies during the late nineteenth and early twentieth centuries of so-called primitive societies, for example, African, Native American and Eskimo, identified ways of life that were not only different from the more industrial and technically advanced parts of the USA and Europe but were very often different amongst themselves. This difference was explained by a society's culture. In a similar way we can identify differences between the culture of organizations.

Organizational culture can be defined as shared values and beliefs which take the form of rules of behaviour. At an elementary level, corporate culture can be viewed as 'the particular way things are done' in organizations. Culture will be influenced by many variables, such as the 'baggage' people bring with them from their educational and social background, or traditions and myths about

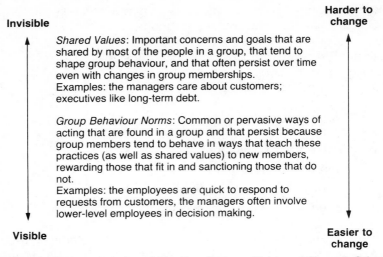

Figure 4.1   Culture in an organization

the management style and worker roles. It is shaped by experience gained over time based on what does and does not work.

Kotter and Heskett, in their book *Corporate Culture and Performance*, propose that it is useful to think of culture at two levels which differ in terms of their visibility and their resistance to change.[5] At the deeper and less visible level, culture refers to values that are shared by people in a group and that tend to persist over time even when group membership changes. At this level culture can be difficult to change, due largely to the fact that people do not recognize these values that they hold. At the more visible level, culture represents the behaviour pattern and style of an organization that new employees are automatically encouraged to follow by their fellow employees. These two levels are illustrated in Figure 4.1.

Culture operates at every level within an organization and can be a cause of friction when two different cultures come into contact with one another. The abandonment of the proposed merger in 1993 between The Leeds Permanent and National & Provincial Building Societies was due to irreconcilable differences in culture between the two and their 'distinct approaches' to business.[6] The hostile bid by Paramount for Time Inc, was blocked by arguments relating to the dramatic consequences that the take-over would have for the culture of Time, and in turn its service to customers and shareholders.[7]

It is important to remember that culture is one ingredient in helping deliver value to customers. Like processes, it must be aligned to the strategy of the organization and managed when change is required. Culture influences behaviour and thus will also influence strategy formulation, but it should not become the driving force. It is important that the behaviour which culture re-inforces is appropriate to the needs of product and service delivery. Clearly a requirement for innovation and risk taking will be called for in some cases, such as in a software house. In others, such as in a nuclear power station, it is likely that one would wish to place as much emphasis on the need to follow exact and laid down safety procedures. Culture will always develop and can either be managed or left to grow. If managed well, culture can enable innovation and development, building on the firm's strengths and avoiding the worst effects of its weaknesses. Illustration 4.1 describes how culture is managed at Hewlett-Packard.

Illustration 4.1 Culture at Hewlett-Packard (HP)

HP has a distinctive culture which is based upon a well-defined set of values and corporate objectives. These values are defined in a document known as *The HP Way*, which is given to all new staff. This document describes the organizational values of trust and respect for individuals; focus on achievement and contribution; business integrity, teamwork, and flexibility and innovation. It also outlines the corporate objectives of profit, providing value to the customer, contributing to fields of interest, growth, allowing employees to share in the achievement, fostering creativity. Induction programmes set aside time to explain these principles.

The document also specifies strategies and practices which include MBWA (Management-By-Walking-Around), MBO (Management-By-Objectives) and an open door policy.

Source: Thomas J. Peters and Robert H. Waterman, *In Search of Excellence* (New York, 1982).

While organizations have an overall corporate culture at some level, they are also composed of a myriad of subcultures. These values may be about seemingly superficial things such as preferred style of dress in that subculture, or their preference for being allowed to take their own decisions rather than being given strict guidelines.

In an organizational context, however these cultural differences may signify the potential for conflict and can pose significant obstacles to communication. This can be especially damaging when these cultural clashes operate between functions that should be working smoothly across processes. Culture management is again crucial to minimizing these clashes yet retaining the positive aspects of each culture within the organization.

Organization – teams

Let us now turn our attention to the organization itself. In recent years there has been a huge swing away from organizations based on individuals performing individual tasks towards team based organizations. The teams work on parts of, or in some cases complete, processes. An example of this emphasis on teams as the bedrock of an organization is Microsoft outlined in Illustration 4.2.

Katzenbach and Smith define a team as a 'small number of people with complementary skills who are committed to a common purpose, performance goals and approach for which they hold themselves mutually accountable'.[8] They suggest that there is a common link between teams, individual behaviour change and high performance.

High-performance teams play a crucial role within Asea Brown Boveri (ABB), the Swedish-Swiss conglomerate. Here, their T50 programme is seeking to reduce cycle times throughout the firm by 50 per cent. Team working resulted from a major change of attitude in the organization. Management by directives was replaced with management by goals and trust; individual piece-rate payment changed to group bonuses; controlling staffs moved to support teams; and there was one union agreement for all employees.

Increasingly, firms are using such teams to co-ordinate development across functional areas and thus reduce product development times. For example, if we look at pharmaceuticals or telecommunications, the traditional sequential flow of research, development, manufacturing, and marketing is being replaced by specialists from all these functions working together as a team. This simultaneous engineering approach typically relies on cross-functional teams and methodologies to integrate marketing, engineering and design and manufacturing. There is a clear focus on goals, the top level plan is robust to change, dependences are less critical as they are dealt with by the team, members develop mutual role acknowledgement

Illustration 4.2 Microsoft

Although Microsoft still promotes itself as a bunch of hackers in T-shirts – out to conquer the world with nothing but a PC and some nifty software – the firm is in fact struggling with many of the problems of sober-suited middle age. With nearly 10 000 employees, Microsoft is having to walk an increasingly difficult line between stifling bureaucracy of a too-rigid management discipline and the chaos of being too loose.

The sheer scale of Microsoft's ambitions increases the problems. It is putting together a range of products, based on a common core of technology, that will compete across virtually the whole of the software industry: from big computers to small ones, and from operating systems in the information-engine room to graphics programs. Nobody in the software industry has yet managed a venture of that complexity – though IBM has tried and failed.

Bill Gates, Microsoft's founder, is aware of the pitfalls ahead 'even if we are a big company, we cannot think like a big company or we are dead'. Big groups of programmers often create bad software more slowly than small ones can write good software. Microsoft is continually subdividing itself into teams of no more than 200 people. But this increases the company's managerial challenge. Not only must its managers keep information flowing smoothly across hundreds of small teams – despite rivalries and differences in focus – they must also choreograph the teams so that they can leap at new opportunities without landing on each other's toes. Technology is widely used.

Microsoft has a three-man 'office of the president'. The division of responsibility reflects what the company sees as the main challenges which it faces in the future: products, relationships and efficiency.

Source: 'Three's company', *The Economist*, 8 February 1992, p. 88; 'Top of the world', *The Economist*, 4 April 1992, pp. 86–90; Louise Kehoe, 'Is Microsoft too big?', *Business Week*, 1 March 1993, pp. 48–55; The hottest act in town, *Financial Times*, 8 March 1993, p. 15.

generating an achievement culture; an example of this is Chrysler's Viper development approach outlined in Illustration 4.3.

Team working is also a feature of product and service delivery. Increasingly, service companies, as well as manufacturing companies, are creating 'cell teams' or 'case teams' to deal with as much of the complete order to fulfilment cycle as possible. These teams often talk to the customer, take orders, schedule and prioritize orders, procure any necessary materials, produce the required product or service, deliver it, obtain payment and continue to support it. Most organizations are realizing great benefits in terms of customer service and productivity, not least because of the significant improvement in co-ordination and co-operation between

Illustration 4.3 Team working at Chrysler

When Chrysler decided to build a sports car to take on Chevrolet's Corvette, it knew exactly what to do. In a warehouse in Mack Avenue, Detroit, it assembled what it calls a 'platform' team of more than 40 of its brightest designers, engineers, manufacturing specialists and managers. Then it left them to their own devices. Liberated from the company's existing hierarchies and able to draw on the cream of Chrysler's resources, the Mack Avenue mavericks produced the Dodge Viper, a rakish ten-cylinder monster with a top speed of 160 mph.

Source: *The Economist*, 5 September 1992, p. 85.

members of the team who previously operated within autonomous departments. To stress the importance of team working, Reuters issue business cards with the name of the account team dealing with a customer and how each member can be contacted. One such business card is reproduced in Figure 4.2.

However, simply throwing people into a room and waiting for results to emerge is not the approach that is likely to guarantee success. Real teams – and not just groups of people with a label attached – will out-perform the same set of individuals operating in a non-team mode. The organization of such a team requires careful thinking and almost certainly a change in a number of organizational features, including:

- **Location** – for best effects teams need to be co-located and, as yet, no amount of IT can substitute for this. Just housing people in the same office is not good enough either – pay attention to the seating layout. We recommend that teams all sit together at a cluster of tables. A conference room can be used to talk confidentially to clients or others as needed but offices are, in our opinion, rarely justified if team working is required. An example of a suggested layout for a team of four persons is shown in Figure 4.3. Communication between all members of the team is facilitated by the layout and all members can see each other as well as speak to each other easily. Be careful in the positioning of computer terminals when constructing desk layouts. Health and safety considerations must be borne in mind as well as the need to enable line of sight communication.

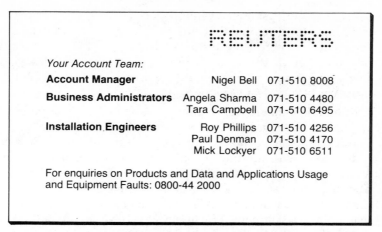

Figure 4.2   An example of a business card for account team at Reuters

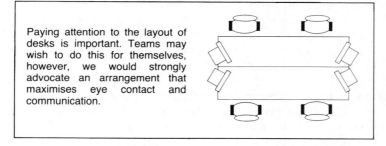

Figure 4.3   Team work layout

- **Pay and rewards** – in moving to team-based working, sales people's pay is often adjusted from payment when the sale is won to when the order is delivered to the customer's satisfaction. While this is a positive move towards increasing customer satisfaction it does not, in our opinion, go far enough. We would like to see the whole team being paid partly according to customer satisfaction not just the sales people.

- **Status** – every member of the team has a role to play and any notion of departmental and hierarchical status should give way to an appreciation of the team as a whole. Reuters gives its 'account teams' a business card with each member of the team shown on the same card with their specific roles. Not only does this break down some of the status symbols within the team as to who is allowed business cards but it also conveys the team sense to the customer. While specific roles are shown it is important to recognize that this may help the customer identify the right member of the team to talk to, but does not mean that any member of the team is not in some way a sales person. Every person who comes into contact with the customer, however briefly, is a sales person.

- **Individual behavioural characteristics** – Not everyone likes working as a team and even those who naturally do may find it hard to adjust to such an environment if they have worked as an individual for some time. People need time and help to adjust, and training and team-building exercises can be very important. The behavioural characteristics of people also become more important than specific skill competency when working as a team and recruitment practices may have to be adjusted to reflect these needs. Team roles should be made clear, as should the fact that team working means working together to support different roles. People's contribution to the team goes beyond the specific expertise that they bring to include supporting, questioning and enhancing the contribution of others. The 'more than my job's worth' mentality should give way to a co-operative, team can-do attitude.

Although team working has become popular it is important to recognize that not everything associated with 'teams' is necessarily true. Table 4.1 shows a few of the myths about teams and highlights what is often the reality.

Table 4.1 Myths and realities of teams

Myth	Reality
• A team is a harmonious group	• Often a diverse group of strong opinions
• Teams work in an atmosphere of co-operation and peace	• Differences are always present and in good teams conflict is seen as the crucible of debate and is managed, not suppressed
• Teamwork is a 'soft' process and full of compromises	• Teamwork is a hard and challenging process, but is rewarding
• Team working works better than individual specialization in all cases	• Teamwork becomes more essential as issues gain in complexity and diversity.

Team members

In constructing any team it is important that a certain level of balance is achieved. Each member may have their own perspective, which could potentially create unbalanced solutions. For example, a design engineer wants engineering innovation, the production manager wants a standard product built to a stable schedule, sales people want instant response to customer demand, and strategists want to change all of these in readiness for tomorrow. These contradictions can be a source of conflict in the team, however it is in enabling these groups to work together despite these conflicts that makes teams so attractive. Without them each would pursue their conflicting objectives independently.

Much work has been done on teams, notably Belbin's work on team roles.[9] In addition psychometric tools such as the Myers-Briggs Type Indicator (MBTI) can be used to help people understand better their preferences and behaviour characteristics.[10] While changing these can be difficult, it can help team members be more aware of their likely impact on others.

Teams and team working, though, are not without their problems. A recent report which explored autonomy and involvement in autonomous workgroups in the UK, Sweden, Germany, Portugal, and The Netherlands concluded that 'team work in itself does not constitute participation' and much more work and investment of time is needed to obtain acceptable social, representational and involvement arrangements in place that offer corresponding rewards to workers.[11] 'Groupthink' can also produce negative results as the team becomes insular and self supporting. A famous example of this phenomenon is the Bay of Pigs invasion, after which President Kennedy asked 'How could we have been so stupid?'[12] Synergy, whereby the team's output is greater than would be achieved by individuals acting alone, also is not universally accepted as being inherent in team work. Indeed, Peter Senge argues that most teams operate at a level of intelligence noticeably below that of each individual in the group.[13] In research for their book *The Wisdom Of Teams* Katzenbach and Smith found that the true high-performance team is very rare. The reason for this is, according to them, that 'a high degree of personal commitment to one another differentiates people on high-performance teams from people on other teams. This kind of commitment cannot be managed, although it can be exploited and emulated to the great advantage of other teams and the broader organization.'[14] It is clear then, that the composition of team members requires careful thought. Table 4.2 contrasts the attributes of winning teams with losing teams.

Table 4.2 Winning teams, losing teams

Winning teams	Losing teams
• Are clear about the goals	• Bring people together because they like each other
• Are in touch with what is going on outside the team	• Focus more on the team itself than the outcome
• Encourage differences	• Encourage similar ways of thinking and sycophancy
• Value input, regardless of rank	
• Are confident in managing and overcoming team conflict	• Accept ideas only from those with equal or greater status
• Encourage competition, providing that it does not undermine individuals	• Suppress conflict
	• Fail to manage competition
• Support other team members in achieving more than they ever thought possible	• Are insufficiently challenging, resulting in individuals losing confidence in their abilities
• Celebrate the success of the team and its members	• Ignore the need for individual recognition

Organization – functions

Although processes have become the focus of attention for many organizations as they strive to make leaps in performance, functions have nevertheless retained some importance. Like all management philosophies the BPR messages of process focus should not be taken to extremes. Functions have, and probably always will have, a role to play in organizational structure. They act as centres of expertise and learning for disciplines which are needed within teams. Teams should not be composed of generalists, but rather a group of team-minded specialists, each of whom brings extra value to the team in the form of their specific knowledge and abilities. Much of this knowledge and skill is fostered within the functions which also act as filters of latest thinking from outside the organization. Functions also provide a mechanism for career development within an organization, though the traditional notion of hierarchically based career progression needs some re-thinking.

Organizations which are moving away from functions towards a process-based organizational structure are relatively few and include most notably the National & Provincial Building Society headed up by David O'Brien who took up his position there after some pioneering work at Rank Xerox UK. It is too early to tell how successful this type of organization is, or how transferable these changes are to larger enterprises, and while we urge caution in destroying functions too much there is no doubt that organizations who have ignored processes for a long time must go a long way towards a process based organization in order to break the existing culture.

Empowerment

It was more than considerate of the Marriott night porter to trace my lost wallet – it meant he had to re-trace my entire journey through Vienna. All I could remember was that I'd been travelling on a Southern District streetcar. Miraculously, from this tiny piece of information, the night porter from the Marriott hotel managed to trace the route I'd travelled, the particular streetcar I was on, and my wallet. I was astonished that he went out of his way so much to help me. But as I now know, everyone at Marriott works this way. Personally assuming responsibility for the needs of every guest. It's called Empowerment. And, thankfully, they never seem to find anything too much trouble.

Based on a true story which took place in Vienna, January 1993.[15]

Empowerment means allowing people the freedom and authority to do their jobs well. It does not necessarily mean letting people decide how to do everything. Rigid standards must be adhered to, for example, by airliner maintenance crews, whereas partners in a consulting practice need considerable discretion in meeting their clients' needs. Empowerment must be effected by recruiting the appropriate people, training them and then giving them the appropriate level of responsibility and authority.

Nothing is more annoying for customers, or indeed staff themselves, than when the person attending to their needs has to continually refer back up the hierarchy to approve a particular request. Lack of empowerment can lead to extended lead times, dissatisfied customers, low morale amongst staff and a general inability to innovate. Harnessing the brain power of the organization cannot be achieved by rigid, hierarchical control. Saying that empowerment is good, however, and that we should all be doing it, is too superficial. We would advocate empowerment in much the same way as we would advocate technology: it should be appropriate. Empowering cabin crew to purchase airliner fleets is not what we mean. Empowering them to serve customers within clear guidelines on customer service and further empowering them to

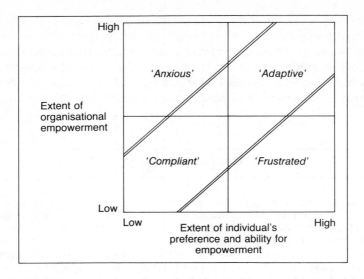

Figure 4.4 The empowerment matrix (after Clutterbuck, Clark and Armistead[16])

improve their service delivery within these guidelines *is* what we mean.

To understand how to examine what is appropriate we suggest the framework put forward by Clutterbuck, Clark and Armistead[16] which we have adapted slightly as shown in Figure 4.4.

The extent of organizational empowerment refers to the extent to which the organization defines systems and procedures which staff must work to. The extent of the individual's preference and ability refers to how comfortable, motivated and able people are to take the initiative and operate without strict procedures. Where people prefer and are able to handle empowerment, and they exist in an organization which empowers them, the organization is characterized as an 'adaptive' one. Further, there is also a match between organizational empowerment levels and individual preferences at the low end of each axis and here organizations are characterized as 'compliant'. There are likely to be situations when elements of both characteristics are required. Airline cabin crew, for example, must be adaptive in dealing with customers and certain situations, yet where safety is concerned they must be compliant. When considering to what extent staff should be empowered it is important to consider the process and circumstances. In some circumstances, particularly in an organization which places great emphasis on individual initiative, people can become 'anxious'. This may be because they have not been adequately prepared to meet this situation, or simply that they feel uncomfortable without any rules and procedures to follow. Similarly, someone who prefers to do it their way and take the initiative will be highly 'frustrated' if they have to work within strict procedural guidelines all the time.

In manufacturing plants there has been a gradual shift away from supervision and quality inspectors to letting those actually doing the work perform their own supervision and quality inspection. Staff are empowered to a greater degree to rectify faults and the movement away from a job being a task to a job being a task and improvement of that task has meant employees now take wider responsibility in many firms. Introducing empowerment, however, can be difficult and it must be more than words. Staff without authority cannot act. Similarly, if the management team are trying to foster initiative they must be careful in handling those early situations when the actions of the newly empowered employee were not felt to be appropriate. Disciplining a member of staff for incorrect initiative early on will send a loud message to the rest of the staff to keep their heads down and avoid risk at all costs; better to have a dissatisfied customer than risk the bosses wrath! The apocryphal story about the transport worker who returned from a customer care programme and within just a few days received an official caution for implementing what he had been taught illustrates the point. Why the caution? There had been a delay and a group of old ladies missed their late night connection. The quick thinking person, fresh out of the customer care programme, immediately booked them into a local hotel and arranged transportation to and from the station enabling them to catch the first connection in the morning. The customers were delighted despite the delay in their arrangements. The company was not happy at all and cautioned the employee.

Just how much is your organization prepared to do to resolve problems and keep customers happy? Does everyone in the organization know the boundaries? They should, as they may have to implement it one day.

Behaviour, skills and development

Culture and the degree of empowerment will be elements to consider when identifying the necessary behaviours and skills which employees must possess and their subsequent training and development needs. The behaviour of employees in the front office will have a direct bearing on the customer's perceptions of the organization as a whole, and will impact customer loyalty and retention significantly. For many firms these front-office staff are key to the organization's financial success, yet often little thought and effort is given to how they should behave and how management can help facilitate that behaviour. Processes are a good place to start. At each point where the customer comes into contact with the organization a clearly identified desired outcome should drive an understanding of what behaviours are needed. This does not stop with the service encounter but works right back through the supply chain, both internally and externally. Few organizations manage to be polite and courteous, committed to their clients, if their own internal organization behaves rudely and with indifference. Similarly the behaviour towards suppliers will determine the perception of the organization and play a part in motivating partnerships between them.

Behaving well towards customer and people is not enough. Customers get fed up with the most attentive staff if they simply cannot actually do what is required of them. Skills are also necessary. In Chapter 3 we outlined service quality as how service and products were delivered and what was actually received. Behaviours and skills map onto these two dimensions and bring processes alive.

In organizing people to work on processes a major change is occurring in industry with regard to the way people are managed. The layers of middle management are perhaps those most threatened by new ways of organizing and their role is undergoing significant change. Middle managers have always handled two main jobs: supervising people and gathering, processing, and transmitting information. But in a growing number of organizations, self-managed teams are taking over such standard supervisory duties as scheduling work, maintaining quality, even administering pay and vacations.

Managerial style

The characteristics of a process oriented organization demand a new type of management style. It is likely that the manager becomes more of a consultant or coach than has typically been the case. Administrative management skills are increasingly less important than leadership skills, i.e. the ability to provide a vision and engage staff in achieving that vision. Table 4.3 distinguishes between the old model of the manager and that of the new leader.

Table 4.3 The new leader

Old Manager	New Leader
Thinks of self as a manager or boss	Thinks of self as sponsor, coach, or internal consultant
Follows chain of command	Deals with anyone necessary to get the job done
Most senior team member	May not be most senior member of team in terms of the firm's hierarchy
Makes most decisions alone	Invites others to join in decision making
Hoards information	Shares information
Tries to master one major discipline, e.g. marketing	Tries to understand the whole process
Demands long hours	Demands satisfied customers

Recruitment and selection

There are broadly three main categories to be considered when recruiting and selecting staff, apart from legal requirements, and these are:

- The qualification of the person for the specific job or jobs that they may be required to undertake.

- The 'fit' with the required organizational culture which the person displays.

- The potential of that person to add value, grow and develop within the organization.

A lot of emphasis has traditionally been placed on a person's qualification for the job they are recruited to perform. This emphasis has continued in many instances but another has risen to equal, and some would say greater, status, and that is how well the person 'fits' within the culture of the firm. Even where people are brought in as part of a culture change there has to be a certain amount of fit, or at least tolerance on both sides. If not, their work situation will become unbearable and they will leave.

Potential is very difficult to assess and remains a rather elusive and subjective quality, although motivation and intellectual ability may provide a guide.

A major decision area for organizations is who should recruit and select employees. Should it be the preserve of management and the personnel function, or should team members be free to choose their colleagues? South West Airlines even goes as far as using its frequent flyers to select cabin crew![17] Traditionally of course managers and personnel staff have performed this function, yet there are an increasing number of instances where teams play an important part in the process. Personnel departments usually contain the necessary expertise to recruit and select staff yet can, in the same way as managers, help and coach team members in performing this function themselves, supported by the professionals.

Pay and rewards

Reward systems are generally believed to be critical to organizational performance. This is not so much in their ability to motivate, for their effects are now believed to be short term, but more in their ability to de-motivate if constructed badly. Deming preached against individual pay for performance for most of his life yet many organizations chose to ignore his message, often just because 'everyone else was doing it' in the words of one of Deming's strongest believers, Donald Petersen, formerly CEO of Ford Motor Company, who believes that further thought should be given to team based performance rewards.[18]

On the factory floor the traditional way of rewarding performance was piece rates, whereby people were paid according to the number of 'pieces' they processed. Piece rates are still found in some firms yet have become increasingly unpopular as they are seen as being a barrier to modern methods:

- Piece rates usually concentrate on individual performance and team working is not supported.

- Inventory reduction programmes are difficult since the motivation of the workforce is to produce as many as possible, not how much is demanded by the customer.

- Different work rates through the process's stages means that balanced production cannot be maintained.

- People are less inclined to spend time working on improvement programmes as this comes straight out of their 'earning' time.

- A concentration on output can lead to poor quality and where penalties are not built in for faulty output workers will not be motivated to work to high quality levels.

Many organizations are moving towards pay and reward systems which support greater flexibility, team working, a customer and quality focus and improvement. Contracts stipulating a steady stream of pay while actually requiring flexible working hours are increasingly common and can operate weekly, monthly and in some cases on an annual basis. Team-based rewards can be given at either an individual team level or at a higher organizational level. Share-based remuneration is not universally accepted as the best means to motivate employees as this can cause a degree of uncertainty which people dislike. Rewards based on customer satisfaction and quality of output can be given yet the trend is towards these aspects, along with improvement, being part and parcel of any job and not something for which a premium will be paid.[19]

Changing people's pay and rewards systems, or constructing new ones from scratch, is a complicated business. Personnel professionals both internally and externally can be used to construct a system which will meet the demands of the processes and the organization. Additional advice can be forthcoming from government bodies aimed at fostering collaboration between unions and employers, such as ACAS (Advisory, Consilidation and Arbitration Service) in the UK.

Training and development

Training and development is seen as a key activity for an organization to maximize the potential of its people resources. Training and development operates throughout a person's career within a particular organization, starting with some form of induction to the firm and continuing throughout their tenure. A number of levels should be considered in evaluating a training and development plan:

- Training programmes.
- On-the-job training.
- Job placement.
- Career moves.

These different types of training can be oriented towards different objectives relating to an employee:

- Skill.
- Behaviour.
- Awareness.

Overall an organization will need to manage these interventions taking into account the profile of its existing people and the demands which will be placed on them in the future. As stated previously a change towards team-based working may require different types of training depending on the nature of the employees and the degree of change.

Training should not be left to chance. Organizations should have a policy of training and development for staff at all levels and many have a minimum number of hours training which must be undertaken as a means of policing this policy. Understanding the training needs of an organization is a first step towards ensuring that they are not left to chance (see Illustration 4.4).

Illustration 4.4 Educating to prevent knowledge obsolescence

> Solectron, the California based assembler of printed circuit boards and other high-tech components is a firm believer in the power of education. Beginning life in 1977 with 15 employees, its revenues have grown an average of 59 per cent per year with the payroll expanding to 3500. In 1991, Solectron won a Baldridge award. In 1992, Solectron employees, from entry-level workers to the Chairman spent an average of 95 hours per year in training rising to 110 hours in 1993 – all training is done during normal working hours. This figure is almost three 40-hour weeks. William Chen, chairman of the company is emphatic in the need for training. 'Technology changes so fast that we estimate 20 per cent of an engineer's knowledge becomes obsolete every year. Training is an obligation we owe to our employees.'

Source: quoted in 'Companies that train the best', *Fortune* 22 March 1993.

Making improvement part of people's everyday jobs has also become a priority for training departments with some notable successes, one example is Motorola (see Illustration 4.5). For new improvement programmes we can learn from past actions. It was once popular to put the whole organization, or division, through a

Illustration 4.5 Education at Motorola

Motorola spends $120 million every year on education, equivalent to 3.6 per cent of payroll. It calculates that every $1 it spends on training delivers $30 in productivity gains within three years. Since 1987 the company has cut costs by $3.3 billion – not by the normal expedient of firing workers, but by training them to simplify processes and reduce waste. For example, the purchasing department at the automotive and industrial electronics group set up a team called ET/VT = 1 because it wanted to ensure that all 'elapsed time' (the hours it took to handle a requisition) was 'value time' (the hours when an employee is doing something necessary and worthwhile). The team managed to cut from 17 to 6 the number of steps in handling a requisition. Team members squeezed average elapsed time from 30 hours to 3, enabling the purchasing department to handle 45 per cent more requests without adding workers

Source: quoted in 'Companies that train the best', *Fortune* 22 March 1993.

training programme as a pre-requisite to a programme of improvement such as TQM. Experience now shows that it is better to train people as they need to use those new skills, not wait for an extended period before utilizing those skills.

Making the most of people: the learning organization

If 'improving' is becoming an equal to 'doing' for each employee, 'learning' as well as 'performing' is becoming a key objective for the organization as a whole. It is in this regard that there has been considerable interest over the past few years in the concept of the learning organization as a way of harnessing the potential of the organization's collective people resource.[20] The learning organization is able to sustain consistent internal innovation or 'learning' with the immediate goals of improving performance. This notion has similarities to the work of Chris Argyris who identified two types of learning which can occur in organizations: *adaptive learning* and *generative learning*.[21] Typically, organizations engage in adaptive or 'single-loop' learning and thus cope with situations within which they find themselves. For example, comparing budgeted with actual figures and taking appropriate action. Generative or double-loop learning, however, requires new ways of looking at the world, challenging assumptions, goals and norms, for example questioning the original budget target.

Quinn-Mills and Friesen[22] list three key characteristics of a learning organization:

- **It must make a commitment to knowledge** – This includes promoting mechanisms to encourage the collection and dissemination of knowledge and ideas throughout the organization. This may include research, discussion groups, seminars, hiring practices.

- **It must have a mechanism for renewal** – A learning organization must promote an environment where knowledge is incorporated into practices, processes and procedures.

- **It must possess an openness to the outside world** – The organization must be responsive to what is occurring outside of it.

Many organizations have implemented information systems in an attempt to improve organizational learning. For example, groupware products such as Lotus Notes or IBM's TeamFocus facilitate the sharing of ideas and expertise within an organization. At Price Waterhouse, they have 9000 employees linked together using Lotus Notes. Auditors in offices all over the world can keep up to date on relevant topics; anyone with an interest in a subject can read information and add their own contribution. By using groupware, Boeing has cut the time needed to complete a wide range of products by an average of 90 per cent or to one-tenth of the time that similar work took in the past.[23]

Over the long run, superior performance depends on superior learning. The key message is that the learning organization requires new leadership skills and capabilities. The essence of the learning organization is that it is not just the top that does the thinking; rather it must occur at every level.

Summary

People are the means by which a process lives. They perform the tasks in a process or support and maintain the machines that do so.

A key element to thinking about how to best utilize the people resource of an organization is to recognize that their tasks now have two dimensions, doing and improving. The improvement comes out of learning which must be facilitated on an organization-wide scale as an integral part of its operations.

For the process to be effective, efficient and adaptable the people must also demonstrate these characteristics. The culture, organization, rewards, empowerment, recruitment and development should all be aligned to the needs of the organization's strategy.

References

1. W.G. Scott, 'Organisation theory: an overview and an appraisal', *Academy of Management Review*, April (1961), 7–26.
2. Fredrick W. Taylor, *Scientific Management*, New York: Harper, 1911.
3. Adam Smith, *The Wealth of Nations*, London: Dent, 1910 (originally published 1776).
4. See, for example, the writings of A.H. Maslow, *Motivation and Personality*, New York: Harper, 1954; Elton Mayo, 'Hawthorne and the Western Electric Company', in *Organisation Theory*, edited by D. S. Pugh, Middlesex: Penguin, 1971; D. McClelland, 'Power as a great motivator', *Harvard Business Review*, May–June (1976), 100–110.
5. John P. Kotter and James L. Heskett, *Corporate Culture and Performance*, New York: The Free Press, 1992.
6. *Financial Times*, 27 October 1993.
7. *Time*, 24 July 1989.
8. Jon R. Katzenbach and Douglas K. Smith, 'Why teams matter', *The McKinsey Quarterly*, Autumn (1992), 3–27.
9. R.M. Belbin, B.R. Aston and R.D. Mottram, 'Building effective management teams', *Journal of General Management*, 3, no. 3 (1976), 23–29.
10. Myers-Briggs Type Indicator tests and information are distributed in the UK by the Oxford Psychology Press.
11. 'Innovative Teamworking in Europe', in *P+European Participation Monitor*, edited by M. Gold, Issue 5, first edition, Dublin: European Foundation for the Improvement of Living and Working Conditions, 1993.
12. Irving L. Janis, 'Groupthink', *Psychology Today*, November (1971).
13. Peter M. Senge, *The Fifth Discipline: The Art and Practice of The Learning Organisation*, New York: Doubleday/Currency, 1990.
14. Jon R. Katzenbach and Douglas K. Smith, *The Wisdom of Teams: Creating the High-Performance Organization*, Boston: Harvard Business School Press, 1993.
15. Advert for *Marriott* hotels, see for example, *Management Today*, March 1994.
16. David Clutterbuck, Graham Clark, and Colin Armistead, *Inspired Customer Service*, London: Kogan Page, 1993.

17. James L. Heskett, Thomas O. Jones, Gary W. Loveman, W. Earl Sasser, Jr., and Leonard A. Schlesinger, 'Putting the service-profit chain to work', *Harvard Business Review*, March–April (1994), 164–174.
18. BBC Education Programme, *Prophet Unheard*, BBC London.
19. For further information on performance appraisal see R. Bretz Jr., G.T. Milkoyich, and W. Read, 'The current state of performance appraisal research and practice', *Journal of Management*, 18, no. 2 (1992), 321–352; I. Kessler and J. Purcell, 'Performance related pay: objectives and application', *Human Resource Management Journal*, 2, no. 3, Spring (1992).
20. See, for example, David A. Garvin, 'Building a learning organization', *Harvard Business Review*, July–August (1993), 78–91; R.H. Hayes, S.C. Wheelwright, and K.B. Clark, *Dynamic Manufacturing: Creating the learning organization*, New York: The Free Press, 1988; *Transforming Organizations*, edited by T.A. Kochan and M. Useem, New York: Oxford University Press, 1992; Ray Stata, 'Organizational learning – the key to management innovation', *Sloan Management Review*, Spring (1989), 63–73; Peter M. Senge, *The Fifth Discipline: The Art and Practice of The Learning Organization*, New York: Doubleday/Currency, 1990; 'The leaders new work: building learning organizations', *Sloan Management Review*, Fall (1990), 7–23; 'Team learning', *The McKinsey Quarterly*, Summer (1991), 82–93; D. Quinn Mills and B. Friesen, 'The learning organization', *European Management Journal*, 10, no. 2 (1992), 146–156.
21. Chris Argyris, 'Single-loop and double-loop models in research and decision-making', *Administrative Science Quarterly*, 21 (1976), 363–375; *Reasoning, Learning and Action: Individual and Organization*, San Francisco: Jossey-Bass, 1982; *Knowledge for Action: A Guide To Overcoming Barriers to Organizational Change*, San Fransisco: Jossey-Bass, 1993.
22. See reference 20.
23. David Kirkpatrick, 'Here comes the payoff from PCs', *Fortune*, 23 March 1992, 51–57.

5

Exploiting information technology

There is no question in my mind that the chip in the form of the computer by January 19th 1985 was a really lethal weapon in the hands of our competitors.

Don Burr, Founder and CEO People's Express[1]

The rate of progress in information technology has been so great that if comparable advances had been made in the automotive industry, you could buy a Jaguar that would travel at the speed of sound, go 600 miles on a thimble of gas and cost only $2.

Randall L. Tobias[2]

Cyberspace. A consensual hallucination experienced daily by billions of legitimate operators, in every nation, by children being taught mathematical concepts ... A graphic representation of data abstracted from the banks of every computer in the human system. Unthinkable complexity.

William Gibson[3]

Introduction

In this chapter we examine the advance of information technology and how it is being used to deliver new and exciting products and services and enable new ways of working and competing. We examine the relationship between processes and information and assess how IT can be combined with process design and the organization of people. The difficulties encountered in exploiting new technology are also briefly reviewed.

The technology snowball

Imagine what it will be like to travel the motorways of the year 2050. Relaxing in a virtual-reality environment while your shuttle cruises only centimetres away from the next at several hundred miles per hour. Finally you decide to stop for a while at one of the multi-service complexes on route and you tell the computer your desire. Entering the complex you place a hand on the palm reader by the insulating barrier door and the entry charge is made to your accounts. Being a financially aware person, of course, you have subscribed to the optimization network and the system has made the payment in the manner most suited to your financial situation, drawing on your selected financial resources and assessing the best one to use. Once inside you make your way to the living quarters and immediately establish the 'virtual family link' which allows you to 'be' with your family even when you are travelling on business. Next you tell the computer to connect you to your mail systems. First up is your boss; he looks happy and says how pleased he was with your market analysis on the buying habits of the rich over 100s. Advances in medical care has transformed this tiny segment into a highly profitable one for a host of companies offering a range of specially developed products and services. Next up is your cousin in The People's Republic of Russia. Thankfully you can hear her voice in clear English and do not have to worry that you do not speak Russian, or for that matter, that she does not speak English. And so on . . .

The point to all this is that the range of products and services which will be around in the future is difficult for any of us to predict with any certainty, yet we can be sure that they will be different from those available today. Oxford BioSciences is developing a needle-less injection device along the lines of that used by Doctor McCoy in the TV series *Star Trek*. The device may be used to inject DNA as well as the more normal drugs and vaccines for those with a phobia of needles. Increasingly, however, as we talk about this advance, people ask 'fine, but who's working on the Starship Enterprises' transporter room: when will I be able to "beam" up?'. One could, of course, hazard a guess as to the only body in the world who might be doing so, but such conjecture would be to obscure the point that increasingly our horizons are being raised to the levels of our wildest dreams and beyond. From telecommunica-

tions to materials sciences many of the latest developments con-
found the sceptics and provide for radically new products and
processes to deliver them. Gaining an understanding of what is
possible with technology and innovatively applying it has always
been a challenge for business. If today's companies are to survive
and prosper in the future they must adapt to the changing
environment at the same pace at which it is changing, and that is
ever faster – just like the proverbial snowball falling down a slope
going faster and getting bigger!

In the previous two chapters we have considered the alignment of
processes and people to the delivery of products and services. In
this chapter, we take a look at the third pillar of the organization,
that of technology. Technology in its widest sense can be thought of
as all facilities, tools, machines and materials which are used by a
firm. We will focus our attention here on information technology
which is, perhaps the most significant technological advance to
impact society and business in the last three decades and indeed is
now an essential part of modern life.

Information as a factor of production

Classical economics proposes four factors of production: labour, raw
materials, capital and land. Operating within this philosophy,
success is seen as the optimum combination of these variables to
maximize shareholder's wealth. While this model may have been
adequate to explain business in days gone by we now need to
consider a fifth factor, that of information.

Companies have always needed information, yet the management
of this key ingredient has been, and still is, too often neglected.
Organizations generate vast amounts of data, but frequently fail to
transform it into anything which could be considered useful for the
conduct of business. The oft quoted phrase 'data rich, information
poor' is illustrative of this situation. A recent study concluded that
the annual US health-care bill could be cut by more than $30 billion
by compiling and transmitting patient information electronically.[4]

Processes, people, information and technology

In developing a process design and considering the people who will
work and support the processes, assumptions about information
requirements and availability will have been made. If, for example,

the process design included a customer-call centre to handle enquiries and complaints, it is important to recognize that the 'material' flowing through this process is information. This information must be processed in the same way that physical material must be processed in a factory. Not only will the information be transformed, transferred or stored but its progress and use will also be monitored and controlled, thereby generating more information. The people in the call centre will collect information from customers and if possible, use the information they have access to in responding to the customer's needs. It is likely that for some customers, the call-centre staff will need to collect further information and possibly initiate action to expedite customer service or product delivery. In order to collect information to serve the customer, the call-centre staff will first have to pass on the relevant customer details to others. Information will flow between the call centre in the front office, other front-office staff and back-office staff and will be both informative and instructional in nature. As an example, imagine the flows of information which result from the need to correct a fault on a telephone system.

So far the information we have considered in the call centre is 'operational' information but there is also another type which is equally important: management information. Information on the volume of calls will determine the number of lines and answering staff to be deployed. The pattern and nature of calls should be monitored to allow decisions on staff scheduling to be made as well as quality improvement efforts to be focused on eliminating causes of failure. Without this management information, the operation of the call centre will deteriorate as changes in its incoming 'material' occur. Another use for management information relates to the collection and analysis of customer data which can be used to better serve the customer in the future. Knowing, for example, that a customer is not happy with a particular product and is thinking of changing it provides the firm with an opportunity. Similarly knowing when the customer last bought your product and when they are likely to re-purchase can help retain custom rather than allow it to be enticed away.

We talk about information as 'material' to illustrate that it should be managed in much the same way as material in a factory. Just as inventory is the lifeblood of production, information is the lifeblood of processes. However, just as excess material is wasteful so excess information can also be wasteful. Organizations need to understand why information is needed and should not process it just because it exists, or has always been processed. Information and its use must be carefully managed and controlled to avoid waste and focus efforts on those areas which are most needed. Some information may be collected on an ongoing basis which only really becomes useful when a problem occurs, a plane's flight recorder black box performs such a function. Such data capture is best performed automatically, if possible, but again it must be designed into the process and its output validated.

The key message from this discussion is that once a process design has been generated and the appropriate staff issues initially considered it is important to examine the requirements for information. What information is required, by whom and where? What form should it take? How much information is needed and how much is available? In addition to information requirements it is also necessary to examine other technological needs. These may take the form of buildings, machines, vehicles and other facilities and tools. These should be written on the process chart along with the information requirements so that a more complete picture can be generated.

Advances in IT mean that information can be collected, analysed, disseminated and updated with a speed and ease only dreamt about by previous generations. Such leaps in power have been accompanied by increasing complexity and people are now faced with a bewildering array of technologies to consider. They are told that these technologies hold the secrets of sustainable competitive advantage, that they must invest in them now if they want to stay ahead of competitors and that totally new lines of profitable business will open up to them if only they would put their money in computers. While these *might* be true, it is also true that a great deal of time, effort and cost has been put into IT programmes which have failed to deliver the promised benefits (as outlined in Chapter 2) and have distracted the organization from the other building blocks of organizations: processes and people.[5]

If we look at the examples in Table 5.1 some of them represent instances where IT solutions have been developed to meet particular requirements, for example, point-of-sale systems and ATMs. There are also examples of where IT has been developed before a particular need was identified and has then 'found' an application, such as neural networks and virtual reality. Most IT implementations will contain elements of both these approaches. Indeed, the ending of the cold war has seen many military technology companies desperately searching for new ways to make money from their products while, at the same time, businesses have needed, more than ever, a means to differentiate themselves; and technology provides one possible answer.

Table 5.1   Examples of using information technology

Retail	• Point-of-sale (POS) terminals provide faster customer checkout, identify customer preferences, and improve inventory control
	• 'Smart' systems are actively being researched to enable the checkout to be dispensed within its traditional role with items being tallied as placed in trolleys
Distribution	• Notebooks or palm-top computers are being used to enhance tracking of deliveries and speed market analysis
	• Positioning systems enable ships and trucks to be tracked and their position identified
Education	• Computer-aided learning through multi-media and interactive video instruction is used for individual education and training
	• International communication networks, such as the *Internet*, link students, teachers and researchers
Financial services	• Automated teller machines (ATMs) support 24-hour banking services
	• Telephone banking relies on rapid information processing for the customer service staff
	• Treasury management systems provide corporations with comprehensive views of their financial position
	• Electronic funds transfer and dealing systems have speeded up deal making and allowed international market operations to be integrated
Manufacturing and engineering	• Computer-Aided Design and Manufacturing (CAD/CAM) and Computer-Aided Engineering (CAE) allow faster development and production of products
	• Computer-Integrated Manufacturing (CIM), Material Requirements Planning (MRP) and Manufacturing Resource Planning (MRPII) enable more effective planning of inventories and plant utilization
	• EDI links enable exchange of design, billing and inventory information
	• Virtual reality and High Definition Television (HDTV) offer gains in new product modelling and decision making
Travel	• Computer Reservation Systems (CRSs) provide current information to agents and travellers; they also assist in analysing demand and altering prices – such systems are even appearing as 'hole-in-the-wall' ATM-type machines
	• Systems enable crew scheduling and give yield and load factor information for better management
General	• Document imaging systems automate data capture and reduce paper usage
	• Telephone systems enable in-coming numbers to be analysed and the appropriate member of staff assigned to take the call (e.g. language preferences detected by area or a customer routed to their account team)
	• Sophisticated pattern recognition software, sometimes based on neural networks enable many organizations to gain more information from their data

One of the most important lessons in managing technology is that there is a level of *appropriate* technology for a particular task, that is, how it delivers particular outcomes measured along the three primary dimensions of effectiveness, efficiency and adaptability. An example to illustrate what we mean is an observation of Boeing's Chief Operating Officer, Philip Condit, on a benchmarking trip to Japan:

> . . . when he visited a Toyota Motor Corporation's engine factory in Japan in 1991, Condit had a sudden insight. At the point in the assembly process where workers needed to turn an engine there was a post. When the engine hit an arm on that post, the arm, set on a turntable, pushed the engine around. A simple device, yet Condit marvelled. 'We would probably have used a set of hydraulic actuators that turn a rotary table when triggered by a fibre-optic sensor,' says Boeing Co.'s new president. 'They just used a little post.'[6]

Often the technology used will reflect the knowledge and expertise of the people chosen to deliver it. Highly skilled technicians are more likely to deliver a high-tech solution than people with little appreciation of technology. Many companies prefer to leave shop-floor workers to design workflow systems than bring in design engineers who will put in sophisticated solutions.

Having said that, it is important to recognize that it may sometimes be necessary to use high-tech, and indeed those companies who successfully utilize leading-edge technology are likely to steal a considerable march on their competitors. Keeping abreast of the latest developments in every area is very time consuming. Some areas to consider are listed in Table 5.2 though this is by no means a complete list of emerging technologies within the IT area.

Artificial Intelligence

Ever since the computer was first invented it has been the dream of scientists to create an intelligent machine. The field of artificial intelligence (AI) seeks to do just this. Yet the term AI is much abused, very often to hype products in the market. The formal definition of AI was expounded by the British Scientist Alan Turing during the 1940s. He contended that a machine has artificial intelligence when there is no discernible difference between the

Table 5.2 Some technologies to watch

Technology	Brief description	Example business applications
Artificial intelligence (AI)	AI is often used as a heading for many technologies such as neural networks, case-based reasoning systems, expert or knowledge based systems. These represent an attempt to go beyond just information provision to perform a degree of analysis previously done by humans.	Applications of AI are increasing and include modelling of the money markets, credit authorization, problem solving and diagnostic systems.
Communications	Communications technologies encompass many different areas ranging from personal communications systems to networks at corporate, national, or international level.	Communications technology has broken out of the office and it is now possible to fax, phone, email and use systems while on the move. Groupware products are having a significant impact on business enabling sharing of data on an enterprise-wide scale.
Multimedia	The combination of text, image, video and sound	Training aids are increasingly popular and multimedia based books are transforming literature study. Entertainment is a major growth area. Geographic information systems also make use of the data processing power of computers coupled with multimedia capabilities.
Virtual reality	The creation of an environment. Flight simulators were an early example, however modern computing tools allow the creation of highly realistic environments electronically using either gloves or wristbands instead of mock-up controls.	The potential for the entertainment industry is enormous with new games to participate in. Business is also finding it useful to speed decision making by 'creating' future products without the need for expensive physical models.
Workflow automation	Arguably an application for IT for many years. Workflow automates the passing of work between people and in some ways resembles a manufacturing type approach to data processing.	Processing of incoming mail with documents 'scanned' on receipt; typically customer service centres use this approach as it enables them to retain the original 'copy' in electronic form and update the customer's data using the same system.

conversation generated by the machine and that of an intelligent person.[7] It was not until late 1991 that the first system ever passed that test, however, and only just. We should not be too pedantic about this, as many AI systems, while less perfect, do exhibit intelligent behaviour and provide real benefits to users.

Today, AI applications can be found in almost every industry from manufacturing to services. For example, when you fill out a life insurance policy, most insurance companies will use a rule-based expert system to evaluate your proposal. In 'conversation' with the client, the system will ask a series of questions. Based on the responses of the client, the system will weigh up the answers and give a response. This is different from an ordinary computer program, in that the AI system will take a probability-based line in response to any particular answer. Thus, the response of the system is conditioned upon weighing up all factors in the client's answers and comparing these to the base of knowledge that the system already has.

Two examples of AI applications are given in Illustrations 5.1 and 5.2. AI suffered from much hype in its infancy and inevitably its failure to deliver caused scepticism. Now, with more realistic expectations companies are beginning to find benefits in applying it to specific problems.

Illustration 5.1 Compaq Computers

Applying rules is not the only way to be clever. Compaq, a maker of personal computers, is trying to improve its customer service by installing automated assistants that work on the principle that reasoning is often just a matter of remembering the best precedent. Using 'case-based reasoning' technology, Compaq is building a compendium of the problems that customers have had with its personal computers and the solutions which Compaq has come up with – a source of corporate collective subconscious.

Computers can remember more precedents than any person. By capitalizing on corporate experience, Compaq's customer-service representatives can answer a broader range of questions before they have to refer the call to a technical specialist. Eventually, Compaq may simply ship its database out to big customers so that they can use it to answer many of their own questions.

Source: While-collar computers, *The Economist*, 1 August 1992, pp. 61–62.

Illustration 5.2 American Express: building knowledge highways

American Express is attempting one of the most ambitious efforts to employ intelligent machines in its credit card operations. The firm is building a 'knowledge highway' in which bright computers will help people with every step of the job of managing credit, from card applications to collecting overdue accounts. The business goal is to use the machines to shield both credit-card holders and employees from the bureaucracy needed to manage American Express's vast business – so leaving employees free to devote their efforts to building relationships with customers.

The machine helps in several ways. The latest addition to the 'knowledge highway' is designed to help with overdue accounts. It leaves humans in charge of collection, but protects them from error at every step. The system automatically pulls together all the information needed to analyse the account. Previously, analysts had to make 22 queries on average – to computers spread across the whole of the company – each time they looked at a problem account. Now they typically make only one. The computer keeps track of which state or national laws might affect the account. It helps to generate a dunning letter. It files all the paperwork. And it automatically reminds the analyst if the account needs to be looked at again.

Communications

Communications technologies have advanced rapidly in the twentieth century. Paper was once the main medium for communication and while it remains an important one, radio, telephone, film, television and computer-based communication are now firmly established.

Radio and telephone

Radio is a means of mass communication which can be used anywhere within the range of the transmitter and is not bound to office or home. Until recently, few applications for individual use existed outside of the military and emergency services. Telephones on the other hand were limited to individual use and were firmly wired into the office or home. These technologies have advanced and in some areas their distinction is now blurred. Mobile telephony can now be used anywhere within the range of the transmitter and transmitter coverage is being extended all the time. People no longer have to go to the phone but the phone can go with the people! Telephones can also be used by more than two people and conference calling is now common.

Whole businesses are now using the telephone as the primary channel to the customer. Examples include, First Direct, Direct Line and the cruelty-free cosmetics firm which delivers outstanding customer satisfaction, Cosmetics To Go. Another example of a company capitalizing on the capability of modern telephone systems is American Transtech, outlined in Illustration 5.3.

Illustration 5.3 American Transtech

American Transtech is a direct marketing service bureau. Key to its ability to answer incoming calls quickly and cost-effectively is sophisticated call management software. Incoming telemarketing call volumes vary widely. There are slow periods in which there is little activity, and peak periods when thousands of calls pour in. Dedicating sufficient telephone lines and agents to handle the peak periods for each period would be prohibitively expensive. To keep labour and capital costs down, agents may work on several telemarketing projects at once. During slow periods of one project, agents can be used to take calls from other projects. But this requires systems that tell agents to which advertising campaign a caller is responding before they answer the phone. Each promotion typically uses a different toll-free telephone number and customers can call to get information, order products, or otherwise participate. The switching equipment records the number that calls are made to and routes them to agents assigned to that project. The name of the promotion corresponding to the toll-free number simultaneously comes up on the agents' screens, as well as a pre-written script.

Source: 'Building marketing information systems', *I/S Analyzer*, April (1990).

Companies are also utilizing the telephone together with computer and communications technologies to dramatically improve their customer service activities. The example Unisys, outlined in Illustration 5.4, clearly demonstrates how customers have benefited greatly from its new service and support operations.

Television

In the same way that radio was once thought of primarily as a mass communications medium and is now being used to facilitate

Illustration 5.4 Customer service and support at Unisys

At Unisys not long ago, calls from customers looking for repairs or advice on their systems were handled in a fairly standard way – or in what Ted Bullock, vice president of operations with Unisys Customer Service and Support, calls 'the old way'.

For years, each of the company's product lines had its own service support centre and customer hotline. 'When the customer called with a request, the operator would take down the information and tell them we'd get back to them,' says Bullock. 'Then, the operator would route that request to the appropriate engineer, who would call the customer back.' If the problem involved two or three kinds of Unisys systems, the customer might have to call two or three numbers to sort things out.

'Over the last three years, Unisys redesigned its support operation in order to make it easier for customers to get the information and help they need', says Bullock. Using interactive phone systems, a computer network and sophisticated call-tracking software, the company created a Call Management System that essentially links its far-flung support facilities into a kind of virtual customer service centre. 'So while actual support personnel are still dispersed geographically, there is just one point of contact for the customer.'

The centralized system is also a valuable source of feedback for Unisys. The system's software keeps track of the company's service performance – how quick calls are answered, how engineers handle problems, etc. These statistics can be used to gauge and continuously hone service.

Source: Peter Haapaniemi, 'Making things happen', *Solutions: The Executive Magazine from Unisys*, Spring, (1993), pp. 6–17.

individual correspondence, so too is television. On-line information services on the TV, such as Oracle and Ceefax, give some control to the user on the information that they wish to see, however, it is only very recently that interactive television services have been tested. The TV is also being integrated with the telephone as companies begin to offer services such as BT's video-on-demand to subscribers. The TV may also be replaced by a multi-use device which combines traditional computer, TV and telephone functions in one unit. Illustration 5.5 describes some of the changes in these technologies which will impact shopping habits in the future.

Computers and networks

Computer communications were once restricted to users on the same computer. The advent of networks has allowed users to communicate with each other all over the world within firms and

Illustration 5.5 Re-inventing shopping

In the next 20 years technology could revolutionize shopping itself. It will change the view of shops as simple repositories for goods to be sold to the public.

The biggest growth area is expected to be TV shopping. In the USA, the cable home shopping industry where customers watch a succession of products on screen and order by telephone generated turnover of $2.3bn last year. So-called 'informercials', advertisements used to sell products directly to the public, pulled in a further £700m. On-line shopping services, in their infancy but expected to mushroom, generated $200m.

As more sophisticated communication networks are developed it is possible that information providers, network operators and transaction companies will group together. That would enable customers to select purchases and transmit orders to retailers via a remote control. An essential part of the growth of such channels is likely to be fast, secure delivery of products to customers' homes, posing new challenges for retailers.

However, shops as physical entities will not die out. Many customers will always want the opportunity to examine or try on products before they purchase. Convenience stores for top-up and impulse purchases are likely to remain indispensable – although they may become more specialized.

But stores will have to ensure they provide a 'value-added' shopping experience and come up with new attractions to lure shoppers away from their TV screens.

Technological advances are expected soon to make shopping, especially grocery shopping, less onerous. One way will be to end queues at checkouts by developing shopping trolleys that can scan purchases as customers make them and automatically deduct the cost from their credit or charge card.

The next step may be using silicon chips or tags which can be read by a radio beam on the trolley. Eventually, however, customers may not need to put goods into trolleys themselves. Supermarkets – and other stores – may display just one example of each product. Customers will walk around the shop and wave a wand across a bar code on the shelf to order and pay for a product. Their order will be assembled behind the scenes by staff.

Source: Neil Buckley, 'A whole new shopping experience', *Financial Times*, 16 March 1994, p. v.

between them. Governments, too, are keen to use networks which they see as critical to the country's competitive position. In the USA, Vice President Al Gore is perhaps the most visible proponent of a national data highway.[8] Gore's father was champion of the interstate highway system and the argument is that, as with the road system, significant economic benefits will quickly follow.

In many countries, knowledge of IT is no longer the preserve of specially trained professionals but is now widespread, particularly amongst the younger generations where computer games mean they become familiar and comfortable with the technology from an early age. At a political level, populations have never had such free access to the outside world, whether it be through telephones or computer networks. The *Internet* network, which spans most countries, now has about 20 million users connected to it, including the White House.[9] The ease with which connections can be established and re-established means that political control of the flow of information is becoming harder and harder. If such growth in information exchange presents the politicians with problems it also offers them and their nations significant potential benefits.

The combination of radio, telephony and computers is transforming the way communications and information can be managed. The personal communications device of the future is likely to enable system use, email, fax, image, video and voice communication all in one small unit. The potential for such devices is enormous and early, focused applications of Apple's Newton are beginning to point the way. Illustration 5.6 outlines how one company, BA, is

Illustration 5.6 BA: Putting the customer first using technology

Between 1990 and 1992 the industry wide losses in the airline business were $9.3 billion. Apart from the slump due to the Gulf war, traffic growth has resumed its interrupted climb. It is estimated that early next century traffic levels will be double what they are today. A critical industry problem is that passenger growth will not wait whilst airports and terminals catch up. Growth must be accommodated within existing constraints.

It was against this background that BA initiated *Airport 95*, a vision of the future based upon what it perceives as the principal need – making the passengers' lives as comfortable, convenient and hassle-free as possible in an increasingly competitive environment.

The changes in passenger handling being studied include:

- the introduction of 'one-stop' service opportunities, such as full self-service check-in facilities, perhaps using touch screen systems
- the choice of multiple off-airport check-in locations, such as airport car parks and eventually underground railway stations and kerb-side check-in
- the convenience of 'fast-track' channels through check-in and security and passport controls for what are called 'premium brands' (first class and business class travellers)

- improved baggage handling, especially speedier baggage at destinations; more directly personalized services for key frequent flyers across a wide range of airline activities, from check-in through to lounges and on-board services.

Much of these will depend on IT. Initiatives which are currently underway include:

Quickres
BA has telephone booking centres located in London, Belfast, Glasgow, Manchester and Newcastle handling up to 1800 calls per hour or over 1 million per month. Quickres is a technique for speedier passenger and agent telephone reservations where telephone calls are automatically routed along 900 lines. A call placed to the London office could be routed to Belfast if no operator is currently free in London.

Aspect
In Newcastle, BA is using a system called Aspect in which a computer selects key words from the caller's request, and uses them to call up data from the airline's main database so that the airline staff can give the desired replies.

Caller responding
Another system which is being tried experimentally involves a caller responding, by pressing numbers on a touch-telephone, to questions about standard items of information, such as flight times, services or fares, and replies being shown on the screen before them.

Queue combing
This technique is currently being used at Heathrow and Gatwick, with ground staff performing 'mobile check-in' for those with hand baggage only. Called Mobile Data, this technique combines recent advances in computer technology with radio telephony to provide a compact PC and a portable, lightweight radio modem. In the future, check-in staff may have small luggage trolleys. This technology also enables airline ground dispatchers to communicate with the airline's mainframe computer database whilst moving around the apron and even aboard parked aircraft.

Automated Ticket and Boarding Pass (ATB)
This is a worldwide 'self-service' handling initiative promoted by IATA. Passengers will purchase a combined ticket and boarding pass, with detailed information about flight arrangements on magnetic strip on the back. The passenger simply inserts this ticket in a self-service machine in the terminal building to check-in and then again when he reaches the boarding gate. The magnetic strip will contain information about seat preferences, desire for privacy, special meal requirements, favourite drinks, etc., allowing cabin staff to improve their levels of service to the passenger concerned.

Source: 'Putting the customer first – again', *Business Life*, May (1993), 50–54.

using a number of technologies to improve customer service. US retailers Kmart have recently pilot-tested an innovative system that uses sensors mounted in ceilings to track customer traffic, which helps in gauging responses to promotions and making sure that staffing is adequate at peak shopping times. The retailer has also armed store managers with hand-held computers that read barcodes of items on shelves and pass that data to an in-store computer via radio signals. This information is then fed through the satellite network and used to trigger reorders, helping to make sure shelves are well stocked with items that customers want.[10]

Business organizations have traditionally exchanged information by exchanging paper. Documents are often printed from one organization's computer system, sent by post, and the data on them rekeyed onto the receiving firm's computer. The obvious inefficiencies in this process led organizations to seek ways of exchanging data electronically. Electronic data interchange (EDI) started as a means to facilitate basic business transactions such as ordering and invoicing. Now many users have become increasingly sophisticated. Retailers Tesco, one of the pioneers of EDI use in the UK, has automated its entire transaction chain for recording sales, amending and checking stock records, re-ordering goods, receiving and checking invoices and making payment. They also exchange 13-week sales forecasts with many suppliers.

In the majority of cases the application of EDI, like internally focused IT projects, merely automated existing business processes without taking into consideration the potential for organizational redesign. An example where IT has been used as part of the overall improvement to a firm's process capability is Beneton. Beneton collects information about sales from all its retail outlets and adjusts its manufacturing schedule based on actual demand for styles and colours in particular regions. One of the inhibitors to effectively achieving this was the traditional manufacturing process where the woven cloth is dyed, the pattern cut and stitched. By moving dyeing to the last activity in the process the time to produce a garment was significantly reduced enabling Beneton to be more responsive to market demands.[11]

Of concern in the longer term is the limited support which today's inter-organizational systems offer the full trading cycle. This cycle is composed of the search for partners, offers, bargaining, contracting, and settlement. In short, markets are becoming dependent on IT and many company's systems lag behind.

Electronic markets

Electronic markets are seen as computer-based co-ordination systems which support or automate the full trading cycle for a large number of legally independent trading partners, as illustrated in Figure 5.1. The search for partners, for example, can be conducted through a database search given the relevant criteria and 'rules' can be established which enable an agreement to be reached at the conclusion of this search. Buying and selling through this mechanism is very different to that of traditional business, not least because price comparisons are immediate. The stock markets have already moved in this direction and this trend looks likely to gather momentum in more traditional areas of commerce in the future.

A major European domestic appliance manufacturer is currently piloting a customer service operation based on the electronic market concept. Customers phone in problems which are entered into a computer system. Points are allocated to each service request depending on the level of attention required. Service engineers dial into the system from their homes and select the jobs they will do based on their points-attractiveness. As jobs remain on the system their points value increases to make them more attractive, ensuring that jobs do not remain unattended for long.

It is expected that through the use of advanced computer and communication technologies markets will become more efficient. Buyers will no longer have to exert great effort to compare products

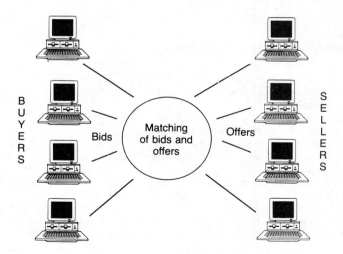

Figure 5.1 Electronic markets

and prices from many different suppliers. Instead, an electronic market can easily and inexpensively collect and distribute such information. These more efficient markets will threaten firms whose strategic advantage rests on market inefficiencies. For example, with the automation of the London International Stock Exchange the cost of matching buyers and sellers declined substantially and reduced the profits of brokers. In addition, the position of jobber or market maker has ceased to exist.

Multimedia

Multimedia is the combination of text, image, video and audio information within a computer and communications environment. Early examples appeared during the 1980s with interactive video aimed primarily at training and these products are fast maturing as leading companies deliver products. According to Bill Gates, a year after its launch in 1993, Microsoft's Encarta electronic encyclopaedia had leapt to the top of the league table, ahead even of the Encyclopaedia Britannica.[12] While multimedia training aids are growing in number the main excitement is in the media world in general with firms in telecommunications, television/film and publishing all positioning themselves to capitalize on future opportunities. A glimpse of how this world might affect the consumer is outlined in Illustration 5.7.

Illustration 5.7 A computerised corner shop

Christmas is coming and your television remote controller has suddenly taken on a new dimension. Press a button and you can select a film; press again and you are one of the first British consumers to be testing an interactive link with a home shopping service, a holiday hotline and a whole range of other retail facilities.

Such is the vision of British Telecom, if as is expected its current employee trials with a new 'video on demand' service are extended to 2,500 consumers in the Autumn.

'The advent of multi-media is not so much a replacement, but an alternative to conventional shopping', says BT. Why, runs the argument, do we need to spend so many hours chasing after essentials such as food and household goods when we can use our television or computer, leaving more time to reflect on the things we really want to own?

Source: Nick Cottam, 'A computerized corner shop', *The Times*, 24 June 1994

Thomas Cook were among the first to launch a multi-media ATM-type machine in the UK which contained video footage of holiday destinations as well as other details. Information on a wide range of holidays is available and the appropriate one can be booked. This sort of technology is bringing a whole new meaning to 'window shopping' as customers can actually use adapted portions of the window itself to enquire about and purchase goods and services.[13]

Virtual reality

Virtual reality (VR) is defined as the simulation of real world events and responses in a computer generated environment. It uses powerful 3-D computer simulations and lets the user 'enter' a computer-generated world. While they are not VR devices by the strictest definition, flight simulators operate along similar lines. The training a pilot receives in a simulator is intended to provide a realistic approximation of the real experience of a flight. The crucial difference between these simulators and a true VR device is that the VR machine would have no real parts, the world would be totally computer generated. VR grew out of a NASA project and became a 'cult' following the publication of *Neuromancer* by William Gibson.

It is early days for VR, however already its potential appears to be enormous. It is easy to envisage the major impact that such devices will have on architects and engineers. They will be able to take clients on full walk-throughs of buildings not yet built, change designs as they 'stand' in the building and generally get client approval without the expensive errors and re-works that are necessary during the physical construction stage of the building. Illustration 5.8 describes how one company is using this technology.

Workflow automation

Workflow automation has close links with BPR as it is a particular type of computer system which seeks to co-ordinate activities. In the past, IT professionals had to construct bespoke systems to achieve this. Now there are a number of specific products available which can be modified to suit particular situations.

Illustration 5.8 Virtual reality at Matsushita

Matsushita Electric Works Ltd. in Osaka Japan manufactures kitchens to customer requirements. In 1994, it will deploy virtual reality decision support systems at its product showroom throughout Japan to help home owners visualize the new kitchens before ordering. With this system, Matsushita hopes to assure a buyer that the planned arrangement of cabinets, counters and appliances really works as the buyer imagines.

The system takes customers into a virtual kitchen generated from their plans. The system lets potential kitchen buyers walk around, open cabinets, check the counter height, turn on faucets and view the room from different angles in 3-dimensional space. Matsushita offers more than 30,000 kitchen products representing an infinite number of layout possibilities. 'The ability to "feel" the room gives the customer confidence that the design is right and helps catch potential problems before the kitchen is built', explained Junji Nomura, senior staff researcher.

Increased customer confidence translates into increased sales. On average, 80% of those who use the virtual reality simulation system place kitchen orders, Nomura claims. For those who do not use VR, the Figure is 35%.

Source: David Kellar, 'Virtual reality, real money', *ComputerWorld*, 15 November 1993, p. 70.

Workflow begins by examining how documents, business forms, and other information wend their way through an organization. This pinpoints bottlenecks and outdated procedures that slow things down and add to costs. New routes are laid out and a workflow system installed to convey information instantly to the right desks – whether it is a digital image of an invoice or an electronic-mail query from a customer.

Workflow software makes the movement of documents automatic, eliminating the need for a human to figure out who should get the information next, collapsing the travel times, and avoiding misrouting. The system can also be programmed to send documents along different paths, depending on content.

The technology has evolved to manage all types of office information, including personal-computer files, incoming phone calls, and even video clips. A frequently cited example of workflow is in processing travel expense reports, as outlined in Figure 5.2. In such a system, an employee fills out an electronic expense form that is automatically routed to his or her manager for approval. After that, the form goes to accounting, or if the expense level is high enough to require additional approval, it is sent to the manager's boss. The routing of the form follows pre-programed rules.

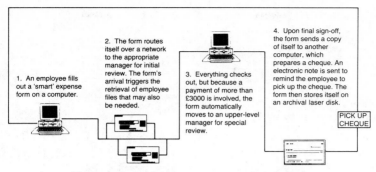

1. An employee fills out a 'smart' expense form on a computer.

2. The form routes itself over a network to the appropriate manager for initial review. The form's arrival triggers the retrieval of employee files that may also be needed.

3. Everything checks out, but because a payment of more than £3000 is involved, the form automatically moves to an upper-level manager for special review.

4. Upon final sign-off, the form sends a copy of itself to another computer, which prepares a cheque. An electronic note is sent to remind the employee to pick up the cheque. The form then stores itself on an archival laser disk.

PICK UP CHEQUE

Figure 5.2 Workflow – a typical application

Figure 5.3 illustrates a shipping process of a company. Orders are received from customers by sales representatives. It then goes through a process of verification, assembling the order and packaging it, and then dispatching it to the customer.

If a workflow system is installed to support the existing process some benefits are gained through the speedier flow of information and the avoidance of any re-input of data into local computers through each stage. Figure 5.4 outlines the new process with each stage using the workflow system.

If the process is redesigned then a number of stages can be eliminated altogether or combined with subsequent steps. Figure 5.5 illustrates an alternative process design with orders being phoned direct to the warehouse who use the system to manage inventories, credit checking and order delivery. When workflow systems are installed it becomes easier to see the flow of information and 'paperwork' between people and some companies use this approach to reach the ultimate goal of a redesigned process. There are mixed messages about whether workflow should be introduced and used as a vehicle for BPR, or, the process redesigned before workflow systems are implemented. We would tend towards the second route although, again, the best approach will depend on the particular circumstances of the company.

Ronni Marshak[14] suggests that to qualify as a true workflow product, the product must offer a way to define and automate the three Rs: routing, rules and roles.

Routing Routing refers to the direction and where objects flow. Objects include documents, forms, data, applications. Routing must also account for the person (or process) to whom the work is being routed.

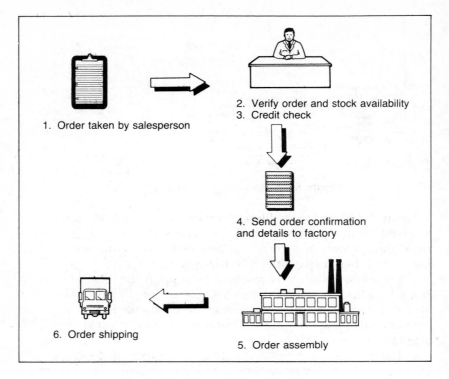

1. Order taken by salesperson

2. Verify order and stock availability
3. Credit check

4. Send order confirmation and details to factory

6. Order shipping

5. Order assembly

Figure 5.3   Pre-workflow operations

Rules   Workflow automation also involves defining rules that determine what information is to be routed and to whom.

Roles   Roles are usually defined independently of the people who carry them out. Defining roles ensures the flexibility of the process; if for example work is to be routed to Susan and she has left the company, the recipient under the new condition would have to be specified.

Roles can be vital when a number of different people have the authorization to do the same work, such as claims adjusters. Any one of them will do; just assign the task to the next available.

Marshak also outlines the three Ps of workflow: processes, policies and practices. The process notion is central to this book and demands no further elaboration.

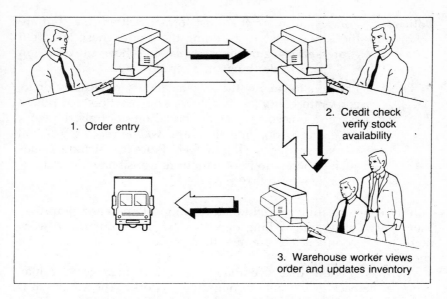

1. Order entry

2. Credit check verify stock availability

3. Warehouse worker views order and updates inventory

Figure 5.4 Initial installation of workflow system

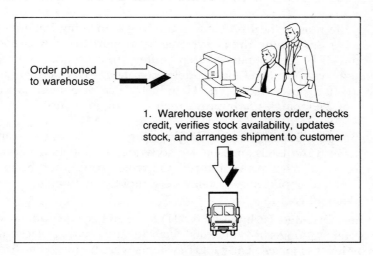

Order phoned to warehouse

1. Warehouse worker enters order, checks credit, verifies stock availability, updates stock, and arranges shipment to customer

Figure 5.5 Redesigned workflow

Policies   Policies are more than just formal written rules but are the actual reasons for doing the work. These are often expressed as guidelines explaining how the decision was made to do things in a certain way.

Practices   Practices relate to the organization's reflections of its corporate culture and values. The practices we put in place in our companies are based on not only the work we have to do, but also how we perceive the actual work experience should feel. Practices include issues such as access to information, responsibility and authority, freedom to take risks.

Simply contemplating workflow automation often sparks improvements. Analysing and writing down an existing sequence of work steps forces companies to examine their procedures – sometimes for the first time.

There is a view that eventually, workflow management may become the backbone of many computer networks. The argument is that once a workflow map is in the network, managers can modify it as often as they like, to squeeze out new efficiencies or accommodate changing work patterns.

Issues surrounding IT

Perhaps the most critical problem in any re-engineering initiative is the issue of developing the IT systems to support the new process architecture. IT departments often suffer from a poor internal reputation with systems being delivered late, over-budget and which do not satisfy users. The IT industry has responded with a number of technologies to improve their own performance:

- **Computer Aided Software Engineering** (CASE) tools became popular in the 1980s and enabled software developers to capture process and data related information which could then be used to generate application systems very rapidly, without the need for detailed coding.

- **Object Oriented Technology** (OOT) has also become popular yet has taken longer to find its way to the market-place and experience is mixed. Early OOT systems were highly specialized, such as the LISP programing language used for early AI applications. OOT systems treat everything as 'objects' which then interact with each other. Many would claim that they represent more accurately the real world and because each object is treated independently, a change to a relationship or another object can be introduced more quickly than in having to change the whole system. One of the major problems of this approach stems from this ease of update in that a small change to an object may have a knock-on effect through the whole system which is very difficult to test out. Today most of the major software developers have products on the market or about to be launched using OOT, however the impact is not yet generally felt by businesses.

- **Rapid Applications Development** is a new model to replace the traditional systems development life cycle. Its emphasis is on the new tools and techniques but also in parallel development, a sort of simultaneous software engineering, using prototypes to speed the validation of system models and specifications.

- **Open Systems** is a drive towards standard, substitutable technology components which can be used in an IT system with reduced cost, complexity and flexibility when compared with multiple proprietary environments. Standards cover operating systems, communications and increasingly other underlying components such as databases and graphical user interfaces. While the drive towards such standards inevitably runs counter to the desire by many vendors to keep customers 'locked' into their systems the shift is clear and continuing, albeit slowly.

Another critical problem area is that of 'legacy systems'. Major re-writes to existing systems can endanger redesign efforts by becoming too large to contain. As Richard Heygate points out 'time after time, the potential value to be unleashed through redesign remains stacked up behind IT bottlenecks, months if not years after implementation should be complete.'[15] Heygate proposes 'filters' as a means to overcome the need to re-write these systems. Indeed, various institutions have done exactly this, building an interface for the user which collects and presents data from a number of old, separate systems. There are still system performance issues to be addressed by such a solution but it does have the advantage of providing systems support for processes quickly and in such a way that modifications, required as the process settles down, are not overly complicated.

In managing IT, and other technologies, one approach which we find useful is the technology management portfolio, based on the

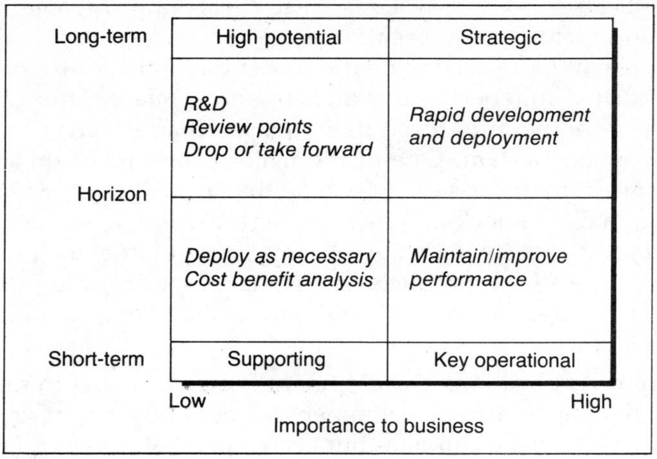

Long-term	High potential	Strategic
	R&D *Review points* *Drop or take forward*	*Rapid development* *and deployment*
Horizon		
	Deploy as necessary *Cost benefit analysis*	*Maintain/improve* *performance*
Short-term	Supporting	Key operational

Low   High

Importance to business

Figure 5.6   The technology management portfolio (after Edwards, Ward and Bytheway[17])

applications portfolio.[16] This is similar to the product portfolio approach proposed by the Boston Consulting Group and treats technology, or applications, as 'products' and classifies them according to the contribution they make (or may make) to the business within the actual and expected competitive environment. This grid, illustrated in Figure 5.6, aids in positioning IT within an organization and relates dependence on IT to its impact on the business. Four types of applications can be defined: supporting, key operational, strategic, and high potential.

Supporting   Applications of IT which improve management effectiveness but are not critical to the business.

Key operational Applications that are critical to sustaining the existing business. In fact, if these systems are not in place the organization will suffer serious disadvantage.

Strategic   Applications which are critical to future business success.

High potential Innovative applications which may be of future strategic importance.

Similar technologies can occupy different positions in different organizations. This is likely to depend on the business strategy of the organization and to some extent on the industry within which the organization competes.

In thinking about the role of IT in an organization we find the following checklist useful:

- What process outcomes is the technology required to facilitate or deliver?
- What forms of technology should be considered for the task?
- What level of technology is acceptable to the people who will encounter it?
- What are the weaknesses of the technology?
- What are the strengths of the technology?
- What additional opportunities does the technology open?
- What threats does a particular technology bring?
- How mature is the technology – is it leading edge, therefore high risk, or is it old but proven?
- Is the technology really necessary or can another solution be found?

Illustration 5.9 outlines the approach of one company in managing IT. We shall return to the subject of IT in later chapters.

Summary of key points

The third pillar of the organization is technology and in this chapter we have focused on information technology, viewing this as most relevant to BPR. Technology plays a leading role, along with processes and people, in success and the appropriate mix of each must be effectively combined to operationalize business strategy. This is not easy as technology is advancing rapidly with new ways of working and living becoming possible at much greater speed.

We started with a quote from Don Burr of People's Express about the importance of IT and we will end with another quote from one of his old business adversaries. Max Hopper argued that technology cannot be management's primary solution because it is every

Illustration 5.9 KPMG Peat Marwick

For service firms, a major challenge of the 90s is how to harness the power of technology in ways that both improve the quality of service and reduce costs. When KPMG Peat Marwick, the largest of the international accounting firms, completed the process of redefining the scope of its client service this year, technology – not surprisingly – was viewed as a critical success factor.

'Information technology is fundamental to our new strategy', says chairman and chief executive Jon C. Madonna. 'As an empowering agent firm-wide, it will enable us to share best information and best practices with our clients and each other on a real-time basis.'

As part of its strategy – revolutionary in the accounting industry – the traditional geographic and functional walls that have divided units of auditors, tax specialists, and management consultants from each other have been eliminated. The firm is creating instead market teams focusing on national lines of business: financial services; government; health care and life sciences; information and communications; manufacturing, retailing and distribution; personal financial planning; energy; education and other institutions; and designated services. Under the plan, partners and managers in each of the firm's ten regional practice areas will report up through the line of business command. Each area will also have its own data processing centre and be responsible for processing practice management, financial, and client information necessary to run the area.

'Implementing our technology vision is a two step process,' says Frank O'Marrs, partner-in-charge, continuous improvement. 'The first step, which is well under way, is to develop a standard computing infrastructure throughout the firm that will allow our professionals to effectively share information and communicate across lines of business. The second step is to build upon this foundation to provide our people with sophisticated knowledge management and analytical tools. That will give us the ability to leverage firm-wide knowledge and deliver the higher valued services our clients demand.'

KPMG Peat Marwick envisions the technology infrastructure as supporting such business applications as client service, knowledge management, practice expansion, practice management, human resource management, and office automation.

One of the applications most advanced in development is a knowledge management system that will allow KPMG professionals easy and immediate access to the vast storehouse of knowledge accumulated by the firm, including firm/staff experience, proposals, studies and reports, company performance comparisons, competitive insights, and reference materials developed by KPMG Peat Marwick as well as by outside sources.

'The major goals of our new technology environment are to support our new organizational structure, leverage the intellectual capital of the firm, and empower our people to serve clients better by making data easily accessible when they need it,' O'Marrs says.

Source: Reprinted with permission from a paid advertising section prepared for *Fortune*, 20 September 1993.

competitors' potential solution.[18] Having been directly responsible for American Airlines SABRE reservations system, he wrote that:

> I do not mean to diminish the pivotal role of information technology in the future or to suggest that technology leadership will be less relevant to competitive success. Precisely because changes in information technology are becoming so rapid and unforgiving and the consequence of falling behind so irreversible, companies will either master or remaster the technology or die. Think of it as a technological treadmill: companies will have to run harder and harder just to stay in place . . . Organizations that stay on the treadmill will be competing against others that have done the same thing. In this sense, the information utility will have a levelling effect. In essence, technological skill is what qualifies a company to play; without it, they can't hope to compete.

References

1. In an interview with F. Warren McFarlan, Harvard Business School. From 1981 to 1985 People's Express enjoyed tremendous growth and was one of the four most profitable airlines in the US. On 19 January 1985, American Airlines and United Airlines took out advertisements across the USA saying they could beat People Express prices in any market they chose. They could do this because they had invested heavily in computerized reservation systems, particularly facilitating sophisticated yield management. People Express went out of business soon afterwards.
2. Randall L. Tobias, then Vice Chairman of AT&T, Henry Ford II Scholar Award Lecture, Cranfield School of Management, 1992.
3. William Gibson, *Neuromancer*, New York: Harper Collins, 1984, 67.
4. 'Hospitals attack a crippler: paper', *Business Week*, 21 February 1994, pp. 50–52.
5. D.P. Douglas, 'The role of IT in business reengineering', *I/S Analyzer*, 31, no. 8 (1993); *The Role of IS in Business Process Reengineering*, P-E Centre for Management Research, November (1993); J.T.C. Teng, V. Grover and K.D. Fiedler, 'Re-design business processes using information technology', *Long Range Planning*, 27, no. 1 (1994), 95–106.
6. Dori Jones Yang, 'Boeing's new president knows how to listen', *Business Week*, 1 March 1993, p. 40.
7. *Electronic Computer Glossary*, The Computer Language Company, 1991.
8. For an excellent discussion on the US National Data Highway, see Blake Ives, 'Ramping up to the US National Data Highway', *MIS*

Quarterly, September (1993), xxxvii–xxxix. See also Paul Craig Roberts, 'Information Highway Robbery', *Business Week*, 21 March 1994, p. 10. For a general review of the information superhighway see 'Building the data highway', *Byte*, March (1994), 46–74 and Philip Elmer-Devitt, 'Battle for the soul of the Internet', *Time*, 25 July 1994, 50–56.

9. Rick Tetzeli, 'The Internet and your business', *Fortune*, 7 March 1994, pp. 56–61.

10. Peter Haapaniemi, 'Making "good things happen"', *Solutions: The Executive Magazine from Unisys*, Spring (1993), 9.

11. *Beneton S.p.A. Industrial Fashion (A)*, Harvard Business School, Teaching Note #5-188-092; *Quick Response in the Apparel Industry*, Harvard Business School Note #9-690-038

12. 'All you ever wanted to know', *The Times*, 24 June 1994.

13. 'Shop Windows that let you look and touch', *Sunday Times*, 22 May 1994.

14. Ronni Marshak, 'Action Technologies' Workflow Products', *Workgroup Computing Report*, 16, no. 5 (1993).

15. Richard Heygate, 'Memo to a CEO: Avoiding the mainframe trap in redesign', *The McKinsey Quarterly*, Autumn (1993), 79–86

16. John Ward, Pat Griffiths and Paul Whitmore, *Strategic Planning for Information Systems*, Chichester: John Wiley & Sons, 1990.

17. C. Edwards, J. Ward and A. Bytheway, *The Essence of Information Systems*, Hemel Hempstead: Prentice Hall International, 1991.

18. Max Hooper, 'Rattling SABRE – new ways to compete on information', *Harvard Business Review*, May–June (1990), 118–125.

Making it happen

Redesigning processes
Realizing the benefits: managing change
Succeeding at BPR

In part two we examined the basic building blocks of organizations: processes, people and technology. For the design of any new process it is important to consider these three elements in relation to the business strategy of the firm and the needs of the market place. In this part of the book we turn our attention specifically to how one might go about re-engineering business processes although these three basic elements are still critical decision areas.

Chapter 6 covers the redesign of processes and the elimination of waste for performance improvement. Chapter 7 presents an overall approach to a BPR programme, how the required change can be managed and the benefits realized. In Chapter 8 we present some dos and don'ts to improve the chances of success for BPR initiatives. initiatives.

6

Redesigning processes

We can lick gravity, but sometimes the paperwork is
overwhelming

Werner von Braun[1]

Reengineering work: don't automate, obliterate

Michael Hammer[2]

Reinvention is not changing what is, but creating what isn't

Richard Pascale[3]

Introduction

In this chapter we examine the main approaches to redesigning
processes for performance improvement, some start points for the
redesign task and a checklist for identifying waste.

In our research we have identified many different methods which
companies use to re-engineer their business processes. A central
area of contention centres around the role that existing processes
should play in BPR:

- Should existing processes be the basis for the new, redesigned,
  processes?
- To what extent should the existing processes be understood?

- Should existing processes be changed at the implementation stage or new processes set up to replace them?
- Should the organization start with a clean sheet?

In our view, ignoring existing processes is high risk, not least because it fails to build on the knowledge and experience which has been built up over time and risks repeating the mistakes of the past. Few companies actually succeed in implementing totally new processes in existing operations. The processes simply bear so little relation to the work that is actually done that workers often cannot relate to the new design and the initiative grinds to a halt. Having said that, we also acknowledge the dangers in analysing existing processes in too great a depth and becoming constrained by them when trying to think of new ways of working. With BPR, as in life, there is no absolute right and wrong and a balance must be struck between gaining knowledge of what currently happens in the process, and new thoughts on how things could be done in an ideal world. Remember, also, that in planning the migration and in managing the required change some understanding is needed of the existing process: after all they are currently in use.

We classify the different approaches to BPR into two broad categories:

1. **Systematic redesign** – identify and understand existing processes and then work through them systematically to create new processes to deliver the desired outcomes.
2. **Clean sheet approach** – fundamentally re-think the way that the product or service is delivered and design new processes from scratch.

There is a great deal of middle ground between these two methods, however, with many organizations choosing a combination of the two. It is worth bearing in mind that many articles and books claim to support the second approach, yet many of the examples they quote actually highlight the first.

The choice between these two approaches will depend on what the organization is most comfortable with, and also on the time scales involved. Whichever alternative is selected, it is important to ensure that the analysis of existing processes is not over done, though the danger of this is higher in the systematic redesign approach. Always remember that the objective, regardless of the approach chosen, is to obtain significant improvements in performance. More attention should be paid, therefore, to the new process rather than the old, which is merely a starting point.

Systematic redesign versus clean sheet

In general, the systematic approach is most often used to implement performance improvements in the short term while the clean sheet approach allows the company to develop new ways to compete in the medium to long term. Systematic redesign tends to require more incremental changes over time, though it can result in significant improvements in the early stages of moving to continuous improvement. The clean sheet approach is more synonymous with making radical changes as the resulting processes usually have no basis in the old. It may, therefore, offer quantum leaps in performance though it does so at significantly greater risk.

We would argue that Western companies usually tend to prefer the clean sheet approach, as the message of radical change is somehow more exciting and indeed more personally rewarding in terms of promotion for the individuals involved. Thus, the increased risk is ignored and perhaps this is the reason for the high failure rate of BPR, which according to some estimates is as high as 70 per cent.[4] It is important to put this into the context that most large scale projects fail to achieve all the targets set for them at the start point. Nevertheless, this is very worrying because often those organizations who have chosen the less risky route of continuous incremental improvements have made considerable gains, and continue to do so while the radical improvement hopes of the others fade. Some organizations recognize that, in their specific situation, talking of radical overhauls to their operations is not appropriate. If customers or shareholders look to the company for reliability, putting that at risk will not be well received unless the firm is under performing and faces a crisis.

The approach adopted by many Japanese manufacturers tends to be more incremental and continuous with the existing processes being constantly refined.[5] The problem with this less risky approach is that it also yields smaller and smaller benefits over time. Eventually, a 'breakpoint' (see Figure 6.1) may be reached where the performance improvement 'wrung' from the process is minimal and a fundamental re-think of how it is performed is required to make further, significant gains. While acknowledging this fact we believe that all too often Western managers leap for the radical change far too early. Many attempts to leap-frog competitors by radical change programmes take so long to deliver the promised performance improvements that the competitors have, through their policy of continuous incremental improvement, passed the target point of the radical change. To quote Dr Len Polizotto, Assistant Director of Research at Polaroid Corporation 'Be careful of the large innovation. The return on investment might be less than the proportionate returns from incremental innovations.'[6] One possible reason why Japanese firms have preferred the incremental continuous route in recent decades could be the relative stability of their economy. The USA and European economies, on the other hand, have been prone to more violent economic swings which may bring an urgency for radical improvements not felt so keenly, until perhaps recently, in Japan. It is also important to recognize that any new process designed from a clean sheet approach may not actually outperform the old process straight away, especially when measured in financial terms. When this is the case it does not mean things have gone wrong; what is important is that new processes have the potential to offer considerably higher levels of performance over the medium term.

Systematic redesign

This approach has the advantage that change can be made incrementally and thus quickly, in small chunks at reduced disruption and risk. Its disadvantage is that its base is the existing process and an innovative new approach is less likely to emerge than with the clean sheet approach, though it can happen. This incremental approach can, however, result in significant step changes in performance when applied on a massive scale, what we refer to as 'massive incremental improvement'. Many European automotive component producers have seen their productivity and quality transformed by the application of JIT methods to their business as they have begun to supply Honda, Nissan and Toyota. Many of these companies have experienced massive incremental change with hundreds of small changes being implemented, adding up to significant improvements in performance as outlined in Illustration 6.1 Not only has their performance improved but they are also applying the continuous improvement philosophy ensuring that they do not get complacent and lose their competitive edge.

The service sector is also embracing this approach and several major banks are undergoing programmes that we would characterize as systematic redesign. These programmes have different labels and often we find that the 'BPR programme' refers to a specific project focusing on more 'radical' change; whether to

Illustration 6.1 Driving out the old regime.

> . . . The Japanese visitor produced 185 Kaizen (continuous improvement) suggestions and Advanced Engineering Systems (AES) teams have come up with half as many again.
>
> The application of TPS [Toyota Production System] principles is already showing in productivity. On the Honda flywheels line, four men were producing 750 flywheels a week on two shifts. Introduction of the U-cells and related improvements, plus a third man lifted output to 1000 a week. The third man has now been re-deployed but output remains at 1000 a week.
>
> Premier [another company] has also introduced the Toyota U-cell system, with reported productivity gains of 30–40 per cent. Perhaps warning other European components groups about the cost and quality benefits deriving from such close links with the Japanese, one leading European vehicle producer is switching to Premier as its exhaust system supplier.

Source: John Griffiths, 'Driving out the old regime', *Financial Times*, 20 August 1993.

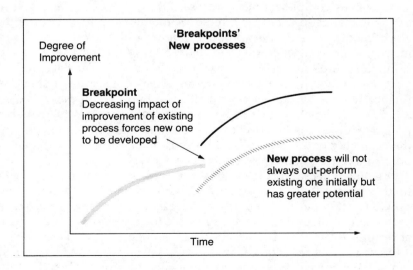

Figure 6.1 Breakpoints and new processes

operate branches or operate a telephone service, for example. If it is useful to distinguish between initiatives in this way then it should be done, but, BPR can be used in a continuous and incremental way and still achieve significant transformations in organizational performance.

Systematic redesign should eventually become an integral part of organizational life as it is, in the form of *Kaizen*, at Toyota.[7] We prefer the term Business Process Management as opposed to Business Process Redesign or Business Process Re-engineering to describe this activity. It has the connotation of a continuous activity rather than a once-off action and avoids the faddish association of BPR and the other 're' words.

Clean sheet approach

This approach has the advantage that it throws away the existing assumptions implicit in the existing process and allows a fundamental rethink in the way business is conducted. Such an approach offers the possibility of a leap in performance; an order of magnitude change in the desired outcome. To obtain a several hundred, or even several thousand per cent improvement in a target, things have to be done very differently. The 'clean sheet' approach is about working back from that target to a design that will make it happen.

As well as completely new processes this approach is also giving rise to a change in products offered. Some newly privatized utilities are hoping to extend their product range based on core capabilities in customer contact, provision and billing. Telephone banking companies are increasingly moving into other financial product areas and may even move into offering a range of services outside of finance, where telephone contact allied to information management are the critical factors for success. Such changes are possible when a process view is combined with a market orientation; understanding the capability of the process as a resource to be exploited as much as other, more traditionally recognized resources.

Organizations adopt a 'clean sheet' approach either because in their opinion they have reached a 'breakpoint', or simply that previous attempts to re-engineer the existing processes through a systematic strategy have failed to result in any significant performance improvement. The main disadvantage of the clean sheet approach is that the required organizational changes can be difficult, though not impossible, to implement incrementally. Overall, with this approach the risk is higher and the pain and disruption greater.

During implementation, a crucial problem faced by many teams who have used this method is that the new processes differ so fundamentally from the existing ones that workers have great difficulty in relating to them. Unless great care is taken and management commitment is solid, workers may refuse to switch to the new methods. Sometimes companies decide a new division or operation is necessary rather than try and change the existing organization. Midland Bank's decision to set up a separate telephone banking company, First Direct, and even General Motors' Saturn business unit are examples of this strategy. This 'greenfield site' approach has a number of distinct advantages, not least, the chance to design the facilities taking into account the latest thinking. Creating the desired culture with a new workforce is also a lot easier than where significant changes must be made to an existing one.

Having designed new processes, organizations will find benefit in then applying the systematic redesign approach prior to implementation and on a continuous basis thereafter. A feature of most new 'greenfield sites' is the commitment to continuous improvement.

Process redesign – doing it

Whatever the approach redesigning processes requires a combination of motivation, attitude, knowledge, creativity and innovation.

Motivation

The motivation to undertake BPR was covered at a strategic level in Chapter 2. At an organizational level, it is necessary to have a clear and coherent argument outlining why improvement is needed and this is a theme that we shall return to in Chapter 7. However, at a deeper level it is necessary to translate these organizational motives into tangible targets which employees can work towards. Setting high targets will set a challenge and build confidence in abilities as the 'impossible' begins to be achieved. Many organizations we come across tell us of outlandishly high targets for performance improvement which when originally set, were thought to be impossible, and which now they are well on their way to meeting. A Motorola advert in 1989 proclaimed what the company called *'the power of belief'*:[8]

> Our formula is a simple one:
> First, banish complacency.
> Second, set heroic goals that compel new thinking.
> Finally, 'raise the bar' as you near each goal. Set it out of reach all over again.

All this from an organization which in 1989 was already held by many to be world-class. At a team level, when 'stretch' targets are set it is not unknown for teams to stretch these targets further as their confidence builds and as they grow to know the techniques better.

This message does take some time to get through though and perhaps it is no accident that it is the Motorola's of this world that preach outlandish targets. In some cultures, notably public sector bodies, it may take some time before 'stretch' targets are accepted and it may be necessary to set what are held to be achievable targets in the first instance to generate a belief in the potential for improvement. These achievable targets should not be cast in stone, however, and should be continually revised and extended as improvements are made, taking care to ensure the teams feel their efforts are rewarded and recognized (if not in a monetary sense).

Attitude

Teams must adopt a questioning attitude. Part of this can be instilled through education and part through the mix of the team. They must question everything, especially assumptions: questioning the sacred cows often yields the best steaks! Probe and obtain facts to support assertions, seek the reasons for something not just the symptoms or results. It is always a good idea to take a 'fresh' look at how work is performed in the process although this can be quite difficult when one is part of the operation. It is important to be creative and innovative in considering how to redesign the process.

Knowledge

In the words of W.E. Deming, 'there is no substitute for knowledge'.[9] Specifically, teams must gain knowledge in two key areas, regardless of their approach to BPR:

- Understand the **service task** and what the customer wants. If the service task is not understood it is likely that any efforts will be misdirected. Knowing your customer, potential customers and lost customers is not easy, particularly in a complex environment where a range of services are being delivered. Those organisations who know their customers best are likely to meet their needs best. Examining existing process outputs might shed new light on the service task and identify what customers really pay for, however these existing outputs may not in themselves be the target outputs for the new process.

- Understand the **potential** in the key areas of **processes**, **people** and **technology**. We like to think of this as a surround to the redesign project. Whatever approach the team takes it will need expertise in all these areas to design a world class process. **Benchmarking** may provide valuable sources of information.

Creativity and innovation

BPR hinges on creativity and innovation applied to processes. Rarely is human kind so creative as in the field of crime. Stories abound of the audacity and daring of simple yet highly successful 'scams' resulting either in stolen riches or the capture of wanted criminals. This natural creativity and ability to innovate exists in all human beings, though it is thankfully not always directed towards crime. It can and should be cultivated and harnessed if an organization is to maximize the value of its people. Despite all this, however, people can become very blinkered within an organizational culture and it is surprising the extent to which a fresh pair of eyes can reveal 'obvious' areas for improvement. People need to develop what is known as 'out of box' thinking – take your mind outside the constraints of the familiar surroundings of the company system and practice lateral thinking. The work of Edward De Bono and Simon Majaro is perhaps best known in this area.[10]

We would see some form of creativity training and idea facilitation as necessary prior to moving on to redesigning the process. An increasing number of software packages aimed at enhancing creativity are available and some organizations have adopted these as a mechanism for improving their learning and creative abilities. These include 'groupware' products, such as the Lotus's 'Notes' product which allows people, whatever their physical location, to view topics and post suggestions or opinions. A group experiencing a problem in a particular area may put up a bulletin board on this topic which can then be read by the entire organization. Someone, somewhere in the organization probably has the solution, but before groupware came along it was extremely difficult to extract their knowledge.

Let us now turn our attention to actually redesigning the process. Although some implementation considerations are discussed, this section concentrates on the redesign activity, not in the implementation of the new processes – this will be covered in the next chapter.

Where to start

One of the problems highlighted to us by companies is that they are often unsure of where to start redesigning. Each organization will have to find its own way, however some guidance can be found by utilizing:

- The performance improvement matrix; see Figure 6.2.
- The learning star – companies can learn about areas for improvement from a number of sources: customers, suppliers, staff and consultants and through a process of benchmarking best practice; see Figure 6.3.
- Evaluate the cost of quality.

Performance/improvement matrix

Martilla and James developed a simple, yet powerful tool called the performance/importance matrix which helps focus attention on those areas which are in most need of improvement.[11] Illustrated in Figure 6.2, the matrix can be used at any level within the organization and can be used to obtain customer feedback as well.

Processes or the outcomes of processes can be plotted on the matrix relative to how well the organization performs them and how important they are. It is often interesting to contrast the data obtained from an organization with that obtained from its customers. Rank the two scales on a 1–5 basis which will allow placement of the items considered in one of the four quadrants.

Additional start points are highlighted in the 'learning star' shown in Figure 6.3.

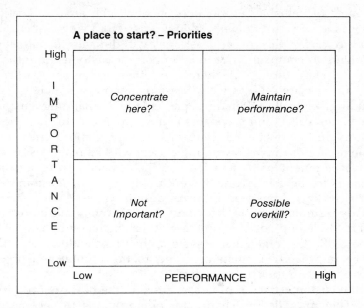

Figure 6.2   Performance/importance matrix (after Martilla and James[11])

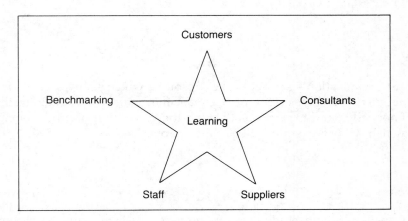

Figure 6.3   The learning star

Customer and supplier feedback

A source of valuable information on how well an organization is performing are customers. Obvious yes, but many organizations seem to forget this or at least make it difficult for dissatisfied customers to complain. The most important customers are the best place to start though if there are others who are particularly innovative or are seen as world class operators these will be worth including as well. Often any particularly demanding customers (sometimes called 'unreasonable') may provide a further view of what might be possible targets for a clean sheet approach.

Boeing, for example, is working closely with its main customers in the development of a new jet, the 777. Seemingly unreasonable demands for flexible layouts have, through a Boeing/customer team approach, been translated into real design success.[12] Suppliers can provide a similar view to customers, and this may not be restricted to the 'back end' of the process either. Better suppliers will be interested in the total delivery system, their part within it and how it can be improved for customers and to the mutual benefit of all organizations in the supply chain.

Often **customer facing processes** provide the best opportunity for BPR. They provide the chance for organizations to become more effective as well as efficient and improvements are thus likely to impact the bottom line more immediately than non-customer facing processes.

Staff

An organization's staff are a key resource which know a great deal about its processes. One of the main mechanisms for utilizing this knowledge and expertise is through the generation of process maps which we will examine later in the chapter.

Consultants

Consultants and academics can provide a useful, 'outsider's' view and act as facilitators for the BPR programme. In our opinion implementation should be undertaken by the organization's own employees who must own the changes, either in partnership with, or supported by, external people.

Benchmarking

Benchmarking can highlight areas for improvement simply by pointing out what is possible. When Ford found out that Mazda had only five people in its accounts payable department versus the 500 Ford had doing the task, it challenged the company's traditional thinking about the process. Knowing it could do better, Ford re-engineered the process and was able to reduce its staff by 75 per cent.

Benchmarking is not new, but like BPR it has received a lot of hype in recent years. In the field of sport, athletes have been benchmarking themselves against their competitors since the dawn of civilization. Today, many businesses seek knowledge and inspiration by benchmarking themselves with others.

Benchmarking can be undertaken at various levels and against a number of bodies. Comparison can be done between:

- different departments within a division;
- different divisions within a company or organization;
- different organizations within the same industry;
- different organizations in different industries.

The comparison can be made across a range of activities and need not be restricted to a limited set of performance measures and processes. Topics could include:

- budgetary or financial performance;
- customer service delivery systems and measures;
- productivity measures;
- use of technology;
- planning and project management practices;
- human resources management;
- financial control systems.

Benchmarking is particularly useful in broadening people's perspectives. Computer company ICL, for example, measured its training methods against those of the Royal Mail. A regional airline in the US strongly improved turnaround time for its aircraft by studying the methods of pit crews at the Indianapolis 500 car race.[13] Often, however, the results of benchmarking projects can be painful to some of the companies taking part in the exercise. No one likes to be

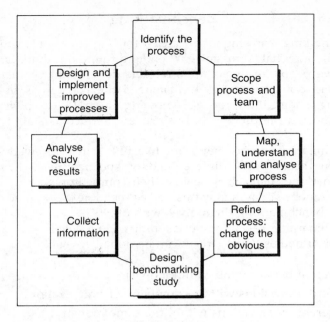

Figure 6.4   Benchmarking framework

told how bad they are and corporate pride is every bit as strong as that of the individual. Once organizations, and the individuals within them, get over this reaction the results can provide a powerful motivating factor in initiating much needed change. Benchmarking also helps at this stage too by providing a chance to view what is possible, through the achievements of others, and how change may be better managed by sharing experiences.

Figure 6.4 outlines an approach to undertaking a benchmarking exercise.

In some ways, benchmarking takes the place of training bodies such as business schools and consultants by putting organizations in touch with each other and eliminating the need for a teacher to pass on the lessons learned. Having said that many business schools and consultancies now make money by acting as the catalyst to benchmarking consortia and facilitating the knowledge transfer. Often companies join a group of other companies to gain exposure to practices and methods outside of their own domain. These consortium groups, many of which exist at the Cranfield School of Management, can be very effective in transferring knowledge from one sector or activity to another. Some of the groups at Cranfield specifically exchange experiences in BPR. These groups have a further advantage in providing those involved in BPR with a network with whom they can discuss problems and share experiences.

Evaluate the 'cost of quality'

Evaluating the cost of quality will highlight a monetary cost of the problems in an organization and highlight areas for improvement. The cost of quality is discussed in Chapter 3.

Understand existing process

One of the most effective ways to gain an understanding of existing processes is to chart them onto a 'map'. Process maps are intended to represent a process in such a way that it is easier to read and understand. In Chapter 3 we drew what were really process maps to represent customer, front-office and back-office processes, and such maps have long been used to design processes in a manufacturing environment. 'Process mapping' has become increasingly popular in recent years and is no longer the preserve of manufacturing, engineers or information systems professionals.

The maps should be living, breathing documents which are 'owned' by the team improving the process. By this we mean that they should be used. We come across so many companies who have hundreds, sometimes thousands, of process maps but have yet to actually make much use of them and are wondering what their value is, having invested a great deal of effort.

During the mapping process it is important to recognize that each task may be viewed differently by people and working methods may vary. These different perspectives may result from a resistance to sharing how things are actually done, particularly if rules are broken, but may also result from the fact that each worker will find the optimum way of working for themselves. The most important things to concentrate on is the input and the output of each step and those ways of working which seem to be best. The experience of the First National Bank of Chicago is indicative of this. During an analysis of customer service employees' work habits, people doing the same job gave different versions of what each did. There was also a gap between what they said they were doing and what was actually happening.[14] The process map provides a focal point for discussions about the way people work and will help create a common understanding of work patterns.

Process maps – advantages

- **Usability** – Maps often give a clearer explanation of a process than words. They should be highly usable, enabling teams to clearly see the process and identify waste and areas for improvement.

- **The mapping process itself** – Much of the advantage lies not with the maps themselves but the process of actually producing them. Where individuals work together to produce an end-to-end map of the processes in which they work they gain an understanding of others' tasks and problems and how they contribute to these. Often the act of mapping spurs teams and individuals into improvement – visibility of wasteful, or plain silly, process steps makes people want to change them.

Process maps – disadvantages and pitfalls

- **Distraction** – Incredibly process mapping can become, to some people, more important than the improvement it is intended to facilitate. We have heard of companies deliberately slowing down or halting improvements altogether just to ensure the maps are accurate. While discipline is needed to ensure actions do not have unforeseen consequences, halting actions to maintain a diagram's integrity seems stupid given its only purpose was to help improvement.

- **Life of its own** – The mapping process can take on a life of its own and lose its relevance to those working on the process. This is particularly true when the mapping is done by central staff functions or specialists using fancy computer packages, of which there are a large number.

- **Misuse for communications** – Maps, contrary to many expectations, do not necessarily make good means of communicating, especially between layers of management. Communication should be undertaken using means appropriate to the audience and this should be borne in mind at all times. Just because the BPR team finds process mapping useful, does not mean that it is a good way of communicating to the board.

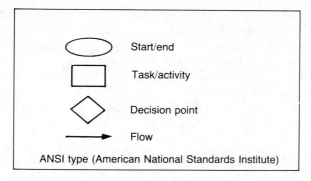

Figure 6.5 Simple flow chart symbols

Mapping

We would recommend that a first process map is constructed by the teams using simple flow-charting techniques. To try and force the use of a standard usually fails or inhibits the teams' flow as they become more 'hung up' on the standard than the knowledge they are documenting. A few simple symbols are sufficient at this stage, and we suggest those shown in Figure 6.5.

It is often useful to put these symbols on *post-it* note type papers so that they can be shuffled around the wall or board as the map begins to take shape. This will save time in constant redrawing of the diagram in the early stages. Different coloured *post-its* can be used to represent the different symbols to add clarity to the diagram, but avoid colour combinations that are a problem for colour-blind people. We have heard of companies using large, pre-printed, *post-its* which can be 'filled in' during the process to capture vital information.

Information which we see as important to note down for each step in the process includes:

- **Lead times** – how long is the process overall, how long does it take to complete each step and in between each step?
- **Dependences** should be clear, i.e. where a task depends on the output of another.
- **Who** is performing each task?
- **Problem areas** should be shown – those tasks that are difficult, dirty or dangerous and those which frequently experience problems.

- **Value adding** – whether a step 'adds value' or merely adds cost. Value adding was discussed in more detail in Chapter 3.

It is necessary to identify 'levels' of processes as outlined in Chapter 1. By having these levels the complete process cycle can be shown in a manageable way with each process step being broken down into more detail on another chart.

IDEF0
The IDEF0 mapping standard (Figure 6.6) is frequently used for BPR initiatives. It was developed by the US Department of Defence during the 1970s and stands for International DEFinition. While it started life as a software development tool, it has found acceptance in a variety of manufacturing and service organizations as a general process mapping tool. It can be used to derive a relationship diagram, if so wished, and some of the computer packages which adhere to it (often loosely) can perform the translation automatically, aiding software development.

A high level map usually identifies the major processes by which the company operates, for example:

- Direction setting.
- Win the customer.
- Deliver to the customer.
- Support the customer.
- Support the organization.

A second level map would then be constructed, breaking each of these processes into a sequence of steps. This second level map can then be further broken down and so on until the appropriate level of detail is identified. Companies should not shy away from the detail of the process as this is necessary to really understand what is happening through the organization, in particular what the staff and customers are experiencing. Having said this it is also important that those constructing the maps do not get bogged down in minute detail. A diagram showing process levels appears in Figure 1.7 in Chapter 1.

For detailed level mapping we would recommend another standard widely used in manufacturing and beginning to be used in office and service environments: ASME (American Society of Mechanical Engineers), as shown in Figure 6.7.

This method has one distinct advantage – inherent in its use is an

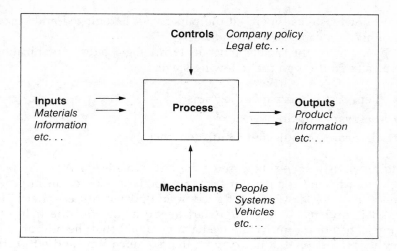

Figure 6.6 IDEF0 process map

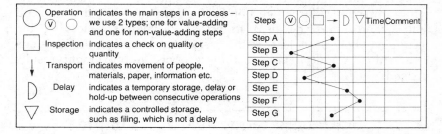

Figure 6.7 ASME mapping standard (after Oakland[15])

evaluation of whether a step is value adding. Only one of the columns contains value adding steps and thus the areas of waste or non-value-adding activity are clear. While the value-adding column's steps may also be improved the chart provides a powerful focus on those areas that definitely should be minimized to improve overall process efficiency.

Tools

There are a number of software products available on the market to produce flowcharts and process maps. These range from simple drawing tools which draw maps to a certain standard, to more elaborate systems which enable the users to monitor and control workflow systems where all the paperwork is digitized and passed around on a computer network.

Even with the availability of technology aids, organizations typically go through the following stages:

- Pen, *post-it* and paper diagrams.
- Software drawing packages.
- Software analysis and simulation packages.

As previously stated, beware of the last two stages. We have been told that in one company it takes up to six weeks for an improvement to the process to be reflected in an updated process chart. This chart is updated by a central staff department, with the help of a large consulting firm. While we have no doubt that the output looks highly professional, it is worrying that so much time and effort, not to say consultancy expenditure, is put into mapping the processes. Because of the lead time to make changes, the improvement effort is hindered and the expertise of the staff department channelled in the wrong direction. Our suggestion to the company – file the lot, send staff experts into the field to act as facilitators – leaving the technology behind (at least in the first instance) and let the divisions return their financial and customer service improvement results instead.

Stationery requests – an example

Now let us look at a process and understand how it can be 'mapped', for this we will examine the process of ordering stationery. This might seem a rather trivial example, but this is a process which all organizations undertake, albeit differently, and for many it accounts for significant cost. The example is based on a real company's actual processes. We start, as outlined in Chapter 3, with an analysis of the service task.

Service task

1. **Customer service dimensions**
   Ideally people would like instantaneous retrieval of stationery items with short lead time if orders are necessary. People would like to know what is available and be able to place orders easily.

2. **Patterns of demand**
   On the whole demand is fairly constant, however when a new

pre-printed form is issued old forms have to be destroyed. At these times demand for new forms is high and the introduction of new forms must be co-ordinated with the stores.

3. **Constraints**

    All purchasing is done centrally thus the stores can only stock 'approved' items. They are also constrained by company policy over who can authorize stationery requests for particular items, though in practice stores' staff exercise a considerable degree of discretion.

4. **Efficiency target**

    Like all areas the stationery stores are under constant pressure to reduce their inventory holding. In addition the overall amount of stationery held by the company is targeted for reduction to minimize cost and mistakes caused by the use of out-of-date forms.

We will map the detail level steps using the ASME method outlined in Figure 6.8.

So we have our mapped process but what now? The map covers a lot of detail and many will think it too much. We would agree, if a clean sheet approach is to be adopted, but for systematic redesign this level of detail will often be necessary. There is a lot of detail because there are a lot of steps. If some of the detail were left out the truly ridiculous nature of the process would be missed. All that time and effort wasted by the organization to get a pencil! We have not mapped any stage as a value-adding process, as in customer terms none are, though we show a step 53 as using the stationery item to satisfy the customer. We know, therefore, that this process is merely a supporting mechanism and thus it should be as simple and as efficient as possible.

Multi-part forms were used to collect orders. These forms then passed through the hands of at least four people if we count only one mail person: the requestor, their manager, the mail person, the store keeper. In all 52 steps were involved in ordering a simple stationery item. On the whole the process was not all bad; the people involved understood each stage and there was no translating of formats from one reference number to another. Typically it took a couple of days (14 hours, and that assumes a maximum wait of one hour for mail at collection stages) for the stationery to come through to the requestor. Although the customers were not singing their praises of the system, it only became a problem if they ran out of something and could not borrow it from their team mates. Because they kept a good local store this rarely happened.

STATIONERY ORDER PROCESS

No.	Steps	V	O	→	D	Time	Who/comment
1	Obtain multi-part stationery request form	1				2	Requestor
2	Open catalogue for reference numbers	1				0.5	Requestor
3	Complete multi-part stationery request form	1				5	Requestor
4	Find envelope		1			0.5	Requestor
5	Write address on envelope	1				0.5	Requestor
6	Enclose stationery request in envelope	1				0.5	Requestor
7	Send request for signature		1			0.5	Requestor
8	Wait in out-tray				1	60	Requestor
9	Collect internal mail	1				0.5	Mail
10	Take to internal mail office		1			10	Mail
11	Wait until all mail arrives				1	30	Mail
12	Sort mail	1				20	Mail
13	Bundle mail for delivery	1				10	Mail
14	Wait until all mail ready for delivery				1	30	Mail
15	Deliver mail	1				0.5	Mail
16	Wait in in-tray				1	30	Manager
17	Open envelope	1				0.5	Manager
18	Manager inspects request			1		1	Manager
19	Signs request	1				0.5	Manager
20	Changes address on envelope to stationery	1				0.5	Manager
21	Send to stationery administration		1			0.5	Manager
22	Wait in out-tray				1	60	Manager
23	Collect internal mail	1				0.5	Mail
24	Take to internal mail office		1			10	Mail
25	Wait until all mail arrives				1	30	Mail
26	Sort mail	1				20	Mail
27	Bundle mail for delivery	1				10	Mail
28	Wait until all mail ready for delivery				1	30	Mail
29	Deliver mail	1				0.5	Mail
30	Wait in in-tray				1	30	Stationery
31	Open envelope	1				0.5	Stationery
32	Check authority and form details			1		1	Stationery
33	Place order on picklist	1				0.5	Stationery
34	Wait for all orders to be processed				1	60	Stationery
35	Consolidate pick list and determine pick route	1				30	Stationery
36	Pick stationery items	1				60	Stationery
37	Bundle order together	1				5	Stationery
38	Wait until all orders bundled				1	60	Stationery
39	Add stationery cost to department budget record	1				1	Stationery
40	Wait while other order details entered				1	30	Stationery
41	Place white copy of order form for filing			1		1	Stationery
42	Send items to requester plus blue copy of form	1				1	Stationery
43	(plus re-order instructions for out-of-stock items)						Stationery
44	Wait in out-tray				1	60	Stationery
45	Collect internal mail	1				0.5	Mail
46	Take to internal mail office		1			10	Mail
47	Wait until all mail arrives				1	30	Mail

No.	Steps	Ⓥ	◯	→	□	D	Time	Who/comment
48	Sort mail		1				20	Mail
49	Bundle mail for delivery		1				10	Mail
50	Wait until all mail ready for delivery					1	30	Mail
51	Deliver mail			1			0.5	Mail
52	Wait in in-tray					1	30	Requestor
53	Use stationery to satisfy customer	▨						
	STEPS	0	27	7	2	15	836	14 hours
	TIMES	0	201	33	2	600	836	

Time measured in minutes

Figure 6.8 A detailed process map of the stationery ordering process

What we have done with this map is what Shapiro *et al.* called 'walking an order'.[16] That is, we have gone through every step that occurs from order to fulfilment, on what is, or should be, a very simple process. We would advise that every redesign team takes the approach of 'walking an order' whether they be mapping an actual order taking process or some other process such as a request for information or query. Having done so, and constructed their map, they should then ask the following questions of the process:

- How are orders taken?
- Is there any pattern, i.e. are there runners, repeaters and strangers?
- How many people are involved through how many stages?
- Do the people involved understand the whole process?
- Are you translating formats?
- How long does it take to process an order and how much time is spent actually working on an order at each step?
- What is your customers' view of your performance?

How would you redesign the process?
Let us start by looking at what is important. In our view, speedy access to stationery for the user and minimization of costs to the company. These two objectives, are, to some extent in conflict with each other and a balance must be achieved. Making the process easier and speeding it up will reduce the tendency for people to

over-order and minimize the number of times they have to go through the process. Over-ordering can be a major problem as it raises inventory costs which may not be very visible or significant per desk, but adding up the desks of, say, 20 000 employees, this cost is not trivial. This is not so far-fetched and after an investigation, one major bank in the UK found its stationery costs ran into millions of pounds per year. Clearly the company needs to keep some control over these costs.

From the map we can see that a great deal of the time is spent by the parties involved in getting the form authorized and sent to the stationery department but is it really necessary to get authorization for everything? How often do managers turn down stationery requests and why? Is it necessary to pinpoint who has initiated the request? Actually as it turned out very few, if any, requests were refused and the requestor information rarely used. What was important was that managers could review their department's use if necessary. In that case, why go through the authorization process at all? Even though it does not consume much management time, it is nonetheless wasteful and does mean a significant delay due to the mail processing required to support it.

One way of redesigning the process would be to allow telephone ordering of stationery, perhaps with certain cut-off times morning and afternoon. These cut-off times would allow stationery department staff to take the orders, pick the items and put them in the outward mail system to the requesting area for delivery within a certain time. For example all orders placed before 12 noon would arrive at the department stock point later that afternoon. All orders phoned in before 3pm would be delivered by the first post the following day. What we have done is to replace steps 1 to 33 with a simpler set of steps, namely:

1. Open catalogue for reference numbers.
2. Phone stationery department.
3. Place order.

Of course it would be necessary to change the working practices of the stationery staff somewhat, and depending on the phone system some queuing mechanism for calls may be required. The benefits however are that all unnecessary management time and disruption is eliminated, stationery forms themselves have been eliminated and thus their handling at each stage saving several hours in the overall cycle. Control of costs can still be effected by making the 'spend' by each department available and visible.

The stationery order process described above is relatively simple and BPR teams will generally face more significant tasks. Gaining a good process understanding of more complex processes takes more time and it is important that the level of detail shown above is not entered into, unless necessary, to point out areas where savings can be made. As stated many times already, it is important to gain an understanding of existing processes but only to help you create a better set. Process understanding is so key to improvement that even the most senior management must get involved to some degree, as Reuters found out, much to its benefit as outlined in Illustration 6.2.

Illustration 6.2 Restoring order from chaos

When Parcell and Sanderson were called in from Reuters' continental European operations to become managing director and deputy at the British company, they discovered that many customers in the City of London – by far Reuters' largest market – were having to wait between three and six months to receive new hardware and services. Even if no hardware was involved, it took a fortnight.

From that point, it often took the company two months just to send the bill, and another three or more to collect payment. The cause of this mess was the slow and fragmented nature of the company's long-standing procedures for taking orders, issuing contracts, processing them, arranging and executing installation, invoicing clients and then taking payment.

'The processes which the staff were trying to operate were highly compartmentalized,' says Parcell. 'Even a simple order would go through up to 12 departments' – and five computer systems. In all, there were about 24 'hand-offs' between different specialists as an order was processed, even if no re-work was required to correct the many errors.

. . . An irate client's telephone call was almost invariably answered by someone who knew nothing about the order in question, but had to pass the inquiry on from one department to another. So many inquiries were never answered.

To anyone who had strayed into Reuters from a halfway modernized factory, even back in the mid-1980s, the whole arrangement would have seemed crazy. But, as Sanderson says, it is far easier to see, and re-design, all the different parts of the physical flow in a factory than it is to analyse all the inputs into a set of white-collar processes.

The Parcell-Sanderson recovery programme involved five consecutive steps, aimed at starting to serve customers promptly, accurately and to their satisfaction:

- The organization was broken into four geographic divisions capable of getting closer to customers.
- Each division was sub-divided into a series of small multi-functional 'account teams', consisting of 'account managers' (former salespeople), planning engineers, and 'business administrators' . . . Each team, of between three and six people, was grouped round an array of desks

and terminals. Each was given a small number of clients: between six and 50, depending on the size of customers.

- The entire 'customer order life-cycle' (order through installation to payment) was redesigned from scratch, in order to allow the new teams to operate smoothly 'from end-to-end' . . . A series of the previous steps . . . were condensed into one, or avoided entirely.

Instead of every step being done sequentially by separate departments, several activities are now carried out in parallel by the team members.

As a result, the number of hand-offs through which the process had to pass was reduced from two dozen to four. A series of timing and other performance criteria was also laid down, in most cases for the first time, so that customers and staff knew exactly what was expected.

Few changes have yet been made to people's incentives, except for the crucial one that sales staff now receive commission once orders are installed, rather than received.

- . . . records have been straightened out. . .
- The reliable and flexible old computer system, which has operated the new order process reasonably well, is in the process of being replaced by a more up-to-date system designed specifically to suit the new process . . .

The impact of the new, team-based process has been striking. More than 95 per cent of installations are now on time: between three and four weeks after ordering if hardware and services are both involved, and barely a day for services alone. Bills are now more than 98 per cent accurate and debt from recalcitrant customers is minimal.

Independent market research studies show that, on almost every category of customer attitudes, dissatisfaction has been brought down to 10 per cent or less.

The way most front-line employees feel about the change is encapsulated by one business administrator, Alan Maguire. The old atmosphere of all-round 'firefighting', and buck-passing between specialists, has been replaced by one of mutual help and 'covering' for each other, he says. 'It is astonishing how much has been achieved by co-locating us not just in the same building or on the same floor, but around the same desk'.

Source: Extracts from Christopher Lorenz, *Financial Times*, 2 June 1993.

Systematic redesign – of an existing process

Redesigning an existing process, or for that matter refining a newly designed one is usually about making it:

Better
Cheaper
Faster

Table 6.1 Areas of attention for systematic redesign

ELIMINATE	SIMPLIFY	INTEGRATE	AUTOMATE
Over-production	Forms	Jobs	Dirty
Waiting time	Procedures	Teams	Difficult
Transport	Communication	Customers	Dangerous
Processing	Technology	Suppliers	Boring
Inventory	Problem areas		Data capture
Defects/failures	Flows		Data transfer
Duplication	Processes		Data analysis
Reformatting			
Inspection			
Reconciling			

Better, in that it delivers higher levels of satisfaction to its stakeholders, particularly customers. Faster in that is does so as quickly as possible to increase responsiveness. Cheaper in that it does the above to the highest levels of efficiency.

The ultimate, if only theoretical, goal for every organization is that all its activities should 'add value' in some way to the customer. When redesigning existing processes the emphasis is on the elimination of all non-value-adding activities and the streamlining of the core value-adding ones. The rule for doing this can best be summarized as ESIA:

- Eliminate.
- Simplify.
- Integrate.
- Automate.

Table 6.1 highlights the main areas of attention within these four steps.

Eliminate

All non-value adding steps in the process should be eliminated, or, as Michael Hammer puts it, 'obliterate' them. Where process thinking is new, a large number of activities are often found to be non-value-adding. Ways of working evolve over the years and few see the waste when working in a functional set up.

Toyota has a rule of thumb estimate that in many traditional manufacturing operations 85 per cent of the workers may not be working at any given time:[17]

- 5 per cent may be seen not to be working.
- 25 per cent will be waiting for something.
- 30 per cent could be building inventory which Toyota does not regard as work as it does not directly contribute to the company.
- 25 per cent will be working according to inefficient standards or methods.

While there may be some disagreement about the definitions, it is important to recognize that Toyota pays a great deal of attention to detail and finds significant efficiency improvements from redesigning the detailed tasks which are performed. It applies these lessons not just in the factory, but also in the office. We use Toyota's seven wastes as a start point to examine candidates for 'elimination'. These are adapted and extended to cover many non-value-adding activities which should be eliminated as far as possible:

- **Over-production/over-provision** – producing more than is needed at any given time is a major source of waste. All such over-production achieves is to build up inventories and hide problems. This does not just apply to manufacturing, many services can suffer from this, for example, too much food prepared in a restaurant which must then be thrown away.

- **Waiting time** – There is a cost to material, paper or persons having to wait for something. We are not just talking about storage depots where the manager proudly tells you how many millions of pounds worth of stock is stored there, but all those moments in the day when for one reason or another you have to wait for something, or someone. Where that wait is so long that work on the next item commences, the effect is worsened. Either the worker will be disrupted when what they have been waiting for arrives, or the item or items will sit in folders or on the floor while the current item is worked on. In a system where this is allowed to happen it is not uncommon for the form or item currently being worked on to also require something for which it must wait. Paperwork or inventories build up, throughput times are increased, tracking and monitoring become more complex and little is actually being released or available for release to the customer. In manufacturing, operator and machine utilization measures have been used for a long time, however just keeping people busy and not actually producing what is required when it is required does not eliminate waiting time as such, it merely passes the problem into inventory. In services, waiting time, either for people or paper, is less visible yet equally as costly.

- **Transportation, movement and motion** – every time people, material and paper move, it costs money. Something or someone must move material and paper around, and the time taken to move it, is time that could be spent on adding value to it. It is not unknown for some components, worth only a few pence, to travel miles during their manufacture, or for paperwork to zigzag its way round and between office floors without anyone really being aware of this cost, especially relative to the value added. Economic factors may have dictated that manufacture take place in different countries; however the complete process must be examined. One hi-tech company found that its semi-conductors travelled 15 000 miles during their transformation from raw material to finished goods delivered to the customer! Manufacture took place in the Far East, testing in the USA and many were sold in Europe. The movement of people is also costly – why are they moving, what value does it add and could the time not be better spent working on the next piece of material or paper, or even with another customer?

- **Processing** – does the process add value – if not why is it being done? Even if it is value-adding it may be inefficient either because the product has been badly designed resulting in poor processing, or, the process has not been fully developed or refined. Where the process is 'out of control', i.e. it is not predictable to any great degree of certainty – the cause of this variability must be eliminated.

- **Inventory and paperwork** – why is inventory or paperwork needed? Is it strictly necessary to ensure immediate customer satisfaction? Perhaps the paperwork is required for the delivery of another part of the service task, say a legal requirement for a signature. As discussed in Chapter 3, excess inventory is the scourge of the factory. Similarly, spurious paperwork and forms tie up armies of bureaucrats, yet contribute little to the services actually being received by the consumer.

- **Defects, failures and reworking** – the goal should be to get all things right first time and avoid the cost of labour, materials, disruption and opportunity cost involved in rectifying problems. In the front office this can be especially critical where systems are overloaded, i.e. load exceeds capacity. Under these conditions, quality is likely to be degraded and as customers complain and seek help this will further exacerbate an already poor situation. A classic example of this is airline overbooking. One experience was where even after Air France flights from Paris to London had been cancelled through strikes for over a week, at least one carrier continued to overbook each flight by 10 people! As all the flights were fully booked and passengers were, on the whole, turning up, this seemed extreme folly. As each flight became due for departure a growing melee of angry and frustrated customers sought to get their seats. As the clock struck the hour before departure time these passengers demanded that no-shows be removed from the manifest and their names added. A few minutes later the no-shows arrived, having been detained by the airline itself in a queue elsewhere in the airport, to find their seats gone. And so the situation got worse. In the back office, rework can also store up problems which later surface with the customer. Where rework is performed by staff at the end of a production line it is unlikely that the work will be completed exactly as it should. Tools which are not calibrated exactly, yet seem to do the job, may be used by these professional 'fixit' people who believe they are reworking the quality back into the item, but may only be delaying failure. The important thing to remember here is that it is the **cause** of the failures that should be eliminated and this is most likely to be a **process problem**, not a people one.

- **Duplication of tasks** – each task that is carried out should add value in some way. If a task is repeated it does not add value but merely contributes to costs. Raising paper work and inputting data to computer systems are often found to be repeated elsewhere in the organization. This search for duplication can be carried beyond the boundary of the individual organization and into the supply chain as a whole. EDI, as discussed in Chapter 5, can mean that information need only be input at one point through the entire supply chain with additional elements of data being added to that already existing. Not only does this eliminate the unnecessary task of inputting the data a second time, but it eliminates an additional source of problems, that of errors and mismatches between first and second, or subsequent, inputs of data.

- **Reformatting or transferring of information** – this is another form of duplication. Quite often data is transferred from one form to another, or printed from one computer system only to be input manually to another. This frequently occurs when information moves across organizational boundaries, but that need not mean it has to continue. We know of one major company which now completes its supplier's order forms direct. Prior to this, information on customer orders was manually transferred to the supplier's own internal document.

- **Inspection, monitoring and controls** – while some may be justified, many exist for historical reasons and have become part of the justification for jobs and management layers. *'Counting all personnel, budget, procurement, accounting, auditing, and headquarters staff, plus supervisory personnel in field offices, there are roughly 700,000 federal employees whose job it is to manage, control, check up on or audit others. This is one third of all federal civilian employees.'*[18] Often monitoring and controls occur where departmental boundaries are crossed. Traditionally this happens a lot through the delivery of products or services and has been an agreed way of apportioning cost to different parts of an operation. Increasingly, as the very structure of the organization is being questioned, many monitors and controls cease to be relevant. It is a good idea to draw a distinction between the different types of monitoring and controls as these must be approached differently:

- Regulatory;
- Customer and consumer bodies or watchdogs;
- Organizational for both quality and productivity.

Clearly the organization must comply with regulatory requirements and there may be every reason to do so, such as with health and safety checks. The organization may be able to influence 'watchdogs' but it has the most scope for redesign in those controls it uses for itself. Organizations should be clear about the necessity of each and every one either for quality assurance or productivity/financial health.

- **Reconciling** – similar to monitoring and controls and a classic bureaucratic pastime. While it is good to ensure that things match it is important to realize the purpose of the process as a whole. It was the significant reduction, and then automation, of the number of details to be matched that led Ford to achieve a 75 per cent reduction in the staffing levels of its Accounts Payable function.[19]

At every point through the process the team should consider what contribution is being made to the service task. Teams are often surprised at the number of steps which do not add value and which have previously been taken for granted. These non-value-adding activities are the first targets in any systematic redesign initiative. How can they be eliminated and/or minimized ensuring that this does not have a negative impact downstream in the process?

Simplify

Having eliminated as many of the unnecessary tasks as possible it is important to simplify those that remain. The search for areas which are overly complex can be aided by identifying areas which match the following:

- **Forms** – Do you know what percentage of your firm's forms are completed incorrectly? You should do, and it is not adequate to point the finger at the person who completed it, and should identify the root cause. The chances are that by redesigning the form, significant improvements can be made thus eliminating the need to go back to the originator and ask for clarification or to provide further explanation.

- **Procedures** – Often procedures are overly complicated and difficult to understand. In some cases this may be so evident that staff simply cannot be expected to get them right all the time. *'. . . we have more than 100,000 pages of personnel rules and regulations defining in exquisite detail how to hire, promote, or fire federal employees.'*[20]

- **Communication** – both to the customer and to staff must be clear and understandable to all. Jargon should be avoided wherever possible and simple, clear language used. Recognizing this, the Prudential Insurance Company in the UK has launched a new drive for many of its products to ensure that the longest word contained in their documents is 'Prudential'.

- **Technology** – It is imperative to ensure that any technology is appropriate to the task being performed – avoid high-tech solutions where low-tech will do. In the form of computer screens, technology also accounts for many delays and mistakes. Poorly designed interfaces which are not appropriate to the job they are used for, are plentiful. Some of the simplest, yet functional interfaces may not receive any software award or run under such and such an operating system, but they may allow for high-speed data capture or validation which is what is most important. Increasingly, software companies are recognizing that as they sought to make ever more functional user-interfaces, they merely made them more user-hostile, and we could name quite a few well-known packages as examples. Many are now blaming the software, not the user, when the user takes the long route to perform something, or does not use a particular function. The aim is for more intuitive, simple to use software that does the job it is required to do, and does it well. Fancy 'bells and whistles' can be added for the 'power user' if required, but are not made standard.

- **Flows** – while most processes are initially designed to have a natural flow or order this can become corrupted or impeded as changes are implemented over time on a piecemeal basis. The order of tasks can be changed to simplify the flow of material or paperwork and make subsequent jobs easier. Sometimes the provision of one further piece of information makes a particular job much easier than having to work out the required data from other information. If a map is made of the 'flow' of material or paperwork through an organization both logically and physically it can reveal opportunities for simplification, as shown in Figure 6.9. This material flow is not untypical of many manufacturing plants. In offices the flow of paperwork is harder to see and often more 'spaghetti'-like. Often departments are located in separate offices and paper is sent between them via an internal mail system. In the same way that manufacturing shop-floors are moving away from areas of specialization in favour of 'cells' so too are offices. By rearranging personnel into customer-focused teams, with people from each department sitting near each other, the unnecessary posting of paper is eliminated. We elaborate further on this point in the Integrate section.

- **Processes** – can also be simplified and streamlined by recognizing when they are trying to serve different products or markets. By breaking down the process and identifying activities which could best be dedicated to a particular customer segment the process can be made simpler in each instance. Sometimes the same process is trying to satisfy customers with quite diverse needs, business and leisure travellers, for example. Either the process will inadequately serve both or it will be weighted to favour one particular segment. If at the crucial stages a different process alternative existed for each customer type then the service to each segment will more closely match the customer's

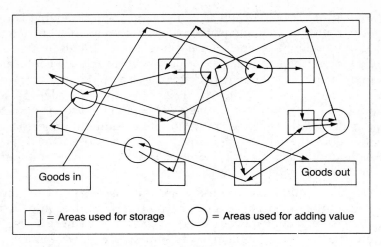

Figure 6.9 The 'spaghetti bowl' syndrome of process flow

need and pocket. The notion of runners, repeaters and strangers, covered in Chapter 3, can be used to identify and manage
different process variants.

- **Problem areas** – we have mentioned some of the possible
  problem areas above, but there may be more. Ask your staff
  what problems they see, your customers and your suppliers too.
  Problems usually mean something is too complicated or ill-
  thought out and thus a candidate for simplification. Jobs that are
  difficult, dirty or dangerous, are less likely to be completed to a
  high standard than those which are simple, clean and safe. In
  one example we are familiar with, a very nasty, dirty job was
  eliminated when it was found that the finished output of this job
  could be bought-in more cheaply than the raw material. Why
  then had it operated for so many years? Some viewed it as a
  management disciplinary option! The task is now much simpler
  – the end product is simply bought in. In general, if people are
  reluctant to do jobs, the reasons should be clearly understood. It
  may not, of course, be that the task itself is wrong. People may
  not have been appropriately trained or developed for it, or, they
  may have been recruited incorrectly. Where a number of
  employees are reluctant however there may be some underlying
  cause. It could be that they end up facing angry customers and
  feel they can do nothing about it?

The use of video is becoming widespread to aid workers' own

efforts in improving their performance. Set-up times for machines have in some cases been dramatically reduced through inexpensive changes by teams analysing in detail what they do through the eyes of a camera. We have not yet seen it done, but office workers could do the same thing with video, describing at each stage what it is that they are doing and why. It is important that the videos belong to the staff and are not viewed, or used, in any way which might cause staff to modify the process. If they are breaking the rules, for example, even with good reason, they may not want management to watch the video.

Integrate

The simplified tasks should now be integrated to effect a smooth flow in delivery of the customer requirement and service task.

- **Jobs** – it may be possible to combine several jobs into one. By empowering one person to complete a range of simplified tasks, rather than have them performed by a chain of people, the flow of material or information through the organization will be speeded up considerably. Whenever work has to be passed between individuals there is opportunity for mistakes to be made and something has to facilitate this transfer. Software to control the flow of work through an office can become extremely complex and serve no other purpose than track the throughput of work. Some organizations have gone as far as making one person responsible for the processing of the complete product or service from order to shipment. This person is called a 'case worker' or 'case manager' in service organizations as they often refer to a client's order as a 'case'. These people act as a 'single point of contact' for the customer.

- **Teams** – a logical extension of combining tasks is to combine specialists into teams where it is not possible for a single team member to undertake the whole range of activity. As discussed in Chapter 4, such teams are known as 'case teams' or sometimes as 'account teams'. While the teams may retain some functional reporting lines, for example to sales and to operations, they combine as a single process delivery team for day-to-day working. The physical proximity means many problems never arise and when they do, they can be quickly dealt with. Information technology enabling physically distant people to co-operate in this way simply cannot replace physical closeness. One day, when virtual reality extends its ability it may be able to do more, however, where possible, teams should be located together and the complex computer systems, that enabled a geographically dispersed group to function as a team, dispensed with. This configuration minimizes the distance that material, information and paperwork must travel and improves communication between those working in the process.

- **Customers** – this can be viewed at two main levels, the integration of the individual consumer and the integration of a customer organization. At the individual consumer level, integration is crucial in certain situations. Customers who do not 'feel' right in a particular place are unlikely to linger and spend money. Those that do feel comfortable can actually be used instead of employees – who, for example, carries the tray of food to the consumers table in a fast food restaurant, and often clears it away as well! Integration between one organization and another is sometimes called **Business Network Redesign** as discussed in Chapter 1.[21] Integrating one's own service provision into the processes of a customer organization can be extremely powerful, such partnership arrangements 'lock in' the customer to your organization and make it very difficult for competitors to gain the business. Baxter Health Care successfully integrate their organization with that of their customers through the just-in-time provision of hospital equipment.[22] Johnson & Johnson do the same with Walmart, delivering the quantities that they believe are needed and stacking them directly onto the shelf. Walmart merely receives the bill and pays.[23] This form of integration is often called *value-added-services*, i.e. they are additional services to the basic need that is purchased, yet provide value to the customer in some way. Value-added-services are becoming increasingly popular as companies find ways to retain customers and keep competitors out of their markets. What value-added-services could your organization offer, and what would you do if your competitors started to offer them?

- **Suppliers** – huge efficiency savings can be made if needless bureaucracy can be eliminated between organizations and suppliers. Trust and partnership are, as with customer integration key, although that does not necessarily mean that there are **no** checks, rather that there are slicker ones. Just-in-time ways of manufacturing have meant that suppliers and manufacturers have begun to work together in an increasing number of ways, integrating, often through IT, the flow of orders, invoices, and even design data. Integration of the activities has also extended to synchronized deliveries in some cases where suppliers make the required parts and deliver them in the sequence required by the assembly schedule of their customers. Someone, somewhere ends up paying for unnecessary inventory or other waste and such synchronized working reduces it to a bare minimum.

Automate

As discussed in Chapter 5, information technology can be a very powerful tool to speed up processes and deliver higher quality customer service. If applied to processes which are basically sound it will enhance that process. If the process is problematic then automation can often make matters worse. It is important, therefore, to apply automation after having eliminated, simplified and integrated tasks in the process. Having reached the automation stage it may be possible to go back through the preceding stages and further eliminate, simplify and integrate tasks. In some instances, the eventual automation of certain aspects of the process may be foreseen from the outset. Many telephone-based businesses rely on information technology to provide their service staff with the necessary customer and product details to provide accurate and speedy service. Clearly when re-engineering these processes IT will be a major factor to be considered. Some 'rules of thumb' for greater success in automation are outlined below:

- **Dirty, difficult or dangerous** – a rule which governs much of Nissan's shop-floor investment. Jobs fitting this category cannot always be automated, yet, where they can significantly higher quality levels are likely to result as machines do not mind such tasks and are unaffected by them.

- **Boring** – any task that is boring or repetitive by nature is a good candidate for automation. This again could be a shop-floor task or it could be adding numbers together or matching items on forms. Machines are untroubled by boredom and are actually best at tasks which are repetitive.

- **Data capture** – clearly if the capture of data can be done by machine rather than a person time can be saved, not to mention increased accuracy. Witness the shift to bar code readers at even small grocery stores.

- **Data transfer** – transferring data from one format to another, or one person to another, or one system to another is another high priority candidate for automation. Different standards of computers has made this task unnecessarily complicated in some cases, yet avoiding the need to input data to one system which has already been put into another one saves not only time at input but a host of problems when the data does not match!

- **Data analysis** – perhaps the City has been the quickest to realize the huge potential of computers for data analysis with neural networks performing pattern matching and trend analysis to support financial traders. Many companies have huge databases containing data but have yet to translate it into information which is actually accessible and valuable to management. Such analysis might be conducted on data collected by service reps who can include details of other company's products in their report yielding analysis on customer repurchase likelihood or intent for the organization's products and services and those of its competitors.

Automation should only be applied to processes which are under control. It is rare that automation actually improves the situation as has been learnt in manufacturing from the application of MRP and MRPII systems. Often the implementation of these systems resulted in problems being exaggerated, inventories increasing and lead times extending, instead of the improvements that had been anticipated. Companies experiencing these problems had usually looked to the MRP systems to sort out basic problems in their processes. In contrast, some other companies, and again notably the Japanese, make very effective use of MRP systems which they use to enhance processes which are under control and performing well.

Our view of automation is that it should be applied using the 80/20 rule. That is that 80 per cent of the functionality should be delivered in 20 per cent of the cost and time, in preference to the 100 per cent solutions long preferred by many companies. 100 per cent systems solutions, catering for every exception condition take a long time to deliver and invariably are less reliable. They are more costly to maintain and organizations are reluctant to throw them away even when big improvements to the process can subsequently be made, as they cost so much in the first place. There is nothing wrong with manual intervention and humans are employed because of their flexibility and innate intelligence. Automation works best in many processes when applied to routine, repetitive tasks or highly complex modelling.

Applying ESIA

Having gained an understanding of a process it is a good idea to hold a brainstorming session to go through each of the ESIA categories so that a list of potential improvements can be generated. Remember to question everything and do not restrict suggestions to the immediate process but to its reason for being or to its contribution to the business as well.

If we return to our **stationery request** example we can apply the ESIA rules to identify further actions.

- **Eliminate** – we have already eliminated many of the steps in the process, but is there anything else we can do? Most certainly. What forms of stationery can we eliminate, thus reducing the need for this non-value-adding process in the first place? It goes further than that. If we can identify, for example, a number of forms which could be eliminated then the bureaucratic burden on the organization, not just this process can be reduced. Other actions could include eliminating stock that is rarely, if ever, ordered yet remains a 'standard' item because it has always been there. Such items take up space, make administration a larger task and are totally unnecessary.

- **Simplify** – It may be possible to simplify the coding system used to describe the stationery and forms so that the number of incorrect orders is reduced. Pictures of items may even help here. An ABC analysis could be applied with type A stationery which is of high value, type B of medium value and type C of low value. Depending on the type of operation, type A items may only account for 20 per cent of those used yet represent 80 per cent of value. Controls are best applied to these items with minimal controls on type C items.

- **Integrate** – For some types of forms, it may be possible to base orders on usage thus the need to consciously reorder stocks is eliminated. This integration is now used by banks to send their customers new cheque books once they have written a certain number of cheques.

- **Automate** – a simple system to capture orders when they are rung in could provide a means of producing pick lists, measuring performance and tracking use by departments. For some stationery items it might even be appropriate to install a simple ordering system which could track orders, usage rates, costs and inventory levels.

Clean sheet – designing a new process

Part 2 of this book deals mainly with the design of processes and how people and technology can be organized and applied to them. Much of the content of Chapters 3, 4 and 5 thus forms the basis for the clean-sheet approach. Essentially the clean-sheet approach requires basic questions to be answered:

- *What* underlying needs are we trying to satisfy and for whom?, i.e. 'The service task.'
- *Why* are we trying to satisfy those needs? – does it fit with the organization's strategy?
- *Where* do those needs need to be serviced? – in the home, the high street and so on.
- *When* are we required to meet those needs? – within what time scales must we operate?
- *How* will we deliver the above? – *what processes* need to be in place, *who* will operate them and *what technological* opportunities exist for enhancing the performance of the processes and the people involved?

As it is likely that those tasked with the design of the new process come from the existing organization it is crucial that the team is able to be creative and innovative in its design of processes, people and technology, having gained a thorough appreciation of the service task. Some questions to ask are:

- 'How would you set up a competitor?'
- 'How would the ideal process look?'
- 'If you had to rebuild the organization from scratch, how would it look?'

Another question which is increasingly being asked in the public sector by managers is 'what would they be expecting from the service if it was contracted out?' In this context we might want to ask some additional questions in considering our stationery request example:

- 'What processes would you plan to operate if asked to take over all stationery provision within an organization?'

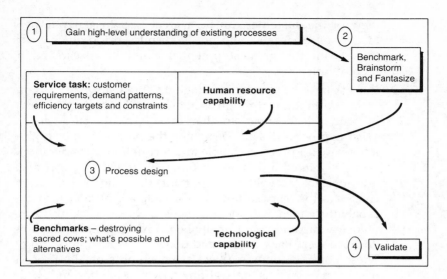

Figure 6.10   The 'clean-sheet' approach

- 'What range of services would you offer?'
- If the organization contracts out stationery provision, how would you measure the contractor's performance?'

As with systematic redesign, organizations should seek out the methodology that best suits their situation. However, as a start point we would suggest the framework outlined in Figure 6.10.

Step 1: Gain a high level understanding of the existing processes. Here it is not necessary to get into anything like the level of detail required for systematic redesign however it is important to identify the core processes. Usually there will be in the region of 6–8 core processes and you may choose to analyse the key stages in each of these before calling a halt to the study. This step will include an analysis of the outcomes which these processes currently deliver.

Step 2: Benchmarking, brainstorming, fantasizing. This is the 'fun' stage which is quite important. Benchmarking is useful, as discussed earlier, to highlight alternative ways of working but should not be viewed as the end of the matter. Brainstorming and fantasizing, particularly from the point of view of the customer can be a great way to generate new ideas. These ideas should not be dismissed too quickly and those with the greatest potential could be researched in more depth.

Step 3: Process design. During this stage the 'brainstormed' process ideas are thought through in more detail. These ideas may be truly 'clean sheet' in that they have no basis in the existing process design. Designing the process will be highly iterative with process, people and technology considerations being examined a number of times. In translating the ideas into designs it will be important that the 'clean sheet' considers the 'service task' in some detail, human resource capability which will include new ways of working, technological capability and finally benchmarks to ensure people do not revert back to the traditional ways of doing things. These considerations may act as constraints on the process designers as well as highlighting new possibilities and while in the final iterations the design must operate within these constraints it is vital that such constraints are themselves fully examined and where possible removed.

Step 4: Validate. Having designed a new process it is important to validate the design by simulating how it will operate in the real world. This does not mean that every single possible exception should be used to declare the process invalid, indeed such exceptions may be best handled as such with the process dealing with the majority of cases. A process map provides an ideal way of representing the new process and aids its overall construction. The ESIA rule should be applied to this new process to ensure it is optimal in terms of delivering the desired outcomes along the dimensions of effectiveness, efficiency and adaptability.

Process maps can be very useful in designing the new processes and should not be considered only when plotting existing processes. Figures 6.11 and 6.12 show examples of new process designs at Mitel Telecom in the UK, starting with the high level process in Figure 6.11 with the order fulfilment process being shown one level down. Note that the process owner is clearly shown and that the owner of the top level processes is the Managing Director who is personally driving Mitel's 'process orientation' programme forward.

Midland Bank's First Direct telephone banking operation is one of the most famous 'clean sheet' examples in the UK. Illustration 6.3 details some of the key points about this business.

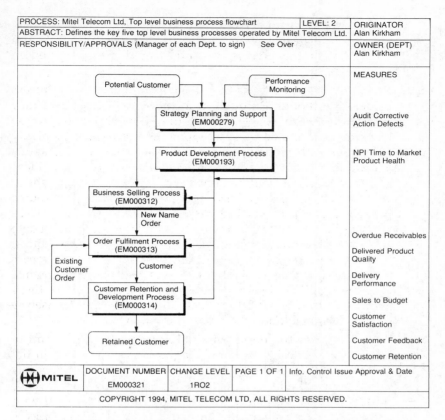

Figure 6.11 Mitel Telecom Ltd: top level business process flowchart

Summary

There are two main approaches to redesigning processes, the systematic redesign approach which starts with the existing processes and works through these eliminating waste, simplifying and integrating tasks and where appropriate automating activities, and the clean-sheet approach which starts from the desired outcomes of the process and works back from those to design a new process from scratch. In most situations a combination of these two approaches will be used at different points for any given process.

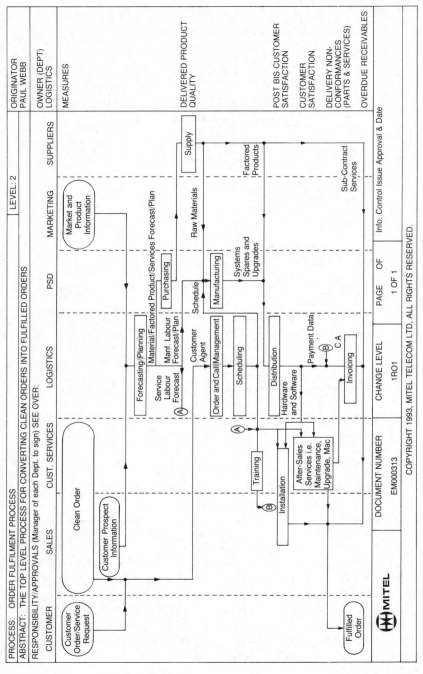

Figure 6.12 Mitel Telecom Ltd: order fulfilment process

Illustration 6.3 First Direct

Midland Bank set up 'Project Raincloud' to look at the future of its banking operations. The team found some surprising results; one in five customers had not visited a branch in the last month, one in ten not in the last six months, over half (51 per cent) said they would rather visit their branch as little as possible. Many customers did not like the appointments systems and 48 per cent had never met their bank manager. The team was tasked with a number of objectives which included: increasing service quality and reducing costs.

After its analysis, the team recommended the 'first direct' concept aimed at providing person to person contact which was highly accessible, fast, competitively priced and with a personal touch. First Direct, Midland's telephone banking operation, was launched in 1989, only a short time after the project commenced.

The team identified the main building blocks of processes, people and technology and designed the operation paying particular attention to these elements.

The approach they adopted was to analyse, map and identify the key processes. Key performance indicators were developed with time profiles and benchmarking used to refine the design. Simulation and walk-throughs were performed on the new designs which made use of many existing information systems. A specially designed interface was developed to give a more friendly and usable 'front-end' to telephone staff.

The operation has experienced tremendous growth and management has been careful to ensure customer service is not degraded. A second centre has been built to accommodate the expansion in the business which is based on high levels of customer satisfaction relative to its competitors.

First Direct remain committed to re-engineering their business and are continually looking for ways to improve.

Source: Presentations by Stephen Mayers and Karen Steele to the Business Process Redesign symposia at Cranfield School of Management, November 1992 and 1993.

Systematic redesign tends to be used to make improvements in the short-term while the clean-sheet approach lays the foundations for competing in the medium to long term.

Gaining an understanding of existing processes can be important for each approach to varying degrees, however teams should avoid getting caught up in overly detailed analysis of the existing order and focus instead on the new. The point of the exercise is performance improvement and this should not be forgotten. Process 'maps' can be useful in gaining an understanding of existing processes and in constructing new ones.

References

1. Quoted by Al Gore, *National Performance Review*, 7 September 1993.
2. Title of Michael Hammer's 1990 *Harvard Business Review* article.
3. Quoted by Christopher Lorenz, 'Change is not enough', *Financial Times*, 12 January 1994, p. 24.
4. This statistic is quoted by Michael Hammer and James Champy in their book *Reengineering the Corporation*, London: Nicholas Brealey Publishing, 1993.
5. A recent Newsweek article suggested that Japanese firms have difficulty in accepting the need for the radical redesign which re-engineering often entails suggesting that this is due to 'management gridlock'. See Douglas T. Shinsato, Japan's Management Gridlock, *Newsweek*, 10 January 1994. For an updated review of BPR developments in Japan, see Allan E. Alter, 'Japan, Inc. embraces change', *Computerworld*, 7 March 1994, pp. 24–25; Frank A. Petro, 'Reengineering Japan', *Focus on Change Management*, July/August 1994, pp. 17–18.
6. Speaking at the *4th International Forum on Technology Management*, Berlin, November 1993.
7. F. Huda, *Kaizen: The Understanding and Application of Continuous Improvement*, Letchworth: Technical Communications, 1992.
8. *Inc.*, September 1989, pp. 50–51.
9. BBC Education Programme, *Prophet Unheard*, BBC London.
10. Edward De Bono, *Serious Creativity: Using The Power of Lateral Thinking to Create New Ideas*, London: Harper Collins, 1994; Simon Majaro, *The Creative Gap: Managing Ideas for Profit*, London: Longman, 1988.
11. J.A. Martilla and J.C. James, 'Importance-Performance Analysis', *Journal of Marketing*, January (1977). For an excellent extension of this model see the work of Nigel Slack, e.g. 'The Importance-Performance Matrix as a Strategic Improvement Priority Tool in Service Operations', *Warwick Operations Papers* (1993).
12. 'The 21st Century Jet', *Equinox*, Channel 4 Television Company Limited, 1993.
13. Roger Trapp, 'Benchmarking moves on to bench-testing', *Independent on Sunday*, 9 January 1994, p. 13.
14. Reported in Lynda Radosevich, 'Evasive action', *ComputerWorld*, 4 October 1993, pp. 83–84.
15. John Oakland, *Total Quality Management: The Route to Improving Performance*, second edition, Oxford: Butterworth-Heinemann, 1993.
16. Benson P. Shapiro, V. Kasturi Rangan and John J. Sviokla, 'Staple yourself to an order', *Harvard Business Review*, July–August (1992), 114–121.
17. John Griffiths, 'Driving Out the Old Regime', *Financial Times*, 20 August 1993.

18. US Vice President Al Gore, *National Performance Review*, 7 September 1993.
19. Michael Hammer, 'Reengineering work: don't automate – obliterate', *Harvard Business Review*, July–August, (1990), 104–112.
20. Gore (reference 18).
21. N. Venkatraman, 'IT-induced Business Reconfiguration', in Morton, editor, *The Corporation of the 1990s: Information Technology and Organisation Transformation*, edited by Michael Scott Morton, New York: Oxford University Press, 1991, 122–158.
22. James E. Short and N. Venkatraman, 'Beyond Business Process Redesign: Redefining Baxter's Business Network', *Sloan Management Review*, Fall (1992), 7–21.
23. George Stalk, P. Evans and L.E. Shulman, 'Competing on Capabilities: the New Rules of Corporate Strategy', *Harvard Business Review*, March–April (1992), 57–69.

7

Realizing the benefits: managing change

It should be borne in mind that there is nothing more difficult to handle, more doubtful of success, and more dangerous to carry through than initiating changes in a state's constitution. The innovator makes enemies of all those who prospered under the old order, and only lukewarm support is forthcoming from those who would prosper under the new. Their support is lukewarm partly from fear of their adversaries, who have the existing laws on their side, and partly because men are generally incredulous, never really trusting new things unless they have tested them by experience. In consequence, whenever those who oppose the changes can do so, they attack vigorously, and the defence made by the others is only lukewarm. So both the innovator and his friends come to grief.

. . .

I also believe that the one who adapts his policy to the times prospers, and likewise that the one whose policy clashes with the demands of the times does not.

Niccolo Machiavelli, 1525[1]

Folks, we're going on a journey. On this journey we'll carry our wounded and shoot the dissenters.

Michael Hammer[2]

Introduction

The scale and scope of the changes often necessitated by BPR mean that many of the challenges exist not so much in understanding

203

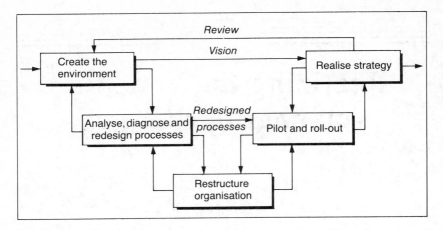

Figure 7.1   An overall approach to BPR

processes and how they can be redesigned, but rather in implementing the change necessary to realize the potential improvement. Organizations tend to be conservative and resistance to change must be turned into active involvement. In this chapter we examine some of the issues associated with managing change and outline a framework which organizations can adapt to re-engineer their business. Some aspects of this framework are new, while others show where topics covered earlier fit into a BPR initiative.

In the previous chapter we presented some practical guidelines for redesigning processes, however, in many ways this is the easiest part of BPR. Actually implementing the new process design is where most projects fail. Realizing the benefits requires changes and these can be hard to bring about. At this point, then, it is necessary to review the overall approach to BPR so that success can be made more likely from the outset of any such initiative. In Figure 7.1 we outline a framework for approaching a BPR programme.

This approach consists of five key phases:

1.   Create the environment.
2.   Analyse, diagnose and redesign processes.
3.   Restructure the organization.
4.   Pilot and roll-out.
5.   Realize strategy.

Each of these is broken down into a number of steps, some of which can be performed in parallel. We shall discuss each of these phases in turn and then discuss the iterative flows between each of the stages as a second step.

Create the environment

Crisis, what crisis?

Consider the analogy of the boiled frog.[3] You can put a frog into boiling water and it will jump out. But if you put a frog into cold water and gradually raise the temperature, the frog will boil to death. The same is true of organizations. They do not always see that they are falling prey to inertia: they fail to read the environment, do not make important improvements and slowly lose their competitive edge. Instead of maintaining their lead or indeed improving on it, many organizations adopt an arrogant attitude of espoused improvement at best. As the competitive waters boil, the organization makes minor adjustments, but it is not until boiling point, when the profits of the organization seem to evaporate rapidly that the crisis is recognized. For organizations in crisis the motivation to improve is often clear, putting pressure on both management and the workforce to do something. It seems few organizations succeed in energizing themselves to make significant improvements unless there is a clear need to do so; unless there is a crisis, it is mainly business as usual. Without a crisis, only a CEO with a vision of a better, more profitable organization can really do very much to provide the necessary motivation.

In achieving this vision or combating a crisis, it is essential to understand how change can be brought about to boost performance. Rummler and Brache highlight three levels which must be addressed in the improvement initiative: the organizational level, the process level and the job/performer level.[4] Implementing change to each of these levels is difficult, not least because it threatens the comfortable *status quo*. In understanding how to manage the organization it is necessary to understand how individuals are likely to react to the proposed changes. While each person will react to the changes differently, there are some discernible phases which people generally pass through as illustrated in Figure 7.2.

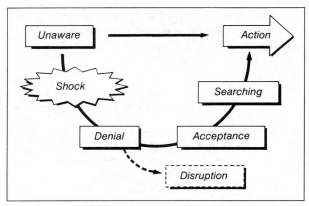

Figure 7.2   General reactions to change

Stage 1: Unaware

Until a crisis is apparent or the need for improvement is recognized, people can be said to be unaware of the need to change the way they work. Sometimes it is through benchmarking programmes, visits or discussions with defecting customers which highlight the fact that performance could improve.

Stage 2: Shock

People are often shocked when confronted with the reasons why they must improve especially if they have being working in the same way for a long time. The end of the 'good times' may be signalled by economic indicators and while people may start to get worried about the security of their jobs, it is still generally a shock when the threat of redundancy and job loss looms on the horizon. For companies that previously thought they were doing well, and indeed may have been celebrating the fact, it can be quite shocking and worrying to find this is not so.

Stage 3: Denial

The denial reaction often comes from a loss of confidence and is the classic reaction of 'if we ignore the problem, it will go away'. This is so easy to criticize in others, yet almost all of us do this at some time in our lives. This stage may also exist where scaremongering has been used to manipulate the workforce previously, and thus people feel they have heard it all before.

Stage 4: Acceptance

When the situation does not go away, and may become clearer, then people start generally to accept the situation and the need for change. Unfortunately some people may never move beyond stage 3 to reach this stage and choose to 'bury their heads in the sand' or worse, attempt to disrupt the process.

Stage 5: Searching
Following an acceptance or belief that things must get better people start searching for answers. They will test out new ideas and begin to experiment. This can be an uncomfortable time when the acceptance of the need to change brings worry yet there are few answers or grounds for hope.

Stage 6: Action
The searching stage will eventually yield some answers and action is the result. Because the searching stage is uncomfortable, some people may want to move to the action stage before the situation is clearly understood and the alternative courses of action thought through. This can be dangerous and 'panic' actions do not usually yield the best results. Nevertheless it is also important that the energy and momentum built up for action is not dissipated or lost through a prolonged period of inactivity.

An important role of management will be to 'pull' people through these stages and ensure that the resistance to change does not overwhelm the initiative. The degree of resistance will depend on the kind of change involved and on how well it is understood, particularly the degree of actual or perceived disruption. Beckhard and Harris describe three conditions that will create significant resistance to change:[5]

- When people are comfortable with the *status quo*.
- When they do not understand why the change is desirable.
- When they have doubts about the company's ability to achieve the desired change.

Workers may also fear that the impending redesign may 'de-skill' them. Fear of de-skilling is more widespread where employees perform many tasks and the new process threatens to 'shrink' their job. Power and knowledge shifts can also cause resistance particularly when, in many organizations, knowledge is a key requirement for power. As sharing knowledge is being seen increasingly as a critical success factor organizations must find ways to overcome this traditional resistance to sharing the knowledge 'power base'.

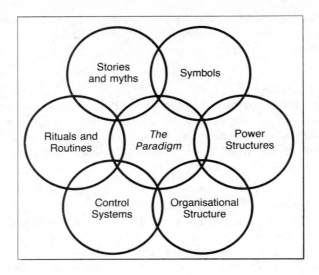

Source: Gerry Johnson and Kevan Scholes, *Exploring Corporate Strategy*, third edition, (Hemel Hempstead, 1993).

Figure 7.3   The cultural web

Cultural audit and levers for change

Culture exerts a powerful influence over individual and organizational perception, behaviour and performance. In a 1993 study of BPR, Delphi Consulting reported that two-thirds of the respondents cited cultural resistance as the major challenge to succeeding at BPR.[6] We discussed in Chapter 4 that while individuals may hold different sets of beliefs, there is at some level a core set of values, beliefs and assumptions commonly held throughout the organization. This has been referred to as the *paradigm* by Gerry Johnson.[7] The paradigm governs and influences an organization's view of itself and its environment. Johnson argues that it is through this paradigm that an organization creates a relatively homogeneous approach to business. As it evolves through time and is reinforced by history, it sets out a repertoire of actions and responses that can be made in certain situations. The paradigm is constructed and protected by a web of what Johnson refers to as 'cultural artefacts'. This web is illustrated in Figure 7.3.

Stories and myths

In every organization there are stories, some true, others either variations of the truth or simply myths. Examples are the big IT failures, the products that flopped, the legendary leaders and mavericks. In particular, new employees hear stories about those who broke the cultural norms and the consequences of their actions. Most have evolved over the years and have become part of the organization's folklore. Like the fisherman's stories of the ever larger fish, these stories can be rapidly distorted by the workings of the grapevine.

Symbols

All organizations have their symbols, although they are often so ingrained that they may not be recognized. The dress code, the furniture, executive parking spaces, the MD's Rolls Royce are all symbols. At one particular insurance company there were five different categories of restaurant and as one progressed up the management hierarchy the quality of both food and dining room decor improved considerably. Symbols also include company specific language which reinforces entrenched attitudes, like addressing managers as 'Mister'.

Rituals and routines

Rituals are those aspects of organizational life that hold a special significance and may include the monthly board meeting, the annual company barbecue, and singing the company song. Routines refer to 'the way we do things here' and incorporate the core activities which the organization traditionally undertakes.

Control systems

Organizations have particular control systems to monitor and encourage performance. Pay and reward systems, budgetary control systems, and the management hierarchy are all examples of such systems. These serve to highlight what is valued by the organization.

Organizational structures

Functions, departments, geographically based business units, product-based business units, flat management hierarchies, large bureaucratic hierarchies, are all examples of how the structure of an organization impacts the paradigm.

Power structures

Power lies with influence, particularly where such influence can reduce uncertainty. The power structures tend to reinforce the paradigm and hence they are often targets for change. This is particularly difficult given that those who may be required to change often hold the power.

In attempting to change their culture many organizations manipulate the 'hard' elements of the web, i.e. the power structures, the control systems and the organizational structures, neglecting to address the more intangible elements. This is a mistake. **All** elements of the web must be examined and acted on if cultural change is to take place and this change translated into tangible action and results.

Illustration 7.1 Cultural change at Renault: focusing on the customer

In the fall of 1986, Renault called a news conference to announce that it had formulated a new commercial policy: 'From now on at Renault,' its official declared, 'the customer is always right; the customer is king.'

The idea seemed strange, if not incomprehensible, to the assembled French journalists, who had come to regard the giant state-owned car marker more as a showcase for French social policy than as a company whose role was to supply products and services that filled and anticipated customer needs.

Today, Renault stands out as a major French company that has restructured not only by drastically reducing its break-even point but also by overcoming an ingrained cultural bias that respected the engineer more than the consumer. In the process, it learned how to meet new standards for products, quality and services in a global marketplace.

This corporate-cultural revolution is given much of the credit for the improvement in the company's fortunes. 'When George Besse took over as chairman in 1985, Renault was a living cadaver', said Paul Horne, an economist with Smith Barney, Harris Upham & Co. in Paris. 'His legacy was to turn it around by being responsive to the customer and producing products people wanted to buy.' In 1992, Renault was the most profitable of Europe's car makers

'They thought about customers, products and finances all together and somehow managed to advance on all three areas relative to their competitors,' said John Lawson, London-based automotive analyst with DRI, and economic forecasting consultancy.

Renault models – the small Clio, the midrange R19, the luxury Safrane and the Espace van – have become leaders in their classes in the French market. Even the Twingo, the odd-shaped minicar launched in April 1993, has generated abundant enthusiasm – about 28 000 orders so far. In Europe, while Renault's market share has improved slightly, a more telling sign is that its R19 and Clio are now strong sellers in Germany, where French cars in general have not been well regarded.

Company officials acknowledge that Renault never used to think much about the customer as it went about its business of designing, building and selling cars. Newly delivered vehicles rattled and came unglued, and the quality of service throughout its dealer network was low, at best.

Renault, of course, was not alone. Many French companies still suffer from a reputation for products that, while well-engineered, fail to meet any identified customer needs, or are accompanied by weak or unprofessional sales efforts and poor after-sales service.

Jean Hoeffner, vice president of Gemini France, a management consultancy group, said France's weakness in sales may be due to top executives' reluctance to believe – because they have not seen it demonstrated – that company earnings could be improved by better salesmanship. Others say that, despite efforts over the past decade to correct it, weakness persists because of an intellectual tradition in which making things has been regarded as an end in itself.

'It's fair to say that French industry for decades and centuries has been dominated by engineers with a production mentality,' said Christian Pinson, president of the French Marketing Association and a professor at the Insead business school in Fontainebleau. 'They believed that if the technical quality was superior, the customer should realize it. If not, the customer was incompetent or stupid. We're behind because we're still dominated by this mentality.'

At Renault, the bias towards production was clear. 'We would say that we built 2 million cars a year, not that we have 2 million new customers a year,' said Philippe Gamba, Renault's director of marketing – a job title that did not even exist in the old regime.

To change course, Renault began introducing the customer into the new-car development process. Customer surveys were ordered to determine what features and equipment were wanted, and the findings were turned into objectives to guide designers and engineers. The sales and marketing departments were brought into the process, as were dealers and garage technicians, who were asked how easy the new models would be to repair. Selected groups of people – such as taxi drivers – were asked to comment on a model's performance and comfort as much as two years before its scheduled unveiling.

'Before,' said Mr. Gamba 'it was our job to sell cars that were given to us by the engineers; but today it's completely different. Today there is a new culture.'

Source: Jacques Neher, Renault wipes out years of deficits with a new idea, please the customer, *International Herald Tribune*, 2 June 1993. Reprinted with permission.

Steps to create the environment

Having reviewed some of the issues around creating an environment it is important to pull them together to form some steps which can be followed. These steps should be treated as building blocks and as stated at the outset of this chapter the exact approach adopted must depend on *your* situation though it is often useful for organizations to start with a method and modify it as their confidence increases and what does and does not work become apparent.

1. Build a vision.
2. Gain the support of the appropriate level of management, if organization wide then the CEO.
3. Formulate a plan and provide necessary training.
4. Identify core processes.
5. Appoint programme team/champion.
6. Communicate vision and goals, the need for the improvement and the plan to get there.

1. Build a Vision

It is necessary for someone senior within the organization, usually the CEO, to build a vision of the future or set targets and provide support for those who develop the vision. A vision should include a notion of what products and services the organization will be offering, how these will be developed in future, how the product and/or service will be experienced by the customer and how the delivery of these will be experienced by staff and suppliers. In short what will it be like to be a customer, work with and work in the organization.

2. Gain the support of management

Not all the BPR efforts we have investigated have been initiated at the top of the organization, yet all of those which proved successful sought approval and sponsorship at the most senior levels early on in the initiative. The level of seniority clearly depends on the scale and scope of the BPR programme. If the vision for the future extends to the whole enterprise or even its supply chain then the top team of each organization must be involved. If however, the BPR programme is more modest in its scope and the vision applies to a small business unit in a large enterprise it is the business unit management and perhaps their immediate superiors who will need to be involved. This senior management commitment is necessary to gain the support of lower levels in the hierarchy and the ultimate success of the project will hinge on this.

3. Formulate a plan and provide necessary training

At this point it is important to formulate a plan of action. What are the main milestones in the project, how will communications be handled, particularly around the area of possible redundancies, and who will lead the BPR programme. Having decided on these aspects some training will almost certainly be required and this should be given immediately before they start. It will be a difficult and uncertain journey anyway and while training does not guarantee success it can certainly boost confidence.

4. Identify core processes

Having formulated a plan it is necessary for the appropriate level of management to identify the core processes of the organization. Again if the scope of the programme is the re-engineering of the entire business then it is the CEO and the board who must participate in this, for if they are not committed the effort cannot be successful. These core processes provide a framework for the process re-engineering effort.

5. Appoint programme team/champion

The board must appoint someone in whom they have confidence, possibly one of themselves, as the sponsor and overall champion of the BPR effort. It is important that this person has their full support and a clear mandate to drive through the improvement programme. A small team may be appointed to aid this champion or czar, though we would urge that the size of this team be kept to perhaps 4–12 people. The best people from the key departments to be affected by the programme should be seconded to the team. Selection of these people should be a joint exercise between the champion and the divisions or departments involved.

The scale of change required by re-engineering is often too great to be handled through the existing management structure. A separate but integrated governance structure is usually needed. Many companies adopt a three-tier arrangement as shown in Figure 7.4. At the top is the sponsor of the initiative who should come from the most senior management level. As already stated, ideally this person should be the CEO. At the second level is the steering group who are responsible for overseeing the transition. The champion should be the chairman of this group which will be made up of key influences in the organization and process owners. Process owners are those people who will be responsible for co-ordinating the activities through the process. The third level is where the actual transition work is done, although it may not be until stage 2 that teams at this level are formed. Here, processes are analysed, mapped, new designs evaluated, and eventually implemented.

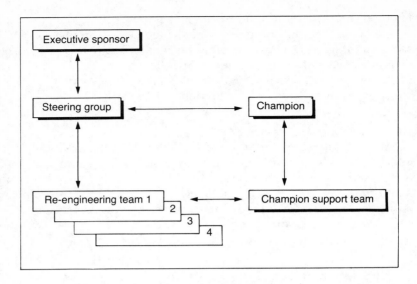

Figure 7.4   The re-engineering team structure

There may be several teams, each charged with a specific task depending on the overall scope of the redesign. Responsibility for assembling the teams usually lies with the process owner. There can be any number between 5 and 10 members on each team. These will come from both inside and outside the organization. Normally employees are assigned full-time to a team though there may be some specialists who are called in on an as required basis.

6.   Communicate vision and goals, the need for the improvement and the plan to get there

The formation of the team and possibly the previous activities will not go unnoticed within the organization and it is important that the board shares its vision, goals and need for improvement with the rest of the organization. Uncertainty eats away at people's confidence like acid through skin and often people imagine the worst possible scenarios. While the truth may not be good news it is likely to be less awful than the grapevine's story, and communicating it early gives people time to come to terms with it. This is by no means to suggest that redundancies will result from BPR as a matter of course, or that change will be greeted by suspicion and fear in your organization. These *tend* to be the reactions but it will depend, like everything else, on your particular situation and culture. It is important to note that communication to the organization as a whole should be maintained throughout the complete programme and indeed beyond. The effectiveness of this communication should be tested frequently by senior management, perhaps at breakfast meetings, to ensure that the right messages are indeed getting through the hierarchy; like everything else, for communication to work senior management must be committed to making it work.

Communication effectiveness or the quality of communication is enhanced through developing shared 'frames of reference', involving critically, shared interpretation of the benefits of the change program and the definition of the underlying problems which the BPR programme seeks to tackle. Communication can help employees see the logic of change and enhance their motivation.

Communication should include:

- A compelling argument for the change.
- The vision for the future.
- Benefits of the BPR project from an organizational and employee perspective.
- Who will be affected.

Hammer and Champy recommend that two key messages must be articulated and communicated to employees:[8]

- Here is where we are as a company and this is why we cannot stay here.
- This is what we as a company need to become.

Analyse, diagnose and redesign processes

At this stage, an organization may decide to pursue the initiative in only a few selected areas, possibly one to begin with. It is important at this stage that the scale of improvement likely to result is clearly understood. As detailed earlier in the book, re-engineering a small part of the organization will, at best, yield only significant benefits to that part of the organization and is unlikely to have a dramatic impact on the bottom line. Other organizations will carve out a more substantial slice of the organizational pie (i.e. greater scale and scope) for re-engineering and in this instance a number of teams must be formed and led. In Chapter 6 we discussed at some length the two main approaches to redesigning processes and we will not repeat these here. We do wish to re-emphasize, however, that our research clearly indicates the importance of gaining a reasonable understanding of existing processes to act as a start point for the redesign, even if a clean sheet approach is to be adopted. Teams should be careful to avoid spending too much time on this, however, and it should always be remembered that the focus is to design *new* processes not build up a comprehensive understanding of today's.

Steps to analyse, diagnose and redesign processes

1. Recruit and train teams.
2. Identify process outcomes and linkages.
3. Analyse existing processes and quantify measures.
4. Diagnose condition.
5. Benchmark best practices.
6. Redesign processes – systematic or clean sheet, or a bit of both.
7. Review people requirements of new process design.
8. Review technological requirements of new process design.
9. Validate new process design.

1. Recruit and train teams

One or a number of teams will be needed to perform the next few stages. Initially, the steering committee may choose to engage in a high level analysis of these steps, supported by the champion's support team. Having selected the pilot process or processes a third level project team should be appointed. At each stage the composition of this team may change somewhat to reflect the needs of the phase of the project and it is important, therefore, that the skills required for each stage are understood. In the initial stage of understanding processes it is important that the team contains the necessary analytical skill to map and understand the processes in sufficient, but not too much, detail. The diagnosis phase requires an overall view of the business and how critical improved performance is in that particular process as well as an assessment of how easy it will be to improve it. The redesign phase requires creative types, though the analytical people used in the analysis phase can be used to validate the designs.

Teams should be trained in the methods and tools outlined in this book. A similar recommendation is made by Harrington who lists ten fundamental tools as shown in Table 7.1.[9]

Table 7.1   Business Process Improvement's (BPI) ten fundamental tools

---

- BPI concepts.
- Flowcharting.
- Interview techniques.
- BPI measurement methods (cost, cycle time, efficiency, effectiveness, adaptability).
- No-value-added activity elimination methods.
- Bureaucracy elimination methods.
- Process and paperwork simplification techniques.
- Simple language analysis and methods.
- Process walk-through methods.
- Cost and Cycle time analysis.

The teams should be drawn from across the organization without becoming too unwieldy. We suggest a facilitator be brought in from another part of the organization to help each team of about six people. Customers and suppliers should be consulted by the teams on a regular basis where possible. The teams should be trained in teamwork and should be managed through the team-building stages. Forming (bringing the people together), norming (when people are still reserved in their communication), storming (arguments and disagreements become apparent as the team gets used to each other and barriers come down – it is necessary to go through this phase to effectively move to the next stage) and performing (when the teams start to work together and realize that they can do great things through co-operation and mutual help). Empathy with 'processes' and the use of simple mapping techniques should also form part of the training programme.

2.   Identify process outcomes and linkages
An important part of the process analysis will be to assess the required outcomes of the process and its linkages to other processes. The required outcome may be defined by using the service task analysis outlined in Chapter 3 as a starting point. Linkages of the process provide a boundary within which staff can redesign the process.

3.   Analyse existing processes and quantify measures
Teams should map and gain an understanding of the existing processes. Measures should be placed against each step in the process and at the process level overall. We suggest teams collect the following information for each stage:

- **Time to perform each step** – which can then be added up to give an overall assessment of the work time in the process. This should only consider the time when work is actually being done and is different from the elapsed time

- **Elapsed time through each step**, and between steps – to give an overall lead time for the process as a whole (combined with work time this will give the throughput efficiency of the process as explained in Chapter 3).
- **Number of 'hand-offs'** through the process, i.e. the number of times material, paperwork or electronic information is passed between different people.
- **Number of computer systems** used through the process.
- Number of customer and supplier **contact points**.
- **Problems** experienced at each stage.
- An assessment of whether the step is **value-adding** or not, i.e. does it contribute directly to the successful delivery of the required outcome (although teams will return to this at a later stage if using a systematic redesign approach).

It may also be useful to gain an assessment of the cost of the overall process, perhaps through activity based costing techniques, however the amount of people and machine time used through the process can give a rough and ready estimate.

4.   Diagnose condition

An important result of the process analysis should be an understanding of the requirement for improvement and the scope for improvement. A process may have enormous scope for improvement, yet if it is not going to yield significant gains to the organization as a whole, the effort required may be better used elsewhere. Organizations need some idea of the priority for action, especially where large-scale changes are required. The whole organization cannot be changed at once and those areas which will have the biggest impact should be addressed first, with some consideration given to the associated risk.

5.   Benchmark best practices

Having prioritized the processes to be re-engineered the organization can focus a benchmarking initiative on those processes which it intends to re-engineer first. As discussed in Chapter 6, benchmarking best practice is a useful way of breaking people's paradigms and helps foster thought on alternative ways of doing things. We do not recommend that organizations then try and 'lift' these best practices and put them into their own processes. Creativity and innovation are key. Today's best practices will not be tomorrow's best practices and it is creating new ways of thinking and breaking the mould of 'what is possible' that is most important.

6.   Redesign processes – systematic or clean sheet, or a bit of both
As outlined in Chapter 6 two main approaches can be used for the redesign of processes. For some elements of the process a complete re-think may be most appropriate, for others it will be systematic redesign. These two approaches should not be viewed as hard choices. The emphasis at this stage is firmly on getting a sound process view and while a high level consideration of people and technology issues may guide certain aspects of the redesign it is important that any detailed discussion be delayed until the process has been outlined.

Where processes cross national boundaries there may be political pressures which must be borne in mind. These issues become particularly sensitive where firms wish to re-locate operations from one country to another. Other issues include culture, language, currency, legal systems, financial reporting standards, all of which add complexity into the redesign task.

7.   Review people requirements of new process design
Having generated a new process design it is vital that the people requirements are analysed in some detail. The main areas to examine are detailed in Chapter 4 and it is likely that changes to one or all of these human resource aspects will be required.

8.   Review technological requirements of new process design
Technological requirements may have been identified at a high level during the redesign phase, with an IT member of staff providing advice as to the feasibility of the requirement. It is necessary, however, at this stage to review in more detail the technological requirements and fix on the approach to be taken in providing any IT systems.

9.   Validate new process design
The combination of new process, people and technology must be validated when combined together. Teams may perform simulations, possibly on computer systems, but most certainly a mock up of real life is needed. If this sounds expensive and time consuming consider just how cheap it is compared with a live launch of the new process which then fails! The lessons learned from the simulations

should be incorporated back into the design and the new process simulated once again, and so on, until teams are confident that the process will perform as required.

Redesign the organization's infrastructure

Before the new processes can be implemented it will be necessary to review and probably change the organization's infrastructure. This infrastructure is made up of people and technology in the widest sense. Management hierarchy, pay and rewards systems, terms and conditions are all examples of infrastructure which impact the human dimension of organizations. The technological infrastructure includes telecommunications networks, site locations, office facilities and plant and machinery. Some of the infrastructure changes needed will have been identified in the previous stage.

Steps to restructure the organization

1. Review the organization's people resource: structure, competences and motivation.
2. Review structure and technological capability.
3. Formulate new organizational form.
4. Define new roles, coach and train employees.
5. Provide outplacement and inplacement services as required.
6. Build new technological infrastructure and applications.

1. Review the organization's people resource: structure, competences and motivation

Knowing the people within the organization is key to knowing how to best use them. The new process may call for quite different roles to be performed than those undertaken at present and who is able and motivated to perform them is a key question. A re-training programme may be one result of this exercise with a new set of skills and behaviours required on the part of a number, if not all, individuals. Management deserve particular attention at this stage. In re-engineering programmes it is often the management, and in particular middle-management, who feel most threatened. Their roles are likely to have changed a great deal along with any 'status' symbols which set them apart and gave them importance. The hearts and minds of all the people, as well as any brawn that is required, must be committed to the new order and most organizations we have talked to have tried hard to know who are supporting the changes, who are not, and most difficult of all, those who say they support the changes but actually fight to stop it.

2. Review structure and technological capability

It will be important to understand the implications of the technological requirements identified in step 8 of the previous phase. The organization will already have an existing technology infrastructure in place and a thorough examination must be made, including its telecommunications network, computer technology, plant and machinery, to determine its capability to support the needs of the new process design.

3. Formulate new organizational form

Having built up a picture of the process requirements, the organization's people resources and technological considerations, a new organizational form can be designed. Re-alignment of hierarchies, terms and conditions, roles and responsibilities are likely to be needed and must be identified and agreed to enable the new process design to be implemented.

4. Define new roles, coach and train employees

As part of this new organizational form the exact nature of the roles must be detailed and employees trained and coached to perform these. The new roles may empower employees to a greater extent than previously and should emphasize not just task roles but also the performance improvement roles to be performed.

5. Provide outplacement and inplacement services as required

If any people are to be made redundant it is important that they are identified and then treated well, not just for their own sakes but for those left within the organization who will react badly to any mistreatment of those who have to go. The use of outplacement services has grown a great deal in recent years, not just for executives, but for all grades of staff who may receive training, counselling, and some resources to use in finding another job. Inplacement services to council the other 'victims' of redundancy programmes – those left – have also become more popular in helping people come to terms with what has happened and look to the future.

6. Build new technological infrastructure and applications

As well as the people infrastructure the technological requirements must also be addressed at this stage, especially if the required applications are significantly different to those available. A strategy for overcoming the 'legacy systems' problem, discussed in Chapter 5, must be detailed and any new 'platform' requirements for telecommunications or computers detailed and a purchasing plan agreed. Consideration should be given to the technological needs of the enterprise as a whole, not just to the individual processes which are currently being redesigned.

Pilot and roll-out

With the new processes and people structures thought through and detailed, it is time to begin the process of implementing the improvements. We suggest that organizations pilot the new processes with selected customers. While this 'parallel running' does create complications and stretches resources we believe it is invaluable in ensuring a successful launch. There is nothing like real life, and all the involvement and simulation in the world cannot replace actual work, though it can make the requirement for the pilot period significantly shorter. It is during this pilot period that organizations will seek to come down the learning curve of the new process quickly so that lessons learned can be incorporated into other areas before the complete overhaul of the re-engineered organization is completed.

Steps to pilot and roll-out

1. Select pilot process.
2. Build team for a pilot process.
3. Engage selected customers and suppliers of process.
4. Launch pilot, monitor and support.
5. Review pilot and feedback learning to other process teams.
6. Prioritize roll-out and begin phased implementation across organization.

1. Select pilot process
The selection of the pilot is crucial for the success of the BPR programme overall. The pilot selected should have the following characteristics:

- The impact of the BPR programme should be visible and significant – success which has no real impact will not prove to people that BPR is worth their efforts.

- The chances of success should be high, the improvements should not involve overly complex changes and the people involved should be of the highest calibre, having the necessary level of experience and be highly motivated to make it work.

- The pilot should contain enough of the ingredients to be implemented across other processes that the pilot is a good test of the roll-out to other parts of the organization.

2.   Build team for a pilot process

As stated the team must be highly capable, experienced and motivated. The team should include the best people from the line functions as well as the supporting areas. Ideally the team should be small, however all the people involved in the operation of the new processes should be involved and engaged by the team throughout the roll-out process. Those tasked with implementing the pilot should be those who will go on to operate the process for some time afterwards. Those in support of these team leaders may go on to support other team leaders during the roll-out, bringing their experiences of the problems encountered to those roll-out areas.

3.   Engage selected customers and suppliers of process

It is important that customers and suppliers play a part in the new process pilot. The organization's best customers and suppliers are good places to start. Customers in particular should be fully appraised of the improvements sought after and the changes which are being piloted to achieve these ends. The customers should have already been involved to some extent and thus be more willing to act as guinea pigs for the new scheme. For redesigning processes within a firm, it may be useful to think of internal customers and suppliers, but we would prefer to talk about *partnership*, which usually represents reality more accurately, instead. This partnership ought to be made meaningful by linking it to outcomes which relate to outside stakeholders. The emphasis should be on the team working together, not the internal supplier just doing what their internal customer tells them to do.

4.   Launch pilot, monitor and support

When it is ready the pilot should be launched and its performance monitored closely. Senior management must ensure that the pilot's leaders can call upon any necessary resources to make things work and failures should be quickly turned into practical lessons which can be applied.

5.   Review pilot and feedback learning to other process teams

The pilot should operate in 'pilot' mode for a specific period of time, long enough for it to achieve results, but not so long that the organizational momentum for improvement and change is lost elsewhere. The teams tasked to implement the next processes in the roll-out plan should be fully familiar with the pilot and the learning fed back to all affected employees.

6.   Prioritize roll-out and begin phased implementation across organization

Having completed the pilot it is now time to plan how to roll-out the re-engineering programme to the rest of the organization. Priorities must be set balancing risk and reward. In an ideal world the first priority would be conveniently highlighted by being high return with minimal risk. Real life is seldom this generous, and time and effort should be put in to ensuring the roll-out proceeds on a path most likely to breed further success.

Training should accompany the roll-out of the newly designed processes and should not take the form of blanket training for all staff. This inevitably takes a long time and unless it is closely linked to implementation will be quickly forgotten. The roll-out plan should be clearly communicated and motivation built up across the organization. Early successes can generate a powerful pull in the organization for improvement, though it must be remembered that to achieve significant performance gains across a large part of the business will take time, can only be brought to fruition by sustained commitment and that senior management must make extra efforts during the roll-out phase to stay a part of the programme and drive it forward. However successful the previous stages are thought to have been it is this stage which will actually transform the organization.

Realize vision

Having transformed the organization it is necessary to use these new capabilities. This may sound obvious but it is not uncommon for organizations to create new capabilities which they then fail to exploit. The classic example is perhaps the lean production facility which can respond to market conditions rapidly, operate at minimum cost and produce high quality output, yet sits within an overall supply chain awash with inventory and its capabilities are never translated into customer or market serving advantages.

Steps to realize vision

1. Assess re-engineered performance.
2. Capitalize on improved performance.
3. Identify new uses for the capability offered by the re-engineered processes.
4. Continually improve.

1.   Assess re-engineered performance
It is important to gain some assessment as to the performance of the re-engineered business as quickly as possible. It may not be possible to translate the gains into bottom-line results early on. People savings for example will only show on the profit and loss account when that saved time is used to add-value in other ways or the people have left the organization and the redundancy payments passed. Time to deliver customer satisfaction, throughput efficiency, hand-offs and staff satisfaction should be easier to gauge and will give an indication as to the success of the initiative.

2.   Capitalize on improved performance
Having identified the successes it is time to make sure they're being used to the full. Hopefully your existing customers will have noticed the leaps in performance and their loyalty should rise. Potential customers however may be ignorant of just how good the organization is now and must be told. Those areas that the organization now excels in, relative to its competitors, should be highlighted and used to differentiate the firm from the rest.

3.   Identify new uses for the capability offered by the re-engineered processes
As well as improved performance delivering today's products and services, and developing replacement products and services it may also be that the capability offers expansion possibilities including new products and services to existing customers, and even new products and services to new customers. Of course a risk assessment should be undertaken before moving in this direction. The

existing reputation of the firm should not be put at risk by ill-thought through moves into new and misunderstood markets sectors. This is not contrary to the saying 'stick to the knitting' but a redefinition of what the knitting is, away from products to capabilities or competencies.

4. Continually improve

Having been through all this upheaval it is important to recognize that while the scale of the changes required in the short term may not be as large, the continuous improvement and thus change of the organization must continue. The scale of the improvements and changes will vary over time, but improvement must take place for organizations to stay with, or ahead of, their competitors.

Flows between the five stages

Broadly speaking, organizations pass through the five main stages in sequence. The movement between these stages involves considerable iteration which must be managed. In addition, the steps outlined within each stage need not necessarily be sequential with some being performed in parallel where circumstances allow.

Create the environment ⟺ Analyse, diagnose and redesign processes

The analysis, diagnosis and redesign phase will throw up aspects of the programme which were not necessarily fully thought through in the first phase and there may be some further environmental work to perform. The scale of improvements and/or changes required may have been underestimated and the approach to be taken may need to be re-visited. It is not unusual for the approach to be changed during the final stages of the second phase and management must be pragmatic in allowing staff to pursue changed directions while not allowing the improvement drive to be diluted.

Analyse, diagnose and redesign processes ⟺ Pilot and roll out

Although the next sequence in the approach to BPR is to redesign the organization's infrastructure, what often happens in practice is that a certain amount of process redesign and role adaptation will take place as a result of the second phase. During this phase, a number of 'silly' aspects of the process, or areas for 'obvious' change will come to light and staff will want to fix them. No one wants to perform a task which they now know is unnecessary, or perform it in such a way that they now know to be wasteful in view of the overall process. These changes should be allowed. If management, or the re-engineering teams, attempt to stop these changes they must know why they are doing so, and the consequences of such action. This does happen but we do not agree that the often given reason, of wanting the documentation of the processes to be accurate, is worth the consequence of killing people's desire to improve and the learning and successes they will derive from it. Keeping documentation up to date yet preventing improvement in performance and the development of people's improvement skills and motivation is not justified in our view. It is also important, however, that management do not rest on their laurels following these initial improvements, this is just the beginning and there is much more to come.

Analyse, diagnose and redesign processes ⟺ Redesign the organization's infrastructure

The redesign of the organization's infrastructure, both its people and technology, will almost certainly have an impact on the design of the new processes. It will be necessary to revisit to redesign stage, possibly carry out further benchmarking on specific issues, and generate a new design which optimizes the organization mix of process, people and technology.

Redesign the organization's infrastructure ⟺ Pilot and roll-out

As the pilot and roll-out phase progress there will be elements of the organizational infrastructure which must be re-thought. Pay and reward systems, budgetary control systems and so on will all have been tested and the unforeseen pitfalls begun to be understood. Adjustment to these infrastructure issues should be brought about quickly, although if this re-hashing is done too many times it can become destructive and sometimes an imperfect system is preferable to an ever changing one.

Pilot and roll out ⟺ Realize strategy

As the capability of the organization is harnessed some changes to the detailed processes may be required. As the potential for the processes and their successes becomes better understood so the roll-out plan can take these lessons into account and build on them.

Realize strategy ⟺ Create the environment

The five main steps should not be seen as a single linear programme, but more as a cycle for improvement. Organizations must continue to re-think how they will conduct business in the future and facilitate continuous improvement day-to-day. The five step cycle will continue as long as the business continues and the business will continue as long as the cycle is continued. In a sense the cycle represents a re-juvenation of the organization, a means of nurturing and developing the next generation on a continuous cycle just as healthy human communities continually regenerate.

Issues of power and politics

Within organizations there are many different interest groups: groups of people with different goals and ambitions. Individuals will align themselves with others who hold similar ambitions or perceive themselves as threatened by similar threats, either individually or by their divisions. In this way coalitions are formed within organizations: these are the alignment of different interest groups with or against each other. They will naturally compete with each other to try to maximize the likelihood of securing decisions and outcomes and resources which are compatible with their goals. The situation is likely to be more acute when resources are limited, for example, given limited investment capital, where investment might be more politically motivated than the contribution it is expected to make to the business. Competition might be overt: wrangling or conflict such as between departments, or covert, where perhaps information necessary for the decision to be made is withheld or massaged.

Such political competition in organizations will pervade the change process. Introducing a new resource or innovation has the effect of creating new alignments and unleashing competition. Change is necessarily destabilizing. Even within the top management team there may also be interest groups. How do their goals differ? Over what might they compete? What resources does each control which will give them power over the other?

Power is the cornerstone of the change management process. The critical perspective on change methodology recognizes that overcoming resistance to reorganization cannot always be resolved through dialogue and that overcoming this resistance may require change in the material and ideological conditions which distort or impede communication. In short, it believes that the underlying structure of power must first be transformed if resistance is to be removed.

Companies are finding novel ways to overcome this problem and one particularly interesting approach is that adopted by GE in America outlined in Illustration 7.2.

In general there are a number of things to bear in mind when planning for change and some are highlighted in Table 7.2. In many cases, the sponsor, acting as change agent, will want to use several

Table 7.2 Some strategies for implementing changes

- Present a non-threatening image. When attempting to introduce innovative programmes such as BPR, it may be effective to be perceived as being conservative and essentially non-threatening to existing organizational activities.

- Present arguments in terms of organization's interests. Do not distort information, but cast arguments for change proposals in terms of the benefits that will accrue to the organization.

- Diffuse opposition and bring out conflict. Rather than stifle opposition, diffuse it through an open discussion of ideas. Conflicts that develop can be dealt with by engaging the opposition in legitimate discussion, answering objections, and allaying fears and facts. Open discussions can also spotlight any die-hard resistors, reducing opportunities for them to covertly thwart the change effort.

- Align with powerful others. In addition to gaining top management's approval, it can be beneficial to build alliances with operating or line managers who are directly affected by the change.

- Bargain and make trade-offs. Change is an on-going activity. Resistors may reduce their resistance if they are assured that other changes, which they favour, will be forthcoming.

- Begin as an experiment. Resistance may be lessened by introducing the change as an experiment. When something is viewed as temporary, it is less threatening. Having the change made permanent is easier once it is already in place.

- Begin small. Start small and slowly expand the change project. If an 'all-or-nothing' stance has a reasonable chance of failing, it may be more effective to 'get your foot in the door' and then expand the project slowly.

Source: Based on V.E. Schein, 'Organisation realities: the politics of change', *Training and Development Journal*, February (1985), 39–40.

Illustration 7.2 GE's work-out sessions

GE in the the USA has a novel way of driving process improvement. Three areas are addressed: processes, best practice and 'work-outs'. Improvement teams are trained at GE's own 'business school' Crotonville in process mapping, benchmarking and the method for implementing improvements which result from these two activities: 'work-outs'.

The 'work-out' is essentially a large meeting with project teams recommending courses for action to improve effectiveness and efficiency. These teams present their suggestions to a senior executive for their approval but the GE way is quite different from usual corporate approval systems. The senior executive is accompanied by their boss, who sits directly behind, and is thus present when decisions are made, but in positions where they are not referred to at every point. The teams 'fire' their action plans in quick succession and the emphasis on the executive is to say 'yes' to the vast majority, though they may ask for further information and may on occasion say 'no'.

This method has, according to GE, proved highly successful in getting a large number of improvements implemented, some of which have been quite significant. In one instance a workforce bid to build new protective shields for grinding machines of $16 000 was accepted saving $80 000 over a vendor's quote as well as maintaining employment within the firm at a time of great worker distrust.

Worker participation has been very strong and 'work-outs' are now being driven by the workforce in many divisions without any senior management intervention. Management must maintain their support and encouragement to this process and not revert to the control centred methods of before if such momentum is to be maintained. In the words of one executive 'when you teach a bear to dance, you'd better be prepared to keep dancing as long as the bear wants to'.

Would GE do anything differently if they were planning this approach from scratch again? Involve middle management more in the process is the suggestion of one insider. They still have considerable power and if they are to use this in a facilitative role they must be made to feel part of the initiative, not left to one side.

Jack Welch, the charismatic CEO of GE, is pleased with the work-outs and can boast to have boosted the stock value of the company by a factor of five or more over the last decade, using this and other approaches.

Sources: Thomas A. Stewart, 'GE Keeps Those Ideas Coming', *Fortune*, 12 August 1991, pp. 19–25; Noel M. Tichy, 'Revolutionize Your Company', *Fortune*, 13 December 1993, pp. 52–54; Robert Slater, *The New GE: How Jack Welch Revived an American Institution* (Homewood, Illinois, 1993).

of these strategies. The one he or she chooses should reflect the political dynamics of the situation.

Vulnerability

The quote from Machiavelli at the start of this chapter highlights the vulnerable position that those attempting to drive change can find themselves in. Understanding the context of this vulnerability is important if senior management is to increase the chances of success and was investigated in a research project undertaken by David Buchanan.[10] Drawing loosely on this work, Table 7.3 outlines some conditions which can increase or decrease this vulnerability.

Table 7.3 High and low vulnerability

High vulnerability	Low vulnerability
Step improvement targets	Incremental improvement targets
Unrealistic expectations	Realistic expectations
Top management 'out of touch' with reality, a 'yes' culture	Top managers 'in touch' and supportive
Fast pace, highly visible results	Slow pace, results not immediately apparent
Diverse motives and understanding	Common vision and understanding
Significant resource required	Few extra resources needed
Little knowledge of how to proceed	Clear method
Complex interdependences	Few interdependences
Dependent on others	Self contained
Large scale, wide scope	Small scale, narrow scope
Dynamic environment	Stable environment
Confused responsibilities of process and outcomes	Clear 'ownership' of process and outcomes

Adapted, based on our own research, from David A. Buchanan, 'Vulnerability and Agenda: Context and Process in Project Management', *British Journal of Management*, 2 (1991), 121–132.

Summary

The success of any BPR initiative will depend on how well the new process designs are implemented. Successful implementation starts right back at the beginning of any BPR programme and must not be left to the end. The five stage framework for a BPR programme presented in this chapter is an attempt to help organizations avoid some of the mistakes of the past and pay close attention to the culture, people and communication issues up front. Implementing new processes will cause 'ripples' of change to spread out across the organization to cover many aspects of people and technology. Trying to win 'hearts and minds' into accepting new processes which have been redesigned without clear communication of the goals of such an initiative, and with little involvement, is a recipe for disaster.

The experiences of Sun Life Assurance Society at re-engineering are described in Illustration 7.3.

Illustration 7.3 Redesign at Sun Life: no pain no gain

Sun Life Assurance Society started re-engineering back in 1990. Now the Bristol-based organization exudes energy, enthusiasm and excitement about its re-engineering experience. An attitude which is indecently attractive in such an un-sexy business.

Managing director, John Reeve is the source of Sun Life's missionary zeal. At the end of the 1980s, recognizing that tough times (more competitors, more regulation, more new products, more recession) were ahead, he ordered a radical business review. The findings were only partially enouraging. 'Industry surveys showed quality of service to be increasingly important to brokers. Our reputation was better than most, but our service levels were still only perceived to be fairly average. We were satisfying, but certainly not delighting our customers,' says Michael Baker, project manager of the customer service review.

Sun Life plunged into turbulent re-engineering waters in its quest for the delighted customer. In came consultants McKinsey and Hay to plumb the corporate soul. 'Where are we going?' 'Where is the industry going?' Next, they reviewed the core processes. The findings were disturbing. Issuing a new life assurance policy was a typical core process involving administrative steps carried out in different departments. No one, it seemed, was in charge of a process from beginning to end; each step was hampered by bottlenecks, ambiguity, delays and errors. A process which should have taken 15 days limped along for 46 days. Once a department has done its bit, the paperwork fell into 'black holes' of inactivity.

In June 1991, Sun Life began re-engineering its core processes in a two year, three-wave programme. All processes were put through a six-stage wringer of documentation; analysis; brainstorming ideas; evaluating solutions; detailed design; and implementation. Tackling processes alone was not enough. Re-engineering without corresponding and supporting organizational change diminishes its potential to deliver. 'Our challenge', says Les Owen, director of the on-going BPR project, 'was to use business process re-engineering as a fresh approach to business needs, processes, organization, people, and finally technology. The objective was to be a pace-setter – to reshape the organization into a more efficient one but vitally, one which has a predominant customer focus.' Sun Life's metamorphosis from an organization based on functional specialists to one based on multi-skilled employees required massive restructuring.

For Sun Life's brave new world, redesigned, streamlined processes were organized in one place around multi-skilled teams to ensure that reponsibility for a complete, end-to-end process was handled in one place. Massive investment in training and communication programmes would broaden and enhance employee roles, responsibilities, skills and competences. Sun Life's historic hierarchical seven layer management structure was transformed. A pilot experiment in the 1200-strong customer-service department slashed the multiple level hierarchy to customer service managers, team leaders and teams supported by two other roles: a dedicated trainer and technical expert. Team members, formally skilled in about one-quarter of a process, familiarized themselves with the other 75 per cent. New reward structures based on pay of competences and customer-related performance measures were introduced. Convulsive change did not engender immediate convulsive delight. 'It was a painful process, especially at the middle management level where people well into their careers were asked to accept radical reform of the job they were doing,' says Baker. 'We had some fall out. Some did not want to be part of this new world' – ultimately a quarter of customer service managers left the company.

Corporate pain was not in vain. Baker is confident of a two or three year payback period. Already Sun Life boasts 40–90 per cent improvements in process turnaround times; 10 per cent reduction in unit costs of some processes, and 50–80 per cent quality improvements (work performed right first time). Sun Life confidently predicts a significant increase in job satisfaction among employees and greater customer satisfaction leading to increased business. Baker reports that the 'black holes' in one process, the Life New Business, have been filled – the process gallops along in 21 days rather than 46. Faults in the company's communication lines are being filled. Employees had a first annual general meeting this year. Peter Sissons has chaired an 'open house' no-holds-barred *Question Time* and videos, focus groups, attitude surveys and training seminars keep momentum high. 'We have an open style of management that was inconceivable three years ago,' says Baker.

Sun Life Assurance's road to re-engineering enlightenment sounds untroubled. It was not. Nor is the journey yet complete. 'Anyone who underestimates the size or difficulty of the task of making the organization transformation will certainly fail,' says Owen. No pain, no gain.

Source: 'Sun Life's new Policy', *Management Today*, August (1993), 22. Reprinted with permission.

References

1. Niccolo Machiavelli, *The Prince*, translated with an introduction by George Bull, Harmondsworth: Penguin Books, 1981.
2. 'ASAP Interview', *Forbes ASAP*, September 1993, pp. 69–75.

3. This example is adapted from J.R. Schermerhorn, J.G. Hunt and R.N. Osborn, *Managing Organisation Behaviour*, fourth edition, New York: John Wiley & Sons, 1991.

4. Geary A. Rummler and Alan P. Brache, *Improving Performance: How to Manage the White Space on the Organization Chart*, San Francisco: Jossey Bass, 1990.

5. R. Beckhard and R. Harris, *Organizational Transitions*, second edition, Reading Massachusetts: Addison Wesley, 1989.

6. Reported in Lynda Radosevich, 'Evasive action', *ComputerWorld*, 4 October 1993, pp. 83–84.

7. Gerry Johnson, 'Managing strategic change – strategy, culture and action', *Long Range Planning*, 25, no. 1 (1992) 28–36, 1992. For further information on the cultural web, see Gerry Johnson and Kevan Scholes, *Exploring Corporate Strategy*, Hemel Hempstead: Prentice Hall, 1993.

8. Michael Hammer and James Champy, *Reengineering the Corporation: A Manifesto for Business Revolution*, London: Nicholas Brealey Publishing, 1993, pp. 148–158.

9. H. James Harrington, *Business Process Improvement: The Breakthrough Strategy for Total Quality, Productivity and Competitiveness*, New York: McGraw-Hill, 1991.

10. David A. Buchanan, 'Vulnerability and agenda: context and process in project management', *British Journal of Management*, 2 (1991), 121–132.

8

Succeeding at BPR

Had I been present at the creation, I would have given some
useful hints for the better ordering of the universe.

Alfonso 'the wise'
King of Castile and León from 1252

Nothing breeds success quite like success

Anonymous

Introduction

Successful re-engineering initiatives bring impressive results. In this
chapter we outline some points which managers should bear in
mind to improve their chances of success.

Improvements brought about by re-engineering of 50–80 per cent,
some even over 100 per cent are widely quoted, as highlighted in
Table 8.1. These are often represented in terms of lower stocks,
shorter lead times, reduced costs, higher productivity. Such reports
have resulted in re-engineering becoming something of a holy grail
to the business world and many managers are earnestly seeking to
repeat this success themselves.

In many re-engineering initiatives lead-time reduction is a key
feature. It is sometimes difficult for people to understand, however,
just what this takes. Figure 8.1 shows one way of analysing
processes and explaining to people the requirement for lead time
reduction: micro-response analysis.[1]

Table 8.1   Some re-engineering results

- Western Provident Association slashed the time taken to process insurance claims from 28 days to 4 days and settles 90 per cent of claims within five working days.
- The Baxi Partnership reduced manufacturing lead times from 9 weeks to an incredible 24 hours.
- Rank Xerox UK reduced the processing time of 'special bills' from 112 days to 24 hours.
- Reuters reduced its debt collection days from 120 to 38 days, increased invoice accuracy by 98 per cent, and can now deliver some new services in just 15 minutes.
- Digital Equipment Corporation cut $1 billion from its manufacturing costs through re-engineering to meet customer needs.
- AT&T Global Business Communications System subsidiary designed from scratch the way it processes orders for customers, cutting delivery times from 8–12 weeks to 'days', even while using 35 per cent fewer people to do the job.
- Pilkington Optronics reduced manufacturing lead times by over 50 per cent, increased delivery reliability to 97 per cent from a poor 10 per cent, slashed stock and work-in-process value by 70 per cent to £6.8m and increased sales per employee by over a massive 285 per cent to approximately £70k.
- Lucas Industries automotive business cut manufacturing lead time by nearly 80 per cent, and reduced overall order-to-dispatch lead time by 70 per cent to 32 days before automation. It doubled inventory turn-around, achieved a 50 per cent increase in productivity, and a 25 per cent reduction in operating costs.
- Compaq Computers cut its costs by more than 30 per cent through a complete re-think of its business.
- Hillingdon Hospital in London, having re-engineered in-patient care, reduced the steps for getting a blood test down to a process which now takes five minutes.
- At another hospital in the UK, outpatients at the neurology clinic now benefit from a reduced cycle time from first consultation to diagnosis. The original time of over 12 weeks has been slashed to less than one day.
- The Mark Twain National Forest in the USA cut the time needed to grant a grazing permit from 30 days to a few hours – because employees could grant permits themselves rather than process them through headquarters.
- Utah's Ogden Internal Revenue Service Centre had more than 50 'productivity improvement teams' simplifying forms and re-engineering work processes. Not only had employees saved more than $11 million, they had won the 1992 Presidential Award for Quality.

Sources: Case study research, various newspaper and journal articles, government publications and conference presentations.

Lead time to work content is the same as throughput efficiency discussed in Chapter 3. Ideally the time taken to complete the process would be the same time as needed to perform the actual work. In reality, lead time is considerably longer. *Process speed to use rate* highlights the fact that there is no point running a particular process or operation at its full speed if subsequent processes or operations cannot work as fast. Stocks and, or, paperwork will merely be built up into an ever growing backlog. Ideally, here again, there should be a ratio of 1:1. On a manufacturing shop-floor in some industries the notion of a 'batch size of one' is recognized as being a theoretical goal and thus an ideal ratio of 1:1 for *pieces to workstation or operator* would be, as with the previous ratios, agreed. In office environments, however, this notion is alien. When we discuss the ideal ratio of 1:1 in relation to an office, the processing of orders using the example shown in Figure 8.1, people usually have trouble accepting this. It simply does not reflect how offices work. The problem, though, is that if offices work with backlogs building up in in-trays, then it is easy to see why ratios of 100:1 or worse are apparent in *lead time to work content*. Figure 8.2 takes a further look at the pieces to work station or operator example of Figure 8.1 to show that there are many people in the process, all with in-trays and using the mail system!

If the ratio for lead time to content is to be reduced anywhere near to the ideal of 1:1 then, a compete re-think of the way that offices are run is needed. The 'case team' approach discussed in earlier chapters is just such a re-think.

Some guidelines for success

In the previous chapter we presented an approach to BPR which can be adapted and used in conjunction with other methodologies to suit any particular situation. No two organizations are the same, however, there are some general principles and guidelines which can increase the chances of success. BPR can learn from the experiences of other improvement philosophies such as TQM and JIT[2] and early BPR projects.[3] Many of the lessons learnt have been covered in previous chapters, however we repeat them here to stress their importance.

Drive from the top

It has become a bit of a cliché to say it but, 'top management commitment is vital'. The level of management required to commit to BPR will depend on the scope, and to a lesser extent scale, of the project. Clearly if a significant portion of the enterprise is to be re-engineered then this commitment must come from the very top. It must be measured by action, not words and some research

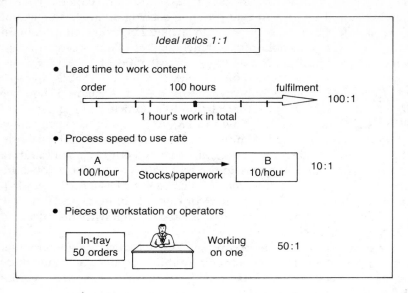

Figure 8.1   Micro-response analysis

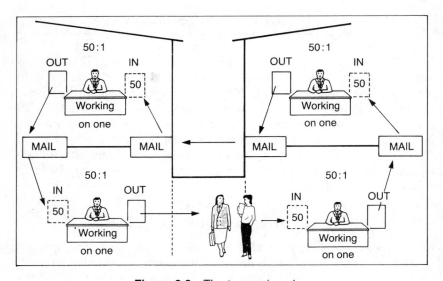

Figure 8.2   The 'paperchase'

findings estimate that as much as 50 per cent of a CEO's time needs to be spent on a BPR project.[4] The support, energy and drive of top management must also be sustained over a long period to ensure things actually get done and that the organization does not fall victim of 'fad' management programmes which come and go regularly.

Communicate, communicate, communicate

People must understand why improvement is needed, the vision of the future and their part in it – even if job losses are likely. Workers are not stupid and will see redundancy coming whatever the management say. Therefore they should communicate this issue up front. Some organizations are now giving as much as a year's notice that offices will be closed and people made redundant to give people a chance to adjust and find alternative employment. Of course, not all situations can be handled in this way but the 'night of the long knives' approach is highly demotivating for everyone, should be avoided and sensitivity demonstrated.

Treat people fairly and with respect

We would all like to think that we treat people as we would have them treat us. Why, then, is this behaviour so often lacking in the context of work? Management, in particular must set a clear example that manners, common courtesy and respect should not be left at home but should brought into work as well.

Ensure that the right sponsor is chosen

In a number of re-engineering initiatives we have seen sponsors coming from too low in the management ranks or who are too technically focused. In other instances, the sponsor lacks credibility and leadership ability. A good sponsor cannot succeed alone but a poor sponsor can kill BPR single handed very quickly. No one is perfect but the best leaders recognize their own failings and recruit others to complement and challenge their skills and abilities.

Be clear about the purpose of the redesign

The vision should be clear and supported by effective research into the 'service task' as outlined in Chapter 3. Customer requirements, patterns of demand, constraints and efficiency targets should all be analysed and understood with the process re-engineering initiative targeted firmly on delivering improvements in performance to these.

Match the scale and scope of the project to the ambitions of the initiative

As highlighted in Figure 1.8 the expectations of the project must match the project's scale and scope. A re-engineering initiative in a single department may have significant impact on the performance of that department and those it deals with but cannot have the same impact as a company-wide initiative. It is important that management looking for big improvements to the whole company's performance focus on those *core* processes through which the company conducts its main business.

Set aggressive re-engineering performance targets

BPR is about achieving radical performance improvements. Setting targets and measuring performance are key to understanding, managing and improving. Particular care must be taken in constructing a performance measurement system. This is notoriously difficult to get right and the truism *what gets measured gets done* means that the 'wrong' measures give rise to the 'wrong' behaviour. Any such system must be aligned to support a process orientation and must not re-inforce functional goals.

It is important to recognize the scale and scope of the project and align expectations based on the potential any initiative holds. Do not expect to create a 'hockey stick' curve effect to the bottom line from a single departmental re-engineering project.

Understand the context of the process being redesigned

BPR, like other philosophies, must be undertaken within the context of the particular firm. The targets and methods of re-engineering must be appropriate to the individual circumstances of the firms involved. Benchmarking can provide a useful way of identifying alternative ways of working but it must be remembered that what works in one company cannot necessarily be made to work 'as is' in another.

Treat BPR as a holistic philosophy

Successful BPR requires action on a broad front, as illustrated by the cultural web. Organizations are composed of interdependent elements. Changing one in isolation is unlikely to produce the required results and may have adverse effects on other elements. One financial institution, for example, redesigned a number of processes but retained its existing budgetary system. To reduce the costs of running branches, an instruction was issued to the effect that no unnecessary phone contact between branches and headquarters was to take place. This resulted in a drop in the phone bill, however the calls were merely replaced by typed memos. These overloaded the mail system and more importantly increased the time customers had to wait for a response from requests made via branches. The functional budgeting system had defeated the purpose of the BPR.

Aim for some quick hits

As we quoted at the start of this chapter, nothing breeds success quite like success. Early, demonstrable successes will help overcome resistance, build momentum and a 'can do' attitude and make people feel confident in their abilities. These 'quick hits', however, should be recognized for what they are and companies must then go on, often through a lot of pain, to achieve the longer term goals.

Ensure that processes 'match' the needs of the markets they are to serve

The importance of a 'match' between the market needs and the processes that are to serve them is paramount. If the market requires high volume, low price and dependable delivery above all else the process must deliver these things and should not be aligned to deliver high design flexibility which has the attendant cost and time penalties. The Lucas notion of 'runners, repeaters and strangers' is particularly useful here, describing the products or services provided in terms of volumes sold.

Involve customers and suppliers in the redesign process as appropriate

As one company's CEO put it 'wear the customers shoes'. Customers should be involved in the BPR programme, especially where the process has direct relevance for them. They, and suppliers too, can give valuable insights and suggest ways in which the process could be redesigned. This may also prove useful in cultivating a closer relationship and have a positive effect on the volume of business conducted with the customer.

Dedicate resources to the project

People cannot do two jobs at the same time and do them well. If BPR is important it is worth the investment of the best people's talents full time. Consultants and academics can help, support and encourage but they should not be the ones to actually 'do' what is required.

Recognize that IT provides opportunities for new designs

While we have emphasized an approach starting with the identifying of processes and then looking at people and technological requirements we again want to stress the iterative nature of this. Technology can be a powerful enabler of new process design and organizations must constantly evaluate how technology both old and new can be used.

Recognize that BPR may be just the beginning

BPR may result in step improvements, after a time, but to stay ahead further improvement will be necessary. *Continuous* improvement must be the goal with periods of incremental and step improvements becoming normal through time. In Chapter 6 we discussed the notion of 'breakpoints' to reflect the fact that incremental change to the existing process suffers from diminishing returns and a re-thinking is required. The new process design, however, is not an end, but merely another beginning. Organizations should seek to constantly 'rejuvenate' themselves to avoid other, younger and more hungry competitors stealing their markets.

Pitfalls to avoid

Business process re-engineering is not easy. It is full of pain and uncertainty. Indeed, many of the companies we have talked to are on their second attempt. Despite this we do not believe that those contemplating BPR should be put off by this. Sure, there is a correlation between risk and return and any company aiming at a complete overhaul runs a significant risk in attempting this. As we have tried to demonstrate in this book though, BPR does not have to be 'all or nothing' as some cosy, ivory tower, academics would have you believe.

As well as some guidelines for success we would like to point out some of the more common pitfalls which should be avoided.

Divorce the re-engineering effort from the main goals of the organization

We have also seen companies undertake re-engineering without reference to their strategic goals and objectives. The initiative is devoid of direction and exists for its own sake. Much effort can be expended and pain endured with little to show for it at the end.

Underestimate the changes required to achieve a process orientation

Lack of understanding about the tremendous upheaval which can result from implementing BPR is one of the main reasons why firms need a second go. BPR requires change, and often lots of it. Too much attention to the process redesign phase and not enough on other aspects as detailed in the framework in Chapter 7 can result in a stalled initiative.

Run before you can walk

Organizations must be 'ready' for BPR. This may be due to a history of TQM, a crisis situation, or a new visionary leader, but whatever the driver there must be a 'readiness' for such a programme. Some organizations would go as far as to say that experience in TQM was vital to preparing themselves for the shake-up of BPR.

Do not expect too much too soon

The real benefits of BPR may take some time to realize. Culture, employee behaviour and attitudes are not something which change quickly. As such, managers should be insulated from any short-term penalties which may arise while waiting for the bigger benefits.

Be wary of the title

BPR has suffered from a tremendous amount of hype in recent years and there is almost bound to be an adverse reaction to it as there has been with other philosophies before. Some of this will be based on ignorance, some from bloody experiences of misdirected, hyped, ideas. In the end it does not matter what it is called, it is the results that count. ABB's experience with the T50 programme to reduce cycle times by 50 per cent bears this out, with many of the best improvements being made in divisions which adopted their own names and ignored the corporate T50 slogan. Senior management at ABB recognized the power of ownership and the inconsequential nature of the name and remained supportive.[5]

Appoint the IT department as BPR agents

Although IT is a enabler of business redesign the evidence suggests that successful BPR projects are driven by the business and not the IT department. Systems people do have certain skills which qualify them for such a role, as they are trained analysts, and often have a cross-functional view of an organization. They do not, however, have responsibility for the business processes and tend to focus their energies on building computer systems.

Do not pilot the new processes

Would you risk your life participating in a process which had never been tried before? You might, but you would have to acknowledge the risk you were taking. So why refuse to run a pilot in your business to prove out a new process design. The usual reasons are cost and time, but as we know all too well, the cost and time involved in clearing up a failed process which has gone live is much greater.

Concentrate on computer packages to do the re-engineering

Quality initiatives have sometimes become bogged down by the over-concentration on technical tools at the expense of involvement and leadership. Complex computer tools might be able to do wonderful things, but usually only in the hands of trained experts. The danger of this approach, as we have highlighted earlier in the book, is that it becomes a 'staff project' and the people working in the process do not have ownership of the analysis.

References

1. Richard J. Schonberger and Edward M. Knod, *Operations Management: Improving Customer Service*, fourth edition, Homewood, Ill.: Irwin, 1991.

2. Colin Armistead and Philip Rowland, *Learning from Operations Management*, paper presented to the Business Process Redesign: Academic Directions Conference, Cranfield School of Management, June 1994. This paper draws together a number of other works including; T.J. Billesbach, 1991, 'A study of the implementation of Just-In-Time in the United States', *Production & Inventory Management Journal*, 32, no. 3 (1991), 1–4; G.S. Easton, 'The 1993 state of U.S. Total Quality Management: A Baldridge examiner's perspective', *California Management Review*, 35, no. 3, (1993), 32–54; A.S. Katz, 'Eight TQM pitfalls', *Journal for Quality & Participation*, 16, no. 4 (1993), 24–27.

3. B. Bashein, M.L. Markus and P. Riely, 'Pre-conditions for BPR success', *Information Systems Management*, 11, no. 1 (1994), 7–13; R.W. Belmonte, and R.J. Murray, 'Getting ready for strategic change: surviving business process redesign', *Information Systems Management*, 10, no. 3 (1993), 23–29; Mark M. Klein, 'The most fatal reengineering mistakes', *Information Strategy: The Executive's Journal*, Summer (1994), 21–28.

4. Gene Hall, Jim Rosenthal and Judy Wade, 'How to Make Reengineering *Really* Work', *Harvard Business Review*, November–December (1993), 119–131.

5. Johan Anckers, Vice-President Customer Focus Programme, Asea Brown Boveri, speaking at the Business Process Redesign conference at Cranfield School of Management, November 1992.

Epilogue

I still haven't found what I'm looking for

U2

Many reading this book may have reached this stage and decided that they have read nothing 'new', that BPR is merely 'old wine in new bottles'. As we said in Chapter 1, this may be so; but to what extent does your organization actually do what BRP proposes? The fact that BPR is not entirely new may also be a good thing. Many of these methods have been tried and tested over the years, and should, therefore, be less risky to use. Where this is not true it is because hype has overtaken common sense, or because people have not taken a step back and looked at the basic principles which underpin BPR.

While BPR as a title may fade somewhat, the fundamental messages are important and will endure. To summarize, BPR has one goal, one focus and one requirement.

- **Goal** – significant improvements in performance.
- **Focus** – processes.
- **Requirement** – management commitment.

The goal

It seems unlikely that businesses will ever be able to relax and enjoy the *status quo*. Continuous improvement in effectiveness, efficiency and adaptability will be the only ways to ensure survival. As new entrants or innovative old timers 'change the rules of the game' step improvements will also be necessary. BPR is about these improvements to business performance. It should not be pursued 'just because it is flavour of the month' and everyone else is doing it. If it is, the initiative is likely to yield lots of change, but little improvement.

The focus

Business *Process* Re-engineering is unquestionably focused on the processes by which an organization works and 'adds value' to its customers (as we have pointed out, sometimes a large part of these processes actually add cost). Processes might be the main focus of BPR but they bring with them the other two organizational pillars of people and technology. Strategy sets the direction for the enterprise. It is through processes, people and technology that this strategy 'lives' for customers, suppliers and staff alike. Operations provides the *do* to complement strategy's *what* and *how*. Without these elements, the search for sustainable competitive advantage is likely to be a fruitless one.

The requirement

Management commitment means many things and we would highlight belief, time and action. If managers do not believe in what they are doing, how can those they purport to lead? A vision cannot be realized by a cold fish following orders, rather it requires an element of religious zeal to get it through the difficult times. Time must be given to the initiative and this is a key indicator as to how important management perceive the improvement to be (note not BPR but the improvements which are its goal). Action in our terms does not mean a hasty, blundering charge following the latest guru but a planned movement towards the goals of the project through a set of planned milestones which the whole organization recognizes and understands. Management commitment does not mean management are alone in performing the above, but rather that they provide genuine leadership for the real teams that they build and join.

BPR is providing a way for many organizations to realize the competitive potential of their operations. It is a particularly 'hot' topic in the USA and UK, although we discern an increasing level of interest in continental Europe and Japan. Wherever you are, we hope you have enjoyed this book and have found value in it.

Further reading

There are a great many books that provide valuable insights into the issues concerned with BPR. We highlight a few of these as being particularly useful for those readers who wish to pursue the subject.

Introduction to BPR

CCTA, *BPR in the Public Sector: An overview of business process re-engineering*, London: HMSO, 1994.

Coulson-Thomas, C., *Transforming the Company*, London: Kogan Page, 1992.

Hammer, M. and Champy, J., *Reengineering the Corporation*, London: Nicholas Brearley Publishing, 1993.

Operations

Bicheno, J., *50 for Quality Q50*, Buckingham, England: Picsic Books, 1994.

Bicheno, J., *Pocket guide to JIT*, Buckingham, England, Picsic Books, 1994.

Harrison, A, *Just In Time Manufacturing in Perspective*, Hemel Hempstead: Prentice Hall, 1992.

Johansson, H.J., McHugh, P., Pendlebury, A.J. and Wheeler, B., *Business Process Reengineering: Breakpoint Strategies for Market Dominance*, Chichester: Wiley, 1993.

Meyer, C., *Fast Cycle Time: How to Align Purpose, Strategy, and Structure for Speed*, New York: The Free Press, 1993.

Slack, N., *Manufacturing Advantage: Achieving Competitive Manufacturing Operations*, London: Mercury, 1991.

Human resources

Kakabadse, A. and Tyson, S., *Cases in European Human Resources Management*, London: Routledge, 1994.

Katzenbach, J.R. and Smith, D.K., *The Wisdom of Teams: Creating High-Performance Organization*, Boston: Harvard Business School Press, 1993.

Salaman, G. (Ed.) *Human Resource Strategies*, London: Sage Publications, 1992.

Tyson, S. and Jackson, T., *The Essence of Organisation Behaviour*, Hemel Hempstead: Prentice Hall, 1992.

Information technology

Davenport, T.H., *Process Innovation: Reengineering work through Information Technology*, Boston: Harvard Business School Press, 1993.
Peppard, J.W. (Ed.), *IT Strategy for Business*, London: Pitman Publishing, 1993.
Scott Morton, M.S. (Ed.), *The Corporation of the 1990s: Information Technology and Organizational Transformation*, New York: Oxford University Press, 1991.
Tapscott, D. and Caston, A., *Paradigm Shift: The New Promise of Information Technology*, New York: McGraw-Hill, 1993.

Approaches

Harrington, H.J., *Business Process Improvement: The Breakthrough Strategy for Total Quality, Productivity and Competitiveness*, New York: McGraw-Hill, 1991.
Rummler, G. A., and Brache, A. P., *Improving Performance: How to Manage the White Space on an Organization Chart*, San Francisco: Jossey Bass, 1990.

Computer tools

Miers, D., *Process Product Watch*, Surrey: Enix Ltd, 1994.
Spurr, K., Layzell, P., Jennison, L. and Richards, N., *Software Assistance for Business Re-engineering*, Chichester: Wiley, 1993.

Index